KU-714-938

T R A V E L E R ' S

THAILAND

C O M P A N I O N

The 1998–1999 Traveler's Companions

ARGENTINA • AUSTRALIA • BALI • CALIFORNIA • CANADA • CHINA • COSTA RICA • CUBA • EASTERN CANADA • ECUADOR • FLORIDA • HAWAII • HONG KONG • INDIA • INDONESIA • JAPAN • KENYA • MALAYSIA & SINGAPORE • MEDITERRANEAN FRANCE • MEXICO • NEPAL • NEW ENGLAND • NEW ZEALAND • PERU • PHILIPPINES • PORTUGAL • RUSSIA • SPAIN • THAILAND • TURKEY • VENEZUELA • VIETNAM, LAOS AND CAMBODIA • WESTERN CANADA

Traveler's THAILAND Companion
First Published 1998

World Leisure Marketing Limited
9 Downing Road, West Meadows Industrial Estate
Derby, DE21 6HA, England
Web Site: http://www.map-world.co.uk
Published by arrangement with Kümmerly+Frey AG, Switzerland

ISBN: 1 899 02678 9

© 1998 Kümmerly+Frey AG, Switzerland

Created, edited and produced by Allan Amsel Publishing
27700 Les Andelys, France. E-mail: aamsel@aol.com
Editor in Chief: Allan Amsel
Editors: Fiona Nichols and Laura Purdom
Original design concept: Hon Bing-wah
Picture editor and designer: Leonard Lueras

ACKNOWLEDGEMENTS
The author would like to acknowledge the kind assistance given him by
many people, but particularly by Aroonsri Srimekhanond and Rungsan Tanvisuth,
both of the Tourism Authority of Thailand.

PHOTO CREDITS
Fiona Nichols: pages 152–153 and 156–157.

Printed by Samhwa Printing Company Limited, Seoul, Korea

TRAVELER'S
THAILAND
COMPANION

by Bradley Winterton

Photographed by Nik Wheeler

Kümmerly+Frey

Contents

MAPS
Thailand   8–9
Bangkok   80
Bangkok Environs   104
Pattaya and the East Coast   115
Pattaya   118
To the South   137
Koh Samui Island   144
Phuket and the South   149
Songkhla   170
Chiang Mai and the North   180
Chiang Mai   182
Southwest Thailand   210

TOP SPOTS   11
Swim in Coral Seas   11
Trek Among the Hill Tribes   11
Ride an Elephant!   12
Sample the Disgusting
(Some Say Delectable) Durian   14
Take a Day-Trip to Myanmar (Burma)   14
Hunt for Hill Tribe Handicrafts   16
Kick a *Takraw*   16
Relax with an Ancient Massage   18
Meander by the Mekong   18
Snack at a Night Market   18

YOUR CHOICE   21
The Great Outdoors   21
Sporting Spree   23
The Open Road   24
Backpacking   28
Living It Up   30
Family Fun   32
Cultural Kicks   34
Shop Till You Drop   38
Short Breaks   40
Festive Flings   42
Galloping Gourmets   44
Special Interests   47
Sports   49
Traditional Performing Arts   51
Taking a Tour   52

THE SIAMESE WORLD | 55
A very Special Place | 57
A Pink Elephant • A Hot Climate
Enter the Thais | 58
Where Do They Come From?
Old Siam | 58
The Sukhothai Period • Naresuan
the Great • Early European
Influences • Decline and
Revival • A Modernizing
Dynasty • King Mongkut •
The French Threat
The Twentieth Century | 64
King Bhumipol
The Many Faces of Buddhism | 66
A Land of Temples • The Light
of Asia • The Language of the
Temples • Other Essences •
The Moslem South
How Do They Live? | 70
Life on Four Dollars a Day •
Upward Mobility • Authoritarian
Ways • A Brightly Lit Future •
Monarchism • A Monastic
Perspective • Prostitution • A
Life in the Hills • A Pastoral Life •
Fishermen of the South

BANGKOK AND AYUTTHAYA
Capitals New and Old | 79
Bangkok | 81
A Bird's Eye View • Major
Communications • Where to
Stay • Where to Eat • Getting
to Know the City • The Grand
Palace and Wat Pho • The River •
Other Temples • Cultural
Attractions • Sukhumvit Road •
In the Snake Pit • Thai Boxing •
More River Trips • Floating
Markets • Weekend Market •
Lumpini Park • Chinatown •
Nightlife • Shopping • Getting
Around • Getting out of Town •
Tourist Information
Day Trips from Bangkok | 104
Crocodiles and Roses • Ayutthaya
and Bang Pa-In • A Once
Gorgeous Ruin • Kanchanaburi
and the River Kwai Bridge

PATTAYA AND THE EAST COAST
RESORTS | 113
The East Coast | 115
How to Get There
Chonburi | 115
Bang Saen | 115
A Free-Range Zoo
Si Racha and Koh Sichang | 116
Where to Stay and Where to Eat •
What to See and Do

Pattaya 116
  Getting There • A Bird's Eye
  View • Where to Stay • Where
  to Eat • After Dark • Getting
  Around Town • What to See
  and Do • Tourist Information
Rayong 125
Koh Samet 126
  Arriving at Nadaan • Where to
  Stay • Sai Kaew • Ao Phai •
  Ao Cho • Wongduan • A
  Viewing Point • Ao Phrao
Chantaburi 132
Trat Province 133

THE SOUTH AND PHUKET 135
Hua Hin 137
  Where to Stay • Where to Eat •
  After Dark • The Beach • Khao
  Takiab • Phetchaburi • Other
  Trips from Hua Hin
Khao Sam Roi Yod National Park 142
  A Wildlife Paradise •
  Uncrowded Pleasures
Koh Samui Island 144
  Getting There • Nathon • A
  Bird's Eye View • Chaweng
  Beach • Lamai Beach •
  Tongsai, Bophut
Koh Pha-Ngan Island 147
  Thong Sala • South Coast •
  Haad Rin • West Coast •
  Koh Tao • A Marine Park

Phuket 149
  A Bird's Eye View • Beach by
  Beach • Phuket Town • Away
  from the Beaches • Diving •
  Phuket's Chinese Vegetarian
  Festival
South from Phuket 160
  Phang-Nga • Krabi Province •
  Phi Phi to Krabi • Krabi Town •
  Krabi to Hat Yai
Hat Yai 166
  Getting There • Where to Stay •
  Where to Eat • Wat Hat Yai Nai •
  Golf • Attractions • Getting
  About • Tourist Information
Songkhla 169
  Samila Beach • Kao Seng •
  The Harbor • Songkhla National
  Museum • Thale Luang
  Waterbird Sanctuary
Yala Province 172

CHIANG MAI AND THE NORTH 175
Hill Territory 177
Phitsanulok 177
Sukhothai 178
  The Sukhothai Era • The Ruins
Lampang 181
Chiang Mai 182
  A Bird's Eye View • Where to
  Stay • Where to Eat • A City
  Tour • Shopping • Nightlife •
  Golf • Exploring by Motorbike •
  Trekking • Festivals • Tourist
  Information • Getting There

Around Chiang Mai 186
  Doi Suthep • A Royal Palace •
  Elephant Camps • Lamphun •
  Shopping for Crafts • Borsang —
  Umbrella Village
Mae Hong Son 190
  A Bird's Eye View • Where to
  Stay • Around Town •
  Trekking • Out of Town
The Far North 194
  Chiang Rai • Chiang Saen •
  The Golden Triangle • Mae Sai •
  Doi Thung • Mae Salong
A Note on the Hill Tribes 203

OFF THE BEATEN TRACK **207**
The Southwest 209
  Koh Jum • Trang Town •
  Trang Province • Koh Taru Tao
The Northeast 211
  Phimai • Phanom Rung •
  Udon Thani • Ban Chiang •
  Nong Khai • Loei • Wat That
  Phanom and Surin • Monsoon
  Country

LASTLY... **217**
A Genial Insouciance 219
Street Theater 220

TRAVELERS' TIPS **223**
Visas 224
Customs Allowances 224
Currency 224
Banks 224
From the Airport 224
Car Hire 225
Health 225
Clothing 226
Traveling Conditions 226
Accommodation 227
Restaurant 227
Security 228
Mail 228
Telephone and Area Codes 228
Newspapers 229
TV and Radio 229
Religion 230
TAT 230
Airlines 230
Etiquette 231
Consulates and Embassies 232
Vocabulary 232
Tax Clearance Certificates 233
Departure Tax 233

FURTHER READING 234

QUICK REFERENCE A–Z GUIDE 235
To Places and Topics of Interest with
Listed Accommodations, Restaurants
and Useful Telephone Numbers

TRAVELER'S
THAILAND
COMPANION

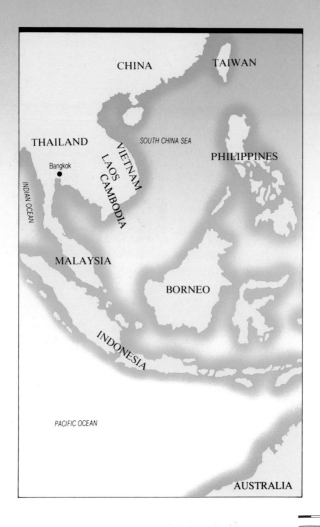

CHINA

TAIWAN

THAILAND

SOUTH CHINA SEA

Bangkok

VIETNAM

LAOS

CAMBODIA

PHILIPPINES

INDIAN OCEAN

MALAYSIA

BORNEO

INDONESIA

PACIFIC OCEAN

AUSTRALIA

Railways
Roads

50 km

TOP SPOTS

Swim in Coral Seas

WHETHER YOU'RE JUST A SIMPLE SNORKELER OR AN EXPERT SCUBA DIVER, you'll find Thailand's waters stunning. The country's long coastline, which borders both the Andaman Sea and the Gulf of Thailand, and its hundreds of islands offer an incredible variety of underwater fish and scenery — coral walls and gardens, huge sea fans and barrel sponges, sharks, rays and barracudas. The water is so warm you don't need a wetsuit and visibility is so good it sometimes extends as far as 30 m (100 ft). Best of all, you can dive year-round in Thailand just by choosing the right area: when the northeast monsoon (October to January) makes popular islands in the Gulf such as Koh Samui unsuitable, simply hop over to the Andaman coast which has its poor season when the southwest monsoon swings through, from May to November. Some areas in the more protected Gulf, such as Pattaya, can be enjoyed year-round.

In fact, despite its sleazy reputation, **Pattaya** is one of the best places to learn to dive. The shallow reefs are perfect for beginners, the standard of tuition and equipment is excellent, and prices are reasonable — about US$300 to $400 for a certified four-day Open Water course. There are more than a dozen dive shops in Pattaya, try the well-reputed **Seafari Sports Centre** ((038) 429253 FAX (038) 424708 (qualified five-star PADI diving facilities).

Phuket and **Koh Samui** are other popular dive centers, especially among more experienced divers. There are so many dive operators here now, prices have become very competitive. You've also got the chance to dive around some splendid nearby island reefs: the Koh Racha islands near Phuket, with their reef slopes, drop-offs and large underwater formations, and the Ang Thong National Marine Park archipelago near Koh Samui which boasts beautiful soft corals. Several Phuket operators, such as **PIDC Divers** (/FAX (076) 381219, also offer five- to ten-day live-aboard dive trips to even more stunning dive sites — the Similan Islands, fabled Burma Banks or Surin Islands. See SPORTING SPREE for more details.

Trek Among the Hill Tribes

THAILAND'S NORTHERN HILLS ARE HOME TO AT LEAST TEN DIFFERENT HILL TRIBES — ethnic minorities of semi-nomadic origin who mostly migrated to Thailand from China, Laos, Myanmar (Burma) and Tibet over the past 200 years. With their distinctive dress, customs and lifestyle they have become the focus of much tourist attention in the past decade: organized treks in the area, including overnight visits to hill tribe villages, are now very popular. You can find hundreds of cheap tour operators in the main trekking center, Chiang Mai, but if you want to avoid being simply a voyeur, it's worth paying a little more for trips run by the longer-established and

OPPOSITE: A beautifully unspoilt beach in the Ang Thong Marine National Park group of islands, west of Koh Samui.

more experienced outfits which have spent years developing a mutually beneficial relationship with the tribespeople and have qualified guides who speak all the local dialects. For a list of recommended trekking operators, contact the **Chiang Mai TAT office ℓ** (053) 248604.

Most treks last three nights, four days and cost around US$60 to US$100, though you can arrange anything from one to ten days if you want. For a little extra cost, elephant rides and river rafting will often be included in the trip, making the outing into quite an adventure. You do have to be prepared for some rigorous walking, as well as simple food and spartan sleeping conditions, but for most visitors the novelty of the experience far outweighs

the discomforts. And if you're really keen you can try trekking in other parts of northern Thailand, too: Mae Hong Son, Chiang Rai, Pai and Thaton are all up-and-coming trekking centers in areas of rolling hills and unspoilt scenery.

Ride an Elephant!

EVER WONDERED HOW THEY TRAIN ELEPHANTS TO PUSH AND PULL LOGS? Or wanted to ride in the wilds on the back of the huge beasts? Thailand is the place to find out what it's all about. There are several elephant training centers in the country where you can watch the pachyderms go through their paces, but

the least commercialized is probably the **Young Elephant Training Centre** (also called the Thai Elephant Conservation Centre) near Lampang in northern Thailand. The training sessions usually start around 9 AM and last until 11 AM. You may also get the chance to ride and feed the animals.

For rides in the wild, your best chance is during an organized trek from Chiang Mai, Chiang Rai or Mae Hong Son: the hill tribe trekking outfits based here often include an hour or two by elephant in the itinerary. Keep an eye out elsewhere, too, for smaller operators offering separate elephant rides: in less-touristy Pai, for instance (near Mae Hong Son), **No Mercy Trek** ((053) 699024, can arrange a

one-to-two hour ride for as few as two people. And in remote Sangkhlaburi, northwest of Kanchanaburi, **P. Guesthouse** ((034) 595061 FAX (034) 595139, gave me the best elephant ride of my life, with the animals climbing astonishingly steep hills and sliding down river banks.

Lastly, if you really want to see the power and glory of the beasts at their best, don't miss the **Elephant Roundup** in Surin in late November, when a hundred or so elephants put on an incredible show, from simple log-pulling to football games and tugs of war.

A typically mountainous backdrop for rice paddies near Mae Hong Son.

Sample the Disgusting (Some Say Delectable) Durian

PITY THE POOR DURIAN: this ugly-looking fruit, about the size of a football and covered in a thick, spiky, pale green shell, smells so awful it's often banned in hotels, buses and airplanes. And the taste? Ah, well, that depends on who you ask. Durian aficionados claim the taste and texture are both delectable, though others may think it reminds them of a rather disgusting cross between custard and cream cheese. But with several different varieties available, you could always keep trying until you come to your own conclusion. The four different kinds are the *mon tong* ("golden pillow"), *gan yeow* ("long stem"), *chanee* ("long-haired monkey") and *grandoom* ("button"). During Thailand's prime durian season — from late April until mid-July — you'll find piles of the prickly fruit in markets and street stalls everywhere. They're at their best, of course, when they are at their most pungent: be prepared to pay several hundred baht per durian, even up to 700 baht for the smelliest and most succulent. And if you really get hooked on the stuff, you can always buy durian flavored chewing gum to take back home with you.

Take a Day-Trip to Myanmar (Burma)

THAILAND SHARES A LONG BORDER WITH MYANMAR (BURMA) but although local Burmese and Thai have long hopped to and fro across the frontiers it's only recently that foreign tourists have been allowed to cross overland to visit the country.

The easiest and most popular border crossing is at Thailand's northernmost point, **Mae Sai**, in the area of the Golden Triangle. This busy trading town faces the Burmese town of **Tachilek** (also spelled Thakhilek) across the narrow Sai River: during the day, a constant flow of local traders and workers crosses the border bridge. For a fee of US$5, foreigners are also allowed across for a day visit (you must leave your passport at the Thai immigration post), though it's arguable whether you'll find enough in Tachilek to interest you for a whole day. More enticing, perhaps, is the chance to stay for the maximum four days and travel 163 km (101 miles) north all the way to **Kengtung** (also called Chengtung), 100 km (62 miles) short of the China border. This will cost considerably more — US$18 for the visa, plus a mandatory exchange of US$100 for Foreign Exchange Certificates plus the cost of the organized tour (officially, foreigners aren't allowed to go alone) — but will certainly give you more of an adventure. An enterprising American tour operator in Mae Sai, nicknamed Kobra Joe, can arrange everything for you. Contact him at **King Kobra Maesai Guesthouse (**/FAX (053) 733055.

There is currently one other entry point where foreigners can cross into Myanmar: the **Three Pagodas Pass**, 235 km (146 miles) northwest of Kanchanaburi. This remote and previously volatile frontier (various insurgent armies used to battle for its control) is now firmly under the control of the Burmese government. The village on the Burmese side, called **Payathonzu**, is a busy little place, with workshops all along the dusty street manufacturing Burmese-style reclining teak chairs for sale in Thailand.

Another crossing point due to open soon for international trade and tourism is at **Mae Sot**, in western Tak province. The border market here on the Thai side of the Moei River is already very popular with visitors, selling cheap Burmese food and teak products, jade and gems. At the time of writing, a highway bridge was being constructed over the river to eventually link up with the road to Rangoon (Yangon). Adventurers, be ready!

A girl of the "long-neck" Padaung tribe near Mae Hong Son; the brass rings actually push down the collarbone rather than lengthen the neck.

Hunt for Hill Tribe Handicrafts

SOME OF THAILAND'S MOST UNUSUAL SHOPPING BARGAINS ARE THE VARIOUS HANDICRAFTS MADE BY THE HILL TRIBES. The northern city of **Chiang Mai** is the undisputed magnet for handicraft-hunters: its proximity to the hill tribes in both Thailand as well as Laos and Myanmar means it can offer a spectacular range of handicrafts, from *yaams* (embroidered shoulder bags) to intricate silver jewelry. The **night market**, off Chang Klan Road, is the place to start hunting, though you'll find a lot of the material here is of low quality, sold to tourists at high prices. Be sure to bargain if you find something you fancy! More reliable are various non-profit organizations (often run by church groups) which channel profits directly back to the hilltribe people. One of the best is **Thai Tribal Crafts** ((053) 241043, on Bamrungrat Road.

Other, less commercial places selling excellent handicrafts are the northern town of **Nan** where the local Thai Lu fabrics and Mien embroidery are good buys (try the non-profit **Thai-Payap Association** ((054) 710230, in Jetraboot Road, and **Chiang Rai**, where the **Population & Community Development Association** ((053) 713410, has a worthwhile little museum and handicrafts center at Thanalai Road.

Kick a *Takraw*

WHEREVER YOU GO IN THAILAND — a noisy city center, a dusty little village, a temple garden or school playground — you're likely to come across a game of *takraw*. This Thai form of football entails kicking a small woven rattan or plastic ball (called *luuk takraw*) around " no hands allowed". At its simplest, it can be played by a bunch of players (the number is irrelevant) who stand in a rough circle, kicking or head-butting the ball from person to person to keep it off the ground. The official version, featured in the South East Asian Games, involves two or three teams and a volleyball net: the rules are

ABOVE: Playing takraw, a Thai form of football popular throughout the country. OPPOSITE: Relaxation, Thai style, with a seaside massage by a blind masseur on Koh Samui where steam baths are also available.

For the best in bodily rejuvenetion the age-old art of Steam bath & Thai massage are experiece not to be Missed when in the country.

similar to those in volleyball, but you can only touch the ball with your head or feet. In the most difficult version of the game players have to kick the ball into a hoop which stands about four meters (12 ft) off the ground.

But even at the simplest village level, style and skill is all-important, with points awarded for the most impressive maneuvers. It may look easy enough from a distance but if you try it for yourself (just ask some kids if you can join in their game) you'll find you need the energy of a football player, the pirouette techniques of a ballet dancer and the dexterity of an acrobat.

Relax with an Ancient Massage

Ancient massage? No, it's not a massage by an old woman, nor anything remotely hanky-panky. It's traditional Thai massage, a healing therapy that's been practiced for centuries. When it's done well you'll feel better than you have done for ages. Combining basic massage techniques with chiropractice and acupressure, Shiatsu and reflexology, *raksaa thaang nuat* or *nuat boraan* (as it's called in Thai) aims to balance the body "elements" (from nerves and tendons to blood and digestion) and relax and soothe the muscles.

Bangkok's Wat Pho is the home of Thailand's oldest massage school and one of the best places in the capital to see for yourself what this traditional massage is all about. For the most therapeutic effects, you should allow 90 minutes to two hours (the cost is usually about 150 baht an hour, though Wat Pho masseurs charge slightly more). The blind masseurs at Bangkok's **Marble House** ((02) 235-3519, are also highly recommended. Beyond Bangkok, you'll find traditional massage available all over the country, especially in the north around **Chiang Mai** which has its own northern version of the therapy (if my experience is anything to go by, you may find that an hour of this kind of hefty pulling and pommeling is quite

enough, thanks). There are also several places where you can take a massage course (usually lasting at least seven days) to learn the techniques yourself. For more information, see SPECIAL INTERESTS, page 47.

Meander by the Mekong

THE MIGHTY MEKONG RIVER — the world's twelfth longest, running 4,200 km (2,625 miles) from its source in Tibet to its mouth in Vietnam's Mekong Delta — forms the 750-km (468-miles) border of Thailand with Laos, to the north and east of Bangkok. If you're the kind of traveler who likes the going to be slow and simple, there's nothing nicer than to meander by this Mekong frontier for a few days.

There are three easy routes for tracing the river. You can either head for Thailand's northernmost point, Mae Sai, in the heart of the Golden Triangle, and curve slowly southeast to Chiang Khong (a charming and little-visited spot), or follow the river north along its route from sleepy Mukdahan in the northeast of the country to booming Nong Khai (the main border crossing into Laos). My own favorite route is to start in Nong Khai itself (an easy overnight train ride from Bangkok) and head west to Chiang Khan, only slightly livelier than its near-namesake Chiang Khong. The reason I like this route so much is because of the laid-back accommodation options (try the guesthouses in Sangkhom and you'll see what I mean).

But wherever you choose, you'll always have the sight of that lazy brown river to soothe you, and plenty of fascinating river life to keep you intrigued: fishermen and gold-panners, kids swimming and farmers working on the river banks, Laotian women on their way to visit Thai markets or traders doing a spot of black marketeering. Sit back, grab an ice-cold beer and let it all drift by.

Snack at a Night Market

THE THAIS ARE INCORRIGIBLE SNACKERS. And considering their snacks are so tasty, it's not surprising. Wherever you go, you'll find street stalls selling noodles, fruit, sate or rice dishes, fresh fruit drinks or savory pancakes. When the sun goes down, entire streets are devoted to food and fruit stalls. These night markets are the places to head for to find the cheapest and often most genuine local specialties, to find a snack to keep you going until dinner-time or just to mix and mingle with the local people.

The food carts are usually trundled into place around 5 or 6 PM. The vendors quickly start firing up their woks in time to serve the stream of customers heading home by motorbike who simply drive right up to the stall to place their order. You can always tell the best cook by the crowd waiting to be served. Each stall specializes in a certain drink or dish — just peer at what's cooking to find out. Tables with stools or benches are usually provided for those who want a sit-down snack, but don't expect any five-star surroundings: more likely than not, you'll be sitting by the gutter beside buckets of washing-up water. Still, who cares when the food is so good, and when you've got the whole night to keep trying more!

A typical array of dishes in a Bangkok street market. Some of Thailand's tastiest (and cheapest) fare is found in markets such as this.

YOUR CHOICE

You can stay overnight at most of the parks — for information and advance reservations, telephone the **Forestry Department's National Park Division** in Bangkok ((02) 579-0529 — though the usually spartan bungalows, sleeping at least five people, don't entice you to stay too long (you can camp if you prefer). Frustratingly for serious independent hikers, both maps and well-marked trails are often in scarce supply at the parks (park rangers can sometimes be hired as guides for a few days). But as long as you don't visit during Thai holidays or weekends, when local Thais love to come on group visits, there's certainly plenty of peace and plenty of space to roam.

The Great Outdoors

When Bangkok's heat and traffic get too much, or Chiang Mai's shopping has exhausted you completely, it's time to head for the nearest national park.

Thailand has over 60 national parks and some 30 wildlife sanctuaries scattered all over the country so you'll never be far from one of them. Together these protected areas cover over 25,000 sq km or 9,500 sq miles (that's some 11 percent of the country's total land area) and host an enormous variety of flora and fauna. You're unlikely to come across the most endangered species — tigers or clouded leopards, Malayan tapirs or Asiatic black bears — but encounters with hornbills or gibbons, wild elephant or barking deer, dolphins or turtles are still a delightful possibility.

Parks to Head For

In central Thailand, the most popular parks are **Khao Yai** and **Erawan** (both fairly easy to reach from Bangkok), much loved by Thais for their waterfalls as much as for their wildlife. In the north, head for **Doi Inthanon** if you want a quick escape from Chiang Mai, or Phu Kradung, near Loei, for a more unusual hiking and climbing adventure. One of the best, though least-visited national parks in southern Thailand, well endowed with both trails and accommodation (in privately-run bungalow resorts), is the **Khao Sok National Park**, just a couple of hours from Surat Thani or Phuket. You can spend days walking through

OPPOSITE: Some of the 40 forested islands which make up the protected Ang Thong Marine National Park near Koh Samui. ABOVE: A floating sampan food stall.

its cicada-throbbing jungle on the fairly well-trodden trails but for tours of its more remote and challenging attractions (monumental caves and rough jungle wilderness) contact any of the resorts about their own guided trips or the Phuket-based **Siam Safari** (/FAX (076) 280107.

Some of the island Marine National Parks have sadly fallen prey to rampant development for the sake of the tourist dollar — Koh Phi Phi and Koh Samet are the most-often cited examples — but others, like the Andaman Sea's Surin and Similan Islands and the Koh Tarutao archipelago are still extraordinarily beautiful and unspoilt areas, renowned for their fabulous underwater attractions. Various diving outfits in Phuket often arrange short trips or longer luxury cruises to the Similans, for example, **Siam Diving Center** ((076) 330936 FAX (076) 330608, but Koh Tarutao (officially only open to visitors from November to May) is much farther off the beaten track and requires determination to reach.

Of course, you don't have to stick to national parks to find your piece of the great outdoors. Hiking in northern Thailand's mountainous wilderness is one of the most popular activities in the country, with organized trips from Chiang Mai, Chiang Rai and Mae Hong Son or from up-and-coming smaller places such as Thaton, Mae Salong or Pai. Although hiking on your own in these areas isn't recommended (there are no detailed maps, the villagers may not even speak Thai, let alone English, and the border with Myanmar is still fairly sensitive), you can easily find a trekking outfit to arrange your own personal trip. Ornithologists, on the other hand, should probably head for southern Thailand where several inland lakes and waterways attract dozens of species of Southeast Asian waterfowl, particularly during November and December. The Khukhut Waterbird Sanctuary and the Thaleh Noi Waterbird Sanctuary are two of the best spots (easily accessible from Songkhla and Phattalung respectively); at both places you can hire a boat for about 150 baht an hour to take

you across the reed-carpeted waters to glimpse bitterns and herons, fishing eagles and falcons, plovers or sandpipers. The Krabi area is another hot bird-watching location (here's your chance to spot the rare Gurney's pitta): check out the **bird book** in Krabi's **May & Mark Restaurant** ((075) 612562, for all the details.

Botanists hardly have to head anywhere in particular to find their outdoor dream. With its tropical climate and ample rainfall, Thailand can provide floral spectacles with enviable ease. Even in Bangkok, there are several rewarding places for plant-lovers, including Rama IX Park, which has been planted by some of Thailand's leading landscape gardeners, and Suan Pakkad Palace where the spacious grounds feature numerous rare plants from all over the world. Beyond Bangkok, head 32 km (20 miles) west to the Rose Garden, or to the Nong Nooch Orchid Wonderland near Pattaya. Up north, in the temperate Mae Sa Valley near Chiang Mai, there are several orchid nurseries, each displaying over 100 species of native and hybrid orchids, while in Chiang Mai itself you can roam happily in the Huai Kaeo Arboretum.

Sporting Spree

Water Sports

With 2,710 km (1,693 miles) of coastline, hundreds of islands, ideal temperatures and year-round accessibility, water sports inevitably top the list of Thailand's sporting activities. Snorkeling and scuba diving are the most popular and rewarding ways to enjoy the fabulous coral blue seas but with the exception of surfing you'll find Thailand's waters suitable for pretty much everything else, too — sailing or sea canoeing, windsurfing or big game fishing, luxury cruising or water-skiing. The Andaman Sea and the Gulf of Thailand have alternating monsoon seasons, so when the diving or sailing isn't at its best on one side you'll find conditions perfect on the other.

Pattaya is a safe bet year-round, and it's here that you'll find the greatest choice of **scuba diving** outfits. In addition to those mentioned in TOP SPOTS page 11, try checking out **Dave's Divers' Den**

((038) 221860 FAX 221618, and **The Scuba Professionals** ((038) 429901. Pattaya's southern beach resort of **Jomtien** is also one of the best places in Thailand for **windsurfing** facilities — the Siam World Cup championships (part of the Asian World Cup Series) have been held here several times. As on Phuket's western beaches, another major windsurfing spot, the windiest times are from November to January, with the waves sometimes reaching a meter and a half or more and the winds racing up to 25 knots. Novices, beware!

Pattaya is also the number one base for **sailors**, with marinas and clubs offering secure year-round moorings and sailing trips. Another big attraction is the close accessibility of the delightful **Koh Chang archipelago** and **Ang Thong National Park islands** — just a day's sail away. Hobie Cats and Prindles can be rented for about 600 baht an hour. Try **Surf House**

OPPOSITE: Sun, sand and coconut shade on Phi Phi Island, one of the most beautiful in southern Thailand. BELOW: Once you've discovered Koh Samui it may be hard to leave.

International ((038) 231029, at Jomtien Beach, or **Wong Amat Hotel** ((038) 426999 in north Pattaya; in Phuket, contact **South East Asia Yacht Charter** ((076) 321292. Pattaya keeps **big-game fishers** happy, too, with the chance to catch sharks, eagle rays, barracuda and sailfish from well-equipped chartered boats (expect to pay around 6,000 baht for the day), although Phuket is really the place to head for if you're serious about your sailfish (July and August are peak biting times). High season for marlin and tuna in the Andaman Sea area is from late-November to May — 200 kg (440 lb) marlins are out there waiting for you.

Divers have a huge choice of places to go. In addition to those areas mentioned in TOP SPOTS, experienced divers looking for novelty may want to consider the less-touristy **Koh Chang National Park archipelago** of 47 islands (November to April is their best time) or the **islands in the Andaman Sea** off the Trang coastline. **Koh Phi Phi** (check out **Scuba Schools International** (/FAX (01) 723-0484), and **Koh Tao** now also have a mushrooming scuba diving business, as well as Koh Tao's jumping-off point on the peninsula, **Chumphon** (the peaceful **Cabana Resort** ((077) 501990 FAX (077) 504442, at Thung Wua Laen Beach, offers qualified diving courses of NAUI and PADI).

Sea canoeing is one of Thailand's more recent water adventures, best done around **Phang Nga Bay, Koh Tarutao** and the **Krabi coastline** where collapsed cave systems in the limestone islands and cliffs offer fantastic fairy-tale worlds at low tide, accessible only by sea canoe. In Krabi, contact **Sea Canoe** ((075) 612173.

Golf
Back on land, golf rates as Thailand's most popular sport among visitors. It's got a long tradition in the country — the first courses were laid out under Royal patronage in the early 1900s. There are now over 50 superb 18-hole courses throughout the country, many created by famous international designers such as Robert Trent Jones and Jack Nicklaus, and often located in exquisitely scenic surroundings. You'll find some of the best in or near **Bangkok, Pattaya, Hua Hin, Rayong, Kanchanaburi, Chiang Mai, Chiang Rai** and **Phuket**. Pattaya alone has some nine courses within 50 km (31 miles) of town (contact **Cherry Tree Golf Tours** ((038) 422385, for organized outings). You might also want to check out Thai Airways International's program of Royal Orchid Golf Holidays which are designed to offer golfers the opportunity to play a selection of the country's finest courses, some of which are usually only available to club members.

Caving, Rock-climbing and River Rafting
For the adventurous and young-at-heart, how about something slightly more unusual — caving, rock-climbing or river rafting? All are available in the new adventure heartland of northern Thailand, near **Soppong** and **Pai** — a four-hour bus ride west of Chiang Mai. Thanks to Frenchman Guy Gorias who operates **Thai Adventure** (/FAX (053) 699111, you can spin down the Pai River to Mae Hong Son in high-tech rubber rafts (July to December only), catching the **Pai Kit gorges** en route and the 20-cascade **Susa Waterfall**. Speleologists will be knocked out by the little-known area nearby known as Pangmapa which has hundreds of kilometers of caves and subterranean passageways, several easily accessible to novices, others for experienced cavers only. For more information, contact John Spies who operates **Cave Lodge** (radio (536-11711 ext. 822) in Soppong. Rock-climbers can scramble around happily both here and even better down south, on the Krabi coastline's spectacular Laem Phra Nang limestone cliffs. Contact Phra Nang Adventures here at Railae Bay Bungalows for half-day or full-day rock climbing and abseiling courses.

The Open Road

Most people who come to Thailand have two goals in mind: to go trekking in the north and swimming in the south. You

can easily do both, even on a short visit, thanks to the country's excellent air, train and bus services. But if you're on a return visit, or keen to have a more in-depth experience of the country you'll want to take things slower, with lots of diversions en route. The itineraries I'm suggesting here can be used by both kinds of visitors: just pick and choose what you have time for.

A detailed 1:1,500,000 map is essential for serious touring — I've found Nelles slightly more accurate than Bartholomew, though no map can keep up to date with Thailand's rapidly changing landscape. Car or motorbike drivers might also find the bilingual *Thailand Highway Map* (1:1,000,000) useful. In the northern Chiang Rai area, be sure to pick up a copy of V. Hongsombud's excellent little map, packed with information, like his one of the Krabi area in the south. And motorbike riders exploring the north will find David Unkovich's booklets (*Motorcycle Touring in North Thailand, The Mae Hong Son Loop*, etc.) full of handy advice and route suggestions. Don't worry if you can't find these publications in Bangkok bookshops — they're usually widely available in the area concerned.

The North

So, let's consider the north first. A flight or overnight train ride from Bangkok gets you to Chiang Mai quickest but for those with more time it's worth considering a stop-over at **Sukhothai**, about half way to Chiang Mai. Thailand's first capital, flourishing during the 13th and 14th centuries, Sukhothai symbolizes the country's Golden Age of art and architecture. Today, its **Historical Park** of ruined Buddhist *wats* (temples), statues and monuments, set amidst lotus ponds and forested hills, are one of the kingdom's cultural highlights. Accommodation is easy to find in the new town of Sukhothai while the train station at Phitsanulok is just an hour's bus ride away. For culture buffs who want more, base yourself in Sukhothai for day-trips by bus to nearby **Si Satchanalai** and **Kampheng Phet** — both sites of ancient cities with wonderfully atmospheric ruins.

Once you're in **Chiang Mai**, there are some excellent touring options. One of the simplest and most popular is to head

Getting around Nathon, Koh Samui's main town, on a *songthaew* pick-up truck.

north on Highway 107 for **Thaton** (direct buses take about five hours so be sure to get an early start), then ride a long-tail boat down the Kok River to Chiang Rai — still an exciting experience despite the number of travelers who do it. But for those with time on their hands, I'd heartily recommend lingering in Thaton a while to enjoy its relaxing riverside location (several guesthouses are situated right by the river) and still uncommercialized trekking experiences: a couple of hilltribe families in the area have recently opened up their homes to visitors and offer short guided treks as well as a unique insight to village life. For more information, pick up the useful little booklet, *The Road from Thaton to Mae Salong from Wat Thaton* (you'll see the Buddhist statues on the hill above the village), which was written by an American resident at Wat Thaton.

Mae Hong Son is an increasingly popular destination in the north, too. The capital of Thailand's most northwest province, surrounded by mountains and set deep in a valley, it still feels delightfully remote, though there are now direct flights four times a day from Chiang Mai, and the trekking industry is picking up fast. Slow-moving travelers can enjoy a rollicking seven hours by bus over the hills from Chiang Mai to get to Mae Hong Son, with a choice of north route (Highway 1095) or south (Highway 108). I'd recommend the northern one for adventurers since there are a couple of worthwhile stopovers half way: small and peaceful Pai with its trekking and river-rafting options, and nearby Soppong for its awesome network of caves. Both places have guesthouses and restaurants geared to the international traveler.

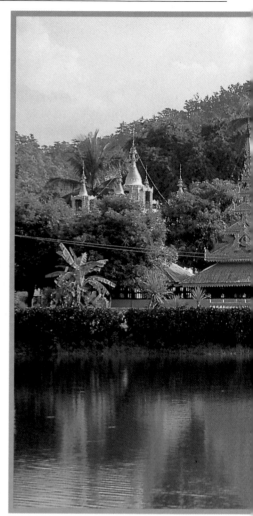

Around Bangkok

If the lure of the sea grows too powerful to ignore you can always fly back to Bangkok and hop on a bus to **Pattaya**, an easy two hours east by bus. Further along the eastern seaboard, following Highway 3, you'll find less crowded seaside options — the island of **Koh Samet**, near Rayong, is one option. Farther still is the far less developed island

of **Koh Chang**, an hour or two by ferry from Laem Ngop, near Trat. And in the opposite direction, heading west from Bangkok, then south down the peninsula, is the royal resort of **Hua Hin**, just four hours by train or bus from the capital and still a relaxing hideaway, despite increasing development.

The South

But undoubtedly the biggest and best choice for seaside escapes is much farther south. Leading the pack in popularity and facilities are the islands of **Phuket** in the Andaman Sea and **Koh Samui** in the Gulf. Both can be reached by direct flights from Bangkok and in the case of Phuket, from several overseas destinations, too. But

dawdling down the coast by train or bus along Highway 4 gives you the chance for some serious sand-and-sea study en route. After Hua Hin you could consider a cultural stop-over in **Prachuap Khiri Khan** before reaching **Chumphon**. This is the jumping-off point for a popular backpackers' island resort, **Koh Tao**, from where you can also reach **Koh Phangan** and **Koh Samui**. Following the western coast to Phuket, there are the fabulous Surin and Similan Islands to tempt you — though these are in fact more easily accessible on organized tours from Phuket.

From either Phuket or Surat Thani (the jumping-off point for Koh Samui), you can hop on a bus to explore the **western**

Krabi coastline — a spectacular area of limestone cliffs and islands similar to Phang-Nga Bay near Phuket but far less touristy. Rock-climbers, snorkellers and beach bums could get held up here for weeks. If culture calls, there's **Nakhon Si Thammarat** on the eastern coast of the peninsula (134 km or 83 miles south of Surat Thani by Highway 401), an ancient city which boasts a fine museum and unique handicrafts. Keep heading south down Highways 41 and Highway 4 for the raunchy nightlife of **Hat Yai** near the Malay border, or the old-fashioned charm

The lakeside Wat Chong Klang temple, at the picturesque heart of Mae Hong Son.

of Songkhla. Thai Airways can whiz you back to Bangkok from Hat Yai in just over an hour (trains take 16 hours).

The Northeast

Take a glance at the map and you'll see one huge area that's gone unmentioned: the **Northeast**. This poor and drought-ravaged region generally has less to offer the tourist than other areas of the country but there are a couple of itineraries that may well appeal to you if you like to keep away from the crowds. From Bangkok, take a train northeast to **Nakhon Ratchasima** to start a tour of 11th- to 13th-century Khmer temple ruins: the most famous is nearby at **Phimai** but the impressive **Phanom Rung** is also easy to reach from other stops on the eastern rail line — Buriram or Surin. If this dip into the undiscovered northeast makes you hanker for more, keep heading east to **Ubon Ratchathani** before taking buses north along Highway 212 which follows the Mekong River border all the way to Nong Khai. En route, be sure to stop at lovely little **That Phanom**, famous for its Lao-style chedi. A shorter, easier itinerary in this area starts at **Nong Khai** and follows the Mekong River some 180 km (113 miles) west on Route 2195 to **Chiang Khan** — an ideal route for motorbike jaunts, or just for dawdling as slowly as you want.

Backpacking

Ever since the first backpackers "discovered" Thailand in the late 1960s and early 1970s, the country has been delighting those who are short on cash but well-endowed with a sense of adventure. Of course, things have changed: the deserted beach in Phuket where I camped under the stars ten years ago has now been developed into a vast five-star resort. And that little-known spot on the map — Mae Hong Son — which took me days of exhiliratingly hard travel to reach and days of deluxe silence to leave now has direct flights from Chiang Mai and a Holiday Inn hotel.

But as a backpacker at heart, I still love Thailand. For a start, you can travel remarkably cheaply — from around US$20 a day or less if you don't mind simple guesthouses (no air-conditioning, and often shared bathrooms), simple food (ah, *khao pat* — fried rice — again!) and local transport. Even the cheapest beach resort or town hotel (as little as 100 baht a double room) is usually kept very clean (if it isn't, keep looking: dirty hostelries are the exception). And another plus: you get to meet the local owners (the family often live in the same premises) on a much more direct level than if you were staying in a large hotel. With prices as low as this, you can also afford to splash out another hundred baht occasionally for your own private bathroom or sea view. Bear in mind, however, that the cheapest rooms are often hard to find at popular destinations such as Chiang Mai and the southern beach resorts during the high season (December to February). Prices can rocket during this time, too. In low season, you can bargain prices way down — but you may also find many of the smaller beach bungalow outfits closed.

Youth hostels are so few and far between in Thailand that you can probably forget them as convenient cheap goals to head for (though I strongly recommend the youth hostel in Phitsanulok, a delightfully artistic hideaway with a huge outdoor teak *sala* (hall) set amidst a rambling garden, and bedrooms featuring antique fans and teak beds). However, camping is well worth considering at the national parks — a far more attractive option than the park's depressing concrete huts (costing around 550 baht and sleeping up to five). You'll only be charged five baht to camp (or around 70 baht if you want to rent a tent); if you're on an island national park you don't even need the tent. Just lie on the beach under the stars and be lulled to sleep by the sound of the surf. Backpackers heaven!

Eating cheaply in Thailand is no problem, either. To get an initial idea of what's available, check out the first night market you come to (see TOP SPOTS page 18). Eating here can provide you with a three-course meal, taken from different food stalls, for less than 60 baht. You'll soon discover that by sticking to foreigners' fare all the time you'll actually be missing out on some of Asia's tastiest, cheapest cuisine. Even simple local restaurants won't break the bank (unless you hit the alcohol: beers aren't one of Thailand's bargains). Many of these restaurants specialize in certain dishes — rice and meat or noodles or curries — but unless it's a seafood restaurant prices will always be reasonable. The only places where you may have to pay slightly higher prices than the locals are at beach resorts (the cuisine tends to be geared to *farang* tastes here, too) or in obviously touristy areas of Bangkok or other cities.

The cheapest ways to get around the country are by train (second or third class), local bus, *songthaew* and *tuk tuk*. Since there's usually little difference in price between the train and bus it's worth choosing, wherever possible, the safest and most comfortable one (even if it's not the quickest) — and that's the train. For long journeys, for instance, from Bangkok to Chiang Mai, Nong Khai or Hat Yai, the overnight sleepers on the train are definitely worth the extra cost (be sure to book ahead in high season). Songthaews and tuk tuks are the cheapest and most convenient transport for short hops — and the most fun, since you'll invariably be crammed in with a crowd of locals. Chartering your own songthaew is worthwhile financially only if you're in a group and know exactly where you want the driver to take you.

Renting your own motorbike, on the other hand, is a very attractive option for backpackers and one that's increasingly popular, especially in the north of the country around Chiang Mai and Chiang Rai where there's an extensive road network, splendid scenery and easily accessible destinations to head for. Here and in other popular tourist areas you'll find it easy to rent a bike for about 120 baht a day for a 100 cc Honda Dream scooter or 450 baht a day for a 250 cc off-road machine. Note that insurance

coverage is rarely offered and that the condition of the bikes can often be poor. You probably won't have to show an international driver's license, though legally it is required. Jeep hire is another attractive possibility, especially in resorts such as Koh Samui and Phuket, though at about 1,200 baht a day it's hardly a choice for budget-bracket backpackers.

Still, who needs private transport to find the hottest spots around? You can party day and night without moving from your beach if you base yourself in lively resorts like Pattaya or Phuket. In Bangkok, Khao San Road is the hub of the backpackers' heartland, crammed with cheap guesthouses, travel agencies, stalls selling cheap cotton clothes and cassettes and cafes offering Western travelers' favorite fare (banana pancakes, muesli and yogurt, fresh brown bread and non-stop music) while in Chiang Mai, backpackers throng around the Thaphae Gate area. The most outrageous, far-out party place going is Haat Rin beach on the island of Koh Pha Ngan. While

From jewelry to Buddhist artifacts, pet parakeets to houseplants, the choice is yours at the Bangkok weekend market.

neighboring Koh Samui grows ever more respectable, the radical New Age traveling fringe have made full moon nights on Haat Rin into a notorious bacchanalia. There are constant rumors that the police will put a stop to it all, but last I heard, the party was still swinging.

Living It Up

Just imagine: you're floating on calm water to the faint sounds of a whale's call at the edge of the Gulf of Thailand. Minutes later you're gazing out over an immaculate Japanese-style garden, dipping your feet into a Jacuzzi and Kneipp foot bath while your masseuse waits to un-tense your muscles with a faint aromatic touch of lavender oil. It may not be your idea of living it up, but there's no denying you get deluxe pampering at **Chiva-Som** ((032) 536536 FAX (032) 511154, Southeast Asia's first international-class spa and health resort which opened in 1994 just outside **Hua Hin**. At US$400 a day (that's including meals but minus any treatments) it ranks as one of Thailand's most indulgent hostelries. But it's certainly not the only place in the country to boast such costly luxury. Indeed, Chiva-Som's strict and sophisticated health regime (no alcoholic binges allowed here!) may be just what you need after living it up elsewhere in Thailand.

Bangkok, for starters, has three of the world's top hotels: the classic and long-established **Oriental** (often ranked as the world's best), the **Regent** and the **Shangri-La**, all with fabulous facilities and restaurants. You'll need to dig deep in your pockets to stay here (room prices start at around US$200) and the experience will spoil you for anything else, but it will certainly show you how Thais can do things in style. Moving south to **Hua Hin**, there's another classic hostelry, the former Railway Hotel, first built in the 1920s. Now called the **Hotel Sofitel Central Hua Hin** it's been restored to all its former colonial-style glory, with shining teak paneling, slowly rotating ceiling fans and spacious balconies and

salons (choose the US$120 rooms in the old wing for the most nostalgic atmosphere or the beach bungalows across the road for a cozier setting).

You'll have no trouble living it up in **Phuket**, Thailand's premier island resort. There are many deluxe hotels such as **Le Meridien Phuket, Chedi Phuket, Phuket Yacht Club, Boathouse Inn, Club Med, Sheraton Grande Laguna Beach**, the **Banyan Tree** and **Dusit Laguna Resort** offer ing international-class facilities for around 3,000 to 5,000 baht a night, while the **Thavorn Palm Beach Hotel** can boast suites for as much as 17,000 baht a night. For something truly special you could splash out at **Amanpuri Resort**, holiday home to celebrities and VIPs who pay

at least 9,000 baht a day for exclusivity. Even little **Koh Phi Phi Don** island has its own sophisticated brand of beach living (hotel rooms with all the trimmings or delightful garden bungalows) at **PP Islands Cabana**, a perfect hideaway for the jet set traveler. And bagging the best spot on Krabi's spectacular **Laem Phra Nang** headland is the discreet but deluxe **Dusit Rayavadee** whose individual circular villas (from US$350 up) are the poshest you'll find on the Krabi coastline.

Up north, in **Chiang Mai**, big spenders should make a beeline for the **Westin Chiang Mai** (rooms start at around US$160) or the **Dusit Island Resort** in **Chiang Rai** which is located on its own island in the Kok River. And if the idea of sleeping rough on a typical hilltribe trek puts you off, consider doing it in style with a soft adventure organized by **Track of the Tiger**, a company based at Maekok River Lodge in Thaton which can guarantee ice and lemon in your gin and tonic at the end of the day.

Living It Up at Night

Living it up at night-time is best done, of course, in **Bangkok** and major tourist resorts such as **Pattaya** and **Phuket**. Bangkok's hottest discos are in top hotels such as the **Shangri-La** and **Dusit Thani**, though the celebrity crowd like to patronize **Diana's** off Charoen Krung Road and the young set the high-tech disco scene of **Paradise** on Arun Amarin Road or **NASA Spacedrome** on Ramkhamhaeng Road. All these places only get truly bopping around 11 PM.

For seriously decadent nightlife, head for Pattaya where dozens of girlie bars pack Beach Road. Discos here are very glitzy (check out the vast Palladium and its crowd capacity of 6,000), though for something truly Pattayan in spirit you shouldn't miss the glamorous transvestite shows at **Alcazar** or **Tiffany's**. On the southern island resorts, the posh hotels all offer their own variety of discos or live music, while open-air bars and nightly videos keep the backpackers happy in the cheaper bungalow outfits. **Chiang Mai's** most popular evening rendezvous is the

OPPOSITE LEFT: Riverside luxury at the Bangkok Shangri-la Hotel. RIGHT: Although often geared specifically for tourists, classical Thai dance performances such as this one at the Bangkok Regent Hotel, are still worth seeing. ABOVE: Book a boathouse and sail away from it all in this unusual villa at the Resort Hotel on Koh Samui.

Riverside Rim Ping on Charoenrat Road; start here before moving on to **The Brasserie** nearby for its late night live Sixties music. If heavy bopping is more your scene, join the crowd at the flashy **Biosphere Spacedrome** disco or the popular **Crystal Cave** disco at the Empress Hotel.

Dining in Style

Deluxe dining is one of the finest ways to live it up in Thailand, especially when the settings are distinctly and elegantly Thai. In **Bangkok**, the dinner theatres where classical Thai dance is performed is a unique experience: the best (and most expensive) is the Oriental Hotel's **Sala Rim Nam** ((02) 437-6211. If you prefer the emphasis to be on the food, try **Bussaracum** ((02) 246-2147, which specializes in traditional recipes once served to Thai royalty. **Chiang Mai**'s top venues for a splurge include **The Gallery** ((053) 248601, whose riverside setting in a beautifully converted old Chinese temple is complemented by a gallery of contemporary pottery, paintings and curiosities. On a similar but more folksy theme is the riverside **Tha-Nam Restaurant** ((053) 275125, a huge teak pavilion chock-a-block with carvings, antiques and rural artifacts.

At the seaside resorts such as Hua Hin, Pattaya, Phuket, Koh Phi Phi or Koh Samui, seafood restaurants are obviously your best bet for wining and dining the

evening away. **Phuket**'s **The Boathouse Wine & Grill** ((076) 330015, actually offers all kinds of Thai (and European) dishes but with such distinction it out-classes almost everywhere else on the island (and its wine cellar has to be seen to be believed). On **Koh Phi Phi**, you'll have to go early to **Mama's** ((075) 620078, to be sure of the best choice of fresh seafood displayed on a table outside, while Hua Hin has so many seafood restaurants you're spoiled for choice: the open-air, seafront **Saeng Thai** ((032) 512144, guarantees a sea breeze and fish of all kinds, from lobsters and crabs to kingfish and perch. In **Pattaya**, queen of the seaside resorts, you'll pay far more dearly for seafood but there's no denying the choice is fantastic. Stick to south Pattaya or Jomtien beach for the best seafood restaurants (for example, **Lobster Pot** on Beach Road or **Nang Nual** in Jomtien).

Family Fun

Child-loving Thais make holidays here heaven for parents: in restaurants and hotels you'll find your exhausting rascals whisked off your hands by doting waiters and waitresses, to be returned at the end of your meal happy and well-fed. And the country itself has a knack of pleasing all ages — beaches with shallow seas keep toddlers content while water sports of all kinds challenge the most adrenalin-charged teenager. Hiking and elephant-riding in the wilds bring out the best in kids of all ages, though packaged amusement parks are also at hand if you don't want to risk the adventure scenario.

Cities are inevitably the most demanding places for keeping everyone happy. In **Bangkok**, cultural sightseeing, traffic and noise can test the patience of the most placid child. Give them a break by taking them to **Dusit Zoo** (there's a lake in the middle of the zoo grounds where you can rent boats) or the famous **Snake Farm** where your girls can prove their bravery by posing with a python. During the kite-flying season (February to April), the place to head for on a Sunday is

Lumphini Park or **Sanam Luang** where you can fly your own kite (sold for about 60 baht each) or just watch the experts. Thai kites are incredibly complex and beautiful works of art and the annual kite competition held at Sanam Luang (check the date with TAT) will keep the kids spellbound for hours. Another unique Bangkok happening that's worth including in your schedule is the weekend **Chatuchak Market**, a vast affair with something to interest everyone (the pet section is always a hit with youngsters). More familiar amusement parks can be found at **Magic Land**, near Central Plaza Hotel, and **Siam Water Park** in the eastern suburb of Minburi, where the water slides are great for cooling off. There's a **Safari World** nearby, too, which features tigers, giraffes and zebras as well as one of Asia's largest aviaries with over 4,000 birds. On the same theme, but more popular, is the **Samphran Elephant Ground & Zoo**, 32 km (20 miles) west of Bangkok and often included in tours to the nearby Rose Garden tourist cultural complex. Samphran features both elephant and

crocodile shows as well as other shows at weekends.

Another day-trip excursion which will appeal to older children is the **Ancient City**, 25 km (15 miles) southeast of Bangkok. It features smaller versions of Thailand's most famous wats and palaces as well as artists making traditional crafts. And a fun, easy trip for this age group right within Bangkok itself is to take a fast, noisy long-tail boat ride along the river and *khlongs* (canals) of the city. Ask at the piers (the one south of the Royal Orchid Sheraton is recommended) about organizing your own private trip or book a tour at your hotel.

Beyond Bangkok, at **Pattaya**, you've got the whole gamut of water sports (see SPORTING SPREE page 23) to wear down the kids' energy. Day tours to nearby attractions are other possibilities: the nearby **Mini Siam** is similar to Bangkok's

OPPOSITE: Dining out at one of Bangkok's open-air restaurants on the banks of the Chao Phraya River. BELOW: Spoilt for choice: a beautifully-landscaped pool at one of Koh Samui's resort hotels, backed by the crystal clear sea.

animal-watching towers in the hope of spotting a tiger. We didn't, of course, but the sound of the gibbons from the surrounding forest and the rustling of the grasslands below us was enough excitement to keep us all awake for hours. The next day, walking along a trail bordered by tall elephant grass, we heard unmistakably large movements; the children yelled, some wild deer leapt into view and the unmistakable large animal moved stealthily away.

Cultural Kicks

Golden Buddhas and intricate frescoes, gleaming *chedis* and towering stupas, marble floors and enameled pillars — they all come together to create a stunning impact in many of Thailand's Buddhist temples. The kingdom's cultural highlights are nearly always to be found in these wats, though several outstanding provincial national museums should also be on your cultural itinerary, as well as ancient Khmer monuments, ruined cities and a couple of private homes and palaces which are treasure-troves of rare and gorgeous artifacts.

Ancient City while the **Khao Khieo "Open Zoo"**, 30 km (18 miles) to the north, features 130 species of birds and 38 different mammals in an attractive forested area. The **Nong Nooch Orchid Wonderland**, 18 km (11 miles) to the south, may not sound immediately appealing to the younger generation but there's actually quite a variety of attractions here, including a small zoo, lakes (with boating) and a twice-daily cultural show which puts on performances of Thai dancing, Thai boxing and even an elephant show.

Ah, elephants. You can't leave Thailand without giving the kids a ride on one (or two, or three...). See RIDE AN ELEPHANT, page 12, for an idea of where to find your ideal elephant. Or consider going to one of the national parks, such as **Khao Yai**, where there's a chance of seeing elephants in the wild. Staying overnight at these parks (see THE GREAT OUTDOORS, page 21) can turn into a great family adventure: the park huts, though unattractive and spartan, can usually sleep up to five (bring your own food supplies), or you can even rent a tent. One of my own most memorable trips with a family of youngsters was staying overnight in one of Khao Yai's

Starting in **Bangkok**, nearly everyone gets a cultural kick out of the **Temple of the Emerald Buddha (Wat Phra Kheo)** and adjoining **Grand Palace**. Housing the tiny but highly-revered Emerald Buddha (it's actually made from a form of jade), the Wat Phra Kheo is a fabulously bright and glittering affair, from its green and orange roof and gaudy guardian demons to its tiled and muralled walls sparkling with colored glass. Originally the private temple for the royal family, Wat Phra Kheo is considered the holiest Buddhist temple in the land — you'll find Thai devotees paying their respects here with the utmost seriousness. The nearby palace buildings open to the public — mostly

ABOVE: Bangkok's delightful Wat Arun, commonly known as the Temple of Dawn, is named after Aruna, the Indian god of the dawn, and is adorned with thousands of pieces of porcelain. OPPOSITE: The striking 14th-century *chedis* of Wat Phra Sri Samphet in the ancient city of Ayutthaya.

audience halls and ceremonial pavilions — epitomize traditional Thai architecture with their soaring and sweeping rooflines and gilded dragon adornments. Feast your eyes as long as you can for you won't see anything else in Thailand as sumptuous as all this.

Nearby **Wat Pho** is a delightful, rambling contrast. Its highlight, the gigantic 46-m- (150-ft)-long reclining Buddha, is definitely worth a visit, but so too are the surrounding grounds which though packed with religious treasures are charmingly unkempt and homely. Several other wats in the capital — notably **Wat Arun** and **Wat Traimit** — should be on your list if you're a serious culture hound, but for a simple taste of what's best, I'd recommend leaving the temples and heading for **Jim Thompson's House**. Once belonging to the American silk entrepreneur who died in mysterious circumstances in 1967 (no-one has yet solved the riddle), the house is the sort you'd yearn to have yourself: a beautiful complex of gleaming teak walls and floors (it's actually a combination of six different houses which Thompson gathered from around the country), set in a quiet and overgrown garden. But the real cultural

delight is Thompson's personal collection of Thai arts and crafts, rare Buddhist pieces and traditional Thai paintings — some of the best in the kingdom.

On a similar note, but grander in scale, is the **Suan Pakkad Palace Museum**. Once the home of Princess Chumbot, the five traditional Thai houses, set in a lovely landscaped garden, are miniature museums of Thai art and antiques. The most outstanding is the Ayutthaya-period lacquer pavilion, wallpapered with intricate gold-leaf murals on a black lacquered background.

Moving out of Bangkok, **Ayutthaya** itself should be first on your cultural itinerary as you trace the kingdom's history through its art and architecture. Now a complex of atmospheric ruins, this once-glorious capital flourished for 400 years, from 1351 to 1767 before it was ravaged by the invading Burmese. If you find the extensive ruins too much to take in all at once you might prefer the similar, but smaller **Historical Park of Sukhothai**, an earlier capital located some 450 km (281 miles) north of Bangkok whose elegant Buddhist statues and temples epitomize the golden age of Thai art and architecture. Lovers of dreamy ruined sites

can take in more historical graveyards nearby, at **Si Satchanalai** and **Kampheng Phet**, both of which can be considered as satisfying cultural diversions off the highway.

Still heading north, **Chiang Mai** is the obvious north-country goal for major cultural kicks. This ancient city, first established in 1296 as the capital of the Lanna kingdom, boasts over 300 temples, many quite different from any you'll see elsewhere, thanks to Burmese influence: the city was under Burmese control for over 200 years and even after it was recaptured by the Thais in 1775 it hosted wealthy Burmese teak merchants who built many temples. **Wat Phra Singh** is the most important, a fabulous display of typical Lanna architecture (don't miss the murals inside the main hall, either: a fascinating revelation of 19th century life). Then there's the **Wat Chedi Luang** with its huge 60-m (197-ft) *chedi* and the city's oldest temple, **Wat Chiang Man**. All these are must-sees before you strike out to Doi Suthep, the mountain west of the city which is culturally notable for its **Wat Phra That Doi Suthep**, the holiest site in the north. It's a glittering, golden complex focusing attention on the central,

gleaming *chedi* and offering distracting views of the plains below, but if you want to concentrate on the artistic merits of the place be sure to arrive early enough to beat the crowds of tourists and pilgrims.

There's another place in the north which Lanna architecture fans shouldn't miss, and that's the **Wat Phra That Lampang Luang** in Lampang. This imposing walled complex houses simple halls with classic drooping rooflines including one of the oldest wooden buildings in Thailand, more than 400 years old. Over 200 km (125 miles) east of Lampang, **Nan** makes a fascinating and little-known cultural diversion which has an excellent national museum charting the provincial capital's strongly-independent history. But it's the 500-year-old **Wat Phumin** which is the city's cultural gem, featuring bright 19th century murals which range from sober Buddhist tales to raunchy moralistic warnings. Particularly handsome are the

Thailand's capital from 1350 to 1767, Ayutthaya OPPOSITE is a World Heritage Site chock-full of magnificent temples such as these 14th-century examples, Wat Raj Burana and the riverside Wat Phra Maha That ABOVE, opposite Wat Raj Burana.

tattooed men on one wall and the gorgeous women with earrings and fancy hairdos opposite.

In the northeast of Thailand, you'll find it's the ruins of Khmer temples which offer the most intriguing cultural journey. Start at **Phimai**, near **Nakhon Ratchasima**, for the best-restored 11th-century Khmer complex in the land, and head east to **Phanom Rung**, a huge and extraordinary hilltop "stone castle" that has more in common with Cambodia's Angkor Wat than anything in Thailand.

Cultural sites down south aren't as thick on the ground as in the center and north of the country, but a few places stand out: **Phetchaburi** for its temples and hilltop palace; **Chaiya** for its ninth-century Srivijayan-era *chedi*; **Songkhla** for its beautiful Chinese-style national museum building and above all, **Nakhon Si Thammarat** for its highly-revered **Wat Mahathat**, the most important religious shrine in the south. If you're a folk art fan you'll be delighted, too, by the excellent **Southern Folklore Museum** at **Koh Yo** (near Songkhla) and **Nakhon Si Thammarat**'s shadow puppet workship where the leading shadow

puppeteer, **Suchart Subsin**, has opened his workshop to the public.

Shop Till You Drop

Thailand is a wonderful place for shopping because it has just attained that magical point in its development where prices are still low but quality is good. There are, it's true, a lot of goods on sale manufactured specially for tourists and of no great interest. But even discounting these, there's no shortage of excellent things to buy if you know what you're looking for — and sometimes, even if you don't.

Thai silk is available everywhere. For top quality, go to **Jim Thompson's Shop** in **Bangkok**; for lengths of rough country silk, and locally-woven cotton go almost anywhere, especially the north and northeast. The silk factories just outside **Chiang Mai** are a good place to inspect the manufacturing process and buy some of the products on the spot. **Nong Khai** has some great outlets for both Thai and Laotian silk and cotton, either in bolts or made up into clothes, bags and furnishings (especially popular are the triangular-shaped pillows). One particularly good shop in Nong Khai is **Village Weaver Handicrafts** on Prajak Road where you can also see the weavers at the back of the shop.

Thai tailors will run you up a suit or a dress in around twenty-four hours — but don't expect such quick service to result in a quality product. I've seen suits literally fall apart after a few weeks! It's best to allow time for at least two fittings. Try the top end of **Bangkok's Sukhumvit Road** (near the Landmark Hotel) for many Indian-run establishments.

Thailand is celebrated for its **gems** and its **gold**: indeed, it's one of the world's largest gem exporters. Great caution is needed, however, if you intend to assay this market. Bargains can be had — especially in jade, rubies and sapphires — but it's rather more likely *you* will be had if you aren't very well informed in the trade. Even so, it's possible to make sound purchases in this field if you insist the retailer comes along with you to an independent assayer for large purchases, and if you have your purchases itemized in detail on your receipt, with gold quality and weight (for example) entered in full, and "subject to identification and appraisal by a registered gemologist" entered and signed for expensive purchases of gems. The main gem centers, where you'll find dozens of shops and dealers, are **Chanthaburi**, **Mae Sot** and **Kanchanaburi**.

Antiques are very tempting but can lead to complications: officially, you need a license from the Department of Fine Arts (which includes certification from one of three national museums — Bangkok, Chiang Mai or Songkhla) to take an antique out of the country. And strictly speaking, neither old nor new Buddha images ("or fragments thereof") can be exported without permission, although obviously plenty of small, cheap reproductions do end up in tourists' luggage. For more information about the procedures, call **Bangkok's National Museum** on ((02) 224-1370.

Clothes are very cheap in Thailand — cotton shirts, for example, of quite

reasonable quality can be bought for around US$4 as well as fake designer t-shirts, jeans and polo shirts. The places to look for these are the stalls of the street vendors in Bangkok's Silom and Sukhumvit Roads or the street market of Pratunam.

In addition, **craft items** that can best be bought locally include Hill Tribe shoulder bags (those made by the Lahu tribe are considered the best), woodcarvings and wickerwork, silverware and ceramics. You can find all these in **Chiang Mai** (try the night bazaar and shops along Thaphae Road, but be sure to shop around and bargain) as well as other northern destinations such as **Nan** (particularly famous for its silverware and embroidered textiles) and **Sukhothai** (for Thai celadon). More unusual is nielloware — engraved silver inlaid with niello, a lead and silver alloy — which can be found all over the country but especially in **Nakhon Si Thammarat** (try the shops along Thachang Road) where it was first

The most famous place in Bangkok to buy top-quality Thai silk is Jim Thompson's shop OPPOSITE in Surawong Road, although glitzy shopping malls such as the one ABOVE offer a wide choice in all kinds of Thai textiles and antiques.

introduced to Thailand from China centuries ago. Nakhon Si Thammarat also specializes in a very fine basketry technique known as *yaan lipao*, using a local reed to make fashionable bags and baskets. Finally, you can come across attractive and unusual small folk objects almost anywhere. Their attraction is that you'd never have conceived of their existence before you saw them — just keep your eyes open, especially in out-of-the-way places.

Short Breaks

With its efficient transport infrastructure and its varied attractions, Thailand makes a great short-break destination. The most obvious plan is to combine a few days in **Bangkok** with somewhere close but quiet, and preferably by the sea. **Hua Hin** or **Koh Samet** could fit that bill perfectly — both only about four hours from Bangkok. Avoid weekends and public holidays if you can, for these destinations are also popular city breaks for Bangkok residents. **Pattaya** is another obvious quick seaside escape from Bangkok (just two hours away by bus) though it could hardly be called quiet. If you need Pattaya's opposite extreme, head further down the eastern seaboard to undeveloped **Koh Chang** (about five hours by bus, followed by an hour's ferry ride).

Remove the seaside combination and you've got plenty of inland choices. One of the most relaxing and interesting destinations is **Kanchanaburi** (famous for its associatin with *Bridge over the River Kwai*), just three hours west of Bangkok by bus. There's a considerable range of attractions here which can keep you occupied for several days, including the fantastic national park of Erawan and war-time eye-openers such as the Hellfire Pass memorial walk. Or you can simply choose the quietest floating raft guesthouse you can find and sit back to the sound of the frogs and lapping waters of the Kwai Yai River.

Taking advantage of flights from Bangkok, you could whiz as far north as **Chiang Mai** or as far south as **Phuket** in just an hour or so (there are also direct flights to both these destinations from several overseas places such as Hong Kong). From Phuket, there are dozens of nearby day-trip possibilities, including the stunning Phang Nga Bay and the surprisingly untouched Koh Yao Noi, although you're unlikely to get bored very quickly by the beaches and water sports of Phuket itself. **Chiang Mai**, meanwhile, has shopping and temples to detain you for a day or so before the northern hills beckon: you could easily book a one- or two-day trek to give you at least a taste of what's there. Alternatively, strike out independently by taking an early-morning bus to **Thaton**, followed by a long-tail boat down the Kok River to **Chiang Rai**; it's possible to do this in a day, though it's more pleasant to stay overnight in Thaton. Renting a motorbike can give you even more flexibility and choice; you'll find plenty of rental outfits in town (see also THE OPEN ROAD, page 24, for more information on motorbike travel in the north).

For even quieter and more remote destinations, you could always fly to **Mae Hong Son** (there are several flights daily from Chiang Mai as well as a daily flight from Bangkok). This puts you in the hills near the Burmese border where there are options for less commercialized trekking than from Chiang Mai, as well as bamboo rafting and day trips to nearby hill tribe villages. On the other hand, just walking around the small town and to nearby villages is pleasure enough for many visitors — or you could really get away from it all and base yourself at one of the resorts a few kilometers outside town such as the **Rim Nam Klang Doi Resort** ((053) 612142 set in attractive gardens by the Pai River (avoid weekends and holidays when groups of Thais often descend on the place). Given a few more

TOP: Mae Hong Son's Wat Chong Klang temple, founded nearly 200 years ago by the local Shan people, reveals Burmese influences in its design. BOTTOM: Deluxe tranquillity at the Resort Hotel's pool in Koh Samui.

days you could even take the bus back to Chiang Mai (around seven hours), stopping overnight in Pai en route.

Overnight train rides are another handy way to make the most of a short trip to Thailand. One of my favorites is to **Nong Khai**, on the Mekong River border with Laos. You arrive in time for breakfast (I usually go to **Mut-Mee Guesthouse** for its scenic riverside garden setting and excellent menu) and can then decide whether to stay a day or so or head straight out along the river to the simple, sleepy guesthouses of Sangkhom (about three hours west on suitably slow, local buses). The trouble with this itinerary is that it's so relaxing it invariably stretches out to more than a few days, especially if you arrive straight from frenzied Bangkok. But after a while you stop caring: I've met backpackers in Sangkhom who have ended up staying months, despite repeatedly trying to leave!

Equally seductive and difficult to leave are the less-developed southern islands such as **Koh Samui**, **Koh Pha Ngan** and **Koh Tao** (fly to Surat Thani from Bangkok and hop on the first boat out). And if you want to combine these with an inland destination, consider the **Khao Sok National Park**, just a couple of hours by bus from Surat Thani. Here you can walk the jungle trails and listen to the gibbons calling before stepping reluctantly back into the world you left behind.

Festive Flings

Every year the TAT publishes a handy booklet, *Major Events & Festivals* which gives their exact dates and is well worth studying before you plan your trip to see if you can include one of the festivals during your travels.

Asian festivals are something very special. They have a vigor and a reality about them that has disappeared from festivals in the West, with the exception of Christmas. With their colorful outdoor processions, their huge crowds and the general air of something that is at one and the same time great fun and of profound

significance, Thai festivals can hold their own with any in the region.

For the poor especially, they are events that help compensate for the restricted opportunities of life, and they also serve to bind the whole of society together in a way that members of more materialistically advanced cultures, Western and Eastern, may envy.

Because the dates of most festivals are calculated according to a lunar calendar, their dates on the international, Western calendar, which is based on the sun, vary from year to year. Only Songkran, the annual New Year ceremony, together with certain modern anniversaries such as Chakri Day and the royal birthdays, occur on fixed dates on the Western calendar.

COOL SEASON (NOVEMBER TO FEBRUARY)
Surin Elephant Round-up. Not really a festival, this tourist-oriented but spectacular event takes place on the third weekend of November in the northeastern town of Surin, 454 km (281 miles) from Bangkok.

Loi Krathong, "floating the leaf-cup". This is the time when Thais everywhere make little boats containing a candle, a

flower, an incense stick and a coin then send them off on the canals. It falls at full moon on the twelfth lunar month. It's one of the big festivals of the Thai year, a joyful occasion marking the official end of the rainy season, and it's celebrated all over the country.

His Majesty the King's Birthday. December 5 and a national holiday. A large military parade is held in Bangkok two days before when the Royal Guards renew their allegiance to the king.

Constitution Day. This celebrates the signing of the first Thai constitution on December 10, 1932.

Chiang Mai Flower Festival. Featuring floral floats and parades, this festival — designed for tourist's cameras — takes place on the first Friday in February (only in Chiang Mai).

Magha Puja is celebrated in February or early March, on the full moon of the third lunar month. It's essentially a religious festival, with sermons, offerings to monks, and freeing of captive birds. In the evening monks and people carry candles, flowers

and incense in procession three times round the temples. The festival commemorates major events in the Buddha's life and is celebrated throughout Thailand.

HOT SEASON (MARCH TO MAY)
Chakri Day is April 6. This is a national holiday to commemorate the founding of the Chakri (the present) royal dynasty.

Songkran begins on April 13 and lasts three days. Songkran is one of the great Thai festivals, celebrated throughout the country, and memorial services dedicated to departed ancestors are held. It's the traditional New Year and apart from the general hilarity, popular entertainments and a traditional skittles game called *"saba"*, it involves the throwing of water as a sign of purification. It's quite possible

OPPOSITE: Devotees in Ayutthaya celebrating the Magha Puja festival, a religious event commemorating the preaching of the Buddha and celebrated nationwide by carrying lighted candles three times round each town's main wat. ABOVE: Elephants at the annual Elephant Round-up at Surin, a cross between a carnival and a rodeo in which elephants "play footbal", march to music and engage in a test of strength with a team of locals via a tug of war — the outcome of which is never in doubt, of course.

to step off a bus in Bangkok in all innocence and have a large bucket of water emptied over you by total strangers. Fortunately, April is the hottest month of the Thai year.

Ploughing Ceremony. This takes place in late April or early May to mark the beginning of the rice-planting season. In Bangkok, the king presides in person over the elaborate ceremonies, usually held at the open space called Senam Luang.

Coronation Day. May 5. This commemorates King Bhumipol's coronation in 1950.

Visakha Puja. Usually in May, this most important of all Buddhist festivals takes place at the full moon on the sixth lunar month. It marks the birth, enlightenment and death of the Lord Buddha. Thais crowd into the temples and take part in candlelit processions.

Bun Bang Fai is the time in May when phallic rockets are let off in the northeast (only) in an attempt to guarantee a plentiful rice crop.

RAINY SEASON (JUNE TO OCTOBER)
Asalha Puja. Usually in July, this festival is at the full moon of the eighth lunar month. It marks the beginning of Thai monks' three-month retreat (called Khao Phansa) during the rainy season and commemorates the Lord Buddha's first sermon to his disciples. Devotees go to the temples with offerings for the monks embarking on a long spell without contact with the rest of the world.

Queen's Birthday. August 12, and a national holiday.

Phuket Chinese Vegetarian Festival. Late September or early October. See pages 156–157 for a description of this spectacular orgy of skewered cheeks, pierced tongues, ladders of knives and walking on fire.

Ok Phansa is the end of the period of retreat during the rains and usually falls

in October. The period is celebrated all over the country with boat races wherever there is a suitable stretch of water.

Chulalongkorn Day. October 23, and a national holiday in honor of Thailand's much loved 19th century monarch.

Public Holidays (when all government offices and banks will be closed):

January 1: New Year's Day
February, full moon day: Magha Puja
April 6: Chakri Day
May 5: Coronation Day
May, full moon day: Visakha Puja
July, full moon day: Asalha Puja
August 12: H.M. the Queen's Birthday
October 23: Chulalongkorn Day
December 5: H.M. the King's Birthday
December 10: Constitution Day
December 31: New Year's Eve

Galloping Gourmets

Many people talk about Thai food as if it's as likely as not to burn the skin off your tongue at the first taste. This is very far from the truth, and although some dishes can indeed be extremely spicy, the cuisine in general is pungent, fragrant and usually made with the freshest ingredients. It's an adventure that shouldn't be missed simply because of some exaggeratedly lurid travelers' tales.

Essentially, Thai food is distinctive and exciting, another experience again from the better-known Indian and Chinese cuisines that flank it to west and north. It is true that these great neighboring civilizations have produced elaborate traditions in eating which the Thais can't in all honesty compete with. Nevertheless, with its simple country flavors, its fresh ingredients and the memorable tastes of its own distinctive herbs and spices, Thai food is a world of its own and an indispensable part of any stay, however short, in the country.

Traditional Thai food as eaten in the home is relatively uncomplicated, compared, for example, with European or Chinese. Rice and vegetables, plus some dried fish (rarely meat), together with a soup and several sauces, add up to a small banquet for the average Thai. And the same thing can be eaten at any time of day. Large restaurants, on the other hand, manage to conjure up specialities as elaborate as any on offer elsewhere in the East.

The basic ingredients of the cuisine are the natural products of the country. The Thais have always been self-sufficient in food produce, and only recently has the population explosion led to local shortages. Thailand produces a huge amount of rice, an abundance of vegetables, and, in its rivers and canals as well as off its coasts, as much fish as its people can eat. The country still manages to export large amounts of food stuffs.

The ingredients tend to be simply and quickly cooked in a wok, Chinese-fashion. The spiced sauces taken with them, though, are hot and sharp in a way not often found in Chinese cooking.

As it's these sauces that are most characteristic of Thai food, it's wise to learn their names first. *Nam* is the Thai word for "water". From this follows *nam prik*, the very hot chili sauce; *nam pla*, fish sauce, made with salted and fermented fish (anyone passing on their way to Koh Samet through Rayong, the port where much Thai *nam pla* is made, will know what it smells like); *nam man*, oil; *nam man oy*, oyster sauce;

OPPOSITE: Exotic Chinese delicacies for sale in Hat Yai — birds' nests and sharks' fins. BELOW: Sampan food stall giving tourists a taste of traditional Thai fare at Bangkok's Regent Hotel.

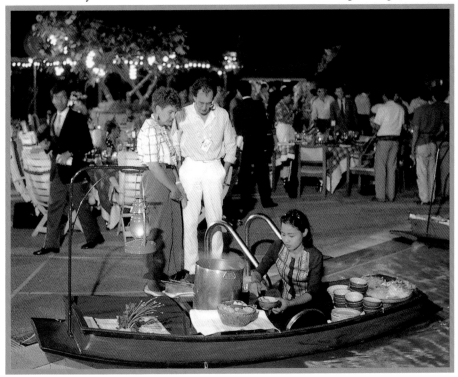

nam manao, lemon juice; *nam som,* vinegar; and *nam oy,* sugar-cane juice. These are usually served mixed with chopped shallots, lemon grass (a very distinctive Thai flavor), chilies, garlic or tamarind.

Finally, soy sauce is *nam si yu,* sticky rice is *khao niaw,* and the short lengths of bamboo you see people buying contain baked rice and are called *putto.*

Dishes You Might Like to Try
TOM YAM — a soup, made sharp and hot with lemon grass and chilies;
TOM YAM KUNG — as above, with prawns;
KAENG JUED — a mild-flavored soup, Chinese-style;
KHAO TOM — a clear white soup;
PLA THORD RAD KHING — fried fish with ginger;
KAENG SOM — sweet sour fish curry;
PLA NUENG JAEW MAKHUA TET — steamed fish with spicy tomato sauce;
PLA THORD PAK THAI — fried fish with garlic and ginger;
LARP NUA — spicy minced meat with mint;
MOU WAN — caramel pork;
KAENG KHIAW WAN KAI — coconut chicken curry;
POD LON — five-flavor duck;
PHAD MAKHUA SAI THUA KHIEW — aubergine with lentils;
KHAI JIEW MANGSAWIRAT — vegetable omelette;
SOM TAM MALAKOR — papaya salad;
YAM HED — mushroom salad.

Dishes for Vegetarians
Vegetarians should be able to find food to suit them even in ordinary restaurants. All the following dishes come without meat:
MASAMAN MANGSAWIRAT — vegetable curry;
PHAD PHAK PRIEW WAN — sweet sour vegetables;
LARB THUA DEANG — kidney-bean salad;
KHAO PHAD THUA SAI KHAI — fried rice with beans and egg;
KHAO PHAD MANGSAWIRAT — vegetable fried rice;
TOM YAM HED MANGSAWIRAT — vegetable and mushroom soup.

The Taste of Home
Western food is on offer in all places where Westerners have ever, even briefly, put in

an appearance. In Bangkok and the other major tourist centers — Chiang Mai, Phuket, Koh Samui — many restaurants have sprung up run by permanent or semi-permanent foreign residents with the result that these places offer a very wide range of food indeed. In Bangkok you can eat virtually any style you can think of, but even in places like Koh Samui, Mexican, Italian and German food can be found. German restaurants are actually particularly common in many places in Thailand.

Western food varies considerably, however, in its relation to the thing back home. The ubiquitous American breakfast, for instance, will usually see you served with two fried eggs, some bacon, cold ham or a sausage, accompanied by lettuce, tomato and cucumber, plus two slices of sweet rice bread, a pat of the world's worst margarine, and some very sweet and chemically flavored pineapple and orange marmalade. Your coffee will be instant, with non-dairy creamer; condensed milk, sweet or unsweetened, will be substituted on demand.

Fruit and Drinks
As for fruit, you'll see it all on display in any market. Don't just stick to the kinds

will have different tolerance levels. It is, though, very hard to avoid. Generally speaking, avoiding crushed ice, and taking a chance with cubes, is a reasonable strategy.

Beer is good, though expensive. Kloster is the best, closely followed by the more strongly flavored Singah. Thai whiskey, Mekong, is very cheap and excellent value for the price. You'll frequently see rows of Mekong bottles standing on shelves behind bars, each with a strip of paper stuck to it. These bottles belong to customers who have bought a bottle from the bar and have left it only partly drunk to be finished off another time. There's no reason at all why you shouldn't do the same. Sometimes the Thais drink their Mekong along with a vitamin tonic such as Liprovitan B, but it's usually — and best — drunk with Pepsi or Coca Cola.

you know — this could prove expensive. Apples, for instance, retail at getting on for one United States dollar *each* as they have to be flown in from such distant sources as New Zealand or North California. Try instead custard apples, luscious mangosteens, fragrantly delicious rambutans, sweet and sticky mangoes, or even the foul-smelling (but fine-tasting) durian.

Thais drink a lot of soft drinks, and you are certain to want to as well. But why not try the fresh local varieties, squeezed citrus drinks, for instance, or, best of all, the deliciously fragrant water of the young coconut, prepared with a chopper before your eyes and served up with a straw for, in the country, as little as five baht?

Tap water is NOT drinkable anywhere in Thailand. Nor is it enough simply to boil it — in Bangkok you have to boil it for *half an hour* before considering taking it into your system, and even then the chlorine will not have been removed, just the content proportionally increased. Far better to buy the inexpensive bottled water marketed under the trade-name Polaris.

For the rest, ice does these days seem to be relatively safe, though different people

Special Interests

Classes and Courses
No one coming to Thailand can fail to be affected, in even the smallest way, by the practice of the Buddhist faith, whether it's simply watching monks glide silently through the dawn streets on their alms-collecting rounds or hearing a ceremony in full chant at some glittering temple. Maybe your curiosity will be piqued enough to start asking some of the monks what it's all about (many like nothing better than to chat with foreign visitors). And maybe you'll decide to find out even more by going on a short course while you're in Thailand or on a return visit. Thailand is one of the easiest places in Asia to do just this — it's been hosting Western students of Buddhism for decades. Particularly popular is the form of meditation known as *vipassana* (roughly translated as "insight" meditation) which is taught at dozens of temples and special meditation centers (usually in Thai, but often in English too). To get the most out of a meditation course you should

Coconuts ABOVE start their journey down river to market and chilies OPPOSITE — both are dominant in Thai cuisine.

consider staying at least a month, though shorter retreats are also possible. There's no official charge for the tuition or the accommodation (which is very basic) but donations of around 100 baht a day are generally expected.

For general information on Buddhism and meditation centers, your first port of call should be the **World Fellowship of Buddhists** ((02) 251-1188, at 33 Sukhumvit Road, **Bangkok**. A regular meditation class in English is also held here. The most famous meditation center in Bangkok (with English-language instruction available) is Wat Mahathat near the Grand Palace. This is where one of the the most important monks' schools in Thailand is located. Classes are held daily and anyone is welcome just to turn up.

Outside Bangkok, one of the most popular places for foreign students is Wat Suanmok near Surat Thani; meditation retreats are held at this rambling forested complex during the first ten days of every month. Closer to the capital is **Wat Asokaram** in **Samut Prakan** about 30 km (19 miles) south of Bangkok or the **Boonkanjanaram Meditation Centre** at Jomtien Beach, **Pattaya**. Further afield, courses given in English are also available at **Wat Ram Poeng** in **Chiang Mai** and **Wat Pa Nanachat Beung Rai** near **Ubon Ratchathani**. Whichever place you choose, it's advisable to write in advance to the relevant temple if you want to be sure to get on the course.

Being able to speak Thai would be a big advantage on such courses, or simply on your travels if you're planning a long trip. Intensive courses are best available in Bangkok at **Union Language School** ((02) 233-4482, or **AUA Language Center** ((02) 252-8170 and in Chiang Mai ((053) 278407. Private tuition is also available through these centers — expect to pay around 250 baht an hour.

Gourmets will be delighted to discover that they can take the secrets of Thai cooking back home with them by going on one of the increasingly popular short cookery courses (I've met several people who have actually come to Thailand just to learn to cook). In **Bangkok**, try

Bussaracum Restaurant ((02) 235-8915, or the Oriental Hotel's **Thai Cooking School** ((02) 236-0400. In **Chiang Mai**, the **Chiang Mai Thai Cookery School** ((053) 278033, even offers a one-day course (700 baht), although the three-day version (2,000 baht) is obviously more rewarding: you learn how to prepare six popular and simple Thai dishes (for example, *tom yam kung* and *phat Thai*) and are given a manual of recipes, with a list of alternative ingredients for those hard-to-find Thai items.

Another uniquely Thai skill which you can study while you're in the country is Thai massage (see RELAX WITH AN ANCIENT MASSAGE, page 18). Chiang Mai is the place to head for if you're keen to come to grips with all those muscles and tendons. The **Old Medicine Hospital** ((02) 275085, has the most famous massage school and offers 11-day courses twice a month for about 3,000 baht. You could also check out the seven-day courses of **Suan Samoonprai** ((053) 252663 or 252706, which are slightly cheaper. At both these places you can also have a massage first yourself (herbal varieties are available at Suan Samoonprai) to find out if you're really prepared for the exertions of the course.

Sports

Thai Games

Very common in Thailand is that wonderful and rare thing, a non-competitive group game. In **takraw** half a dozen young men in a circle try to keep a light ball made of braided rattan in the air by any means other than their hands. You see this game played everywhere — in courtyards, on waste ground or in parks. There are competitive forms too, though. One has teams on either side of a net, and another is very similar to basketball. Both retain the rule forbidding touching the ball with the hands.

Rather less common is **krabi krabong**, sword fighting with two swords. This is almost invariably nowadays put on as part of a public display by accomplished professionals.

Kite Flying

The Thais, like the Chinese, have been flying kites for at least as long as records go back. In olden times kites were used in war, carrying explosives over, and then down onto, enemy fortifications. In more recent times, the art reached its zenith as a popular sport during the reign of King Chulalongkorn (Rama V) when the palace was forced to promulgate laws to curb the practice of kite flying in the capital as kites were becoming entangled on the turrets of public buildings.

Your best chance of seeing formal kite-flying contests nowadays in Bangkok is at **Senam Luang** (a grassy open space opposite the National Theatre and National Museum) during March and April. The Large "male" kites (*chula*) battle with smaller but more nimble "female" ones (*pakpao*), each group of enthusiasts attempting to ensnare the others' kites and drag them across to enemy territory.

Thai Boxing

But the sport most beloved by Thais is their own national form of boxing. There are two major venues in Bangkok, and of these it's the Lumphini Stadium that has more atmosphere and gives a stronger feeling of this most Thai of sports.

The Lumphini Stadium is slightly difficult to find. Coming on foot along

Thai games — OPPOSITE: Kites in the April sky; ABOVE contestants pay their respects to their patrons before a bout of Thai boxing.

Rama 4 from Lumphini Park, it's immediately after the Royal Thai Armed Forces Preparatory Academy, the large formal building behind railings, just by where the shops begin. It's set back a few meters from the road but is immediately recognizable by the mass of food stalls that cluster round the entrance.

The stadium itself has a corrugated iron roof, wooden seats, and barbed wire above the wire-mesh barricades separating the second and third class areas. Neon lights and fans are fixed to the roof. It's all rather rough and ready, old and well-used. There are a few simple advertisements for Coca Cola and other trade marks. Boys aged about ten walk round selling Liprovitan D, a very popular vitamin tonic, served on ice. Framed black and white photos of famous fighters hang by the entrance to the ringside enclosure.

If you go into the third class area early, just before 6 PM, you can join the enthusiasts looking over the back row of seats at the boxers being prepared for the fights.

A NIGHT AT THE RINGSIDE — A FIGHT REMEMBERED

The two being made ready for the first bout lie on tables, their heads on their kit-bags, while two masseurs apiece work over them energetically using embrocation the color of orange-juice. They bind their hands tightly with white bandages, securing the ends with masking tape.

Compared with Western boxers these all seem featherweights. One of them looks about 17. The smell of the embrocation is everywhere. A girl comes forward carrying a pair of red and yellow shorts newly emblazoned with a motto. These are now put on, preceded by a jockstrap and a guard. The assistants then secure their gloves with more white tape. Tight, toeless pink socks follow. A rose-colored towel is then placed over the fighter's slender shoulders, followed by a magnificent red and gold cape.

Finally, round his head goes the *mongkun*, a rigid headband with a long protruding tail. Before he puts this on, one of the two assistants blesses it by holding it momentarily to his lips. The boxer then leaves down a corridor, like a lion at a circus, and emerges moments later by the ring. He takes his place in a sort of iron pen, accompanied by one assistant.

The stadium is now beginning to fill up. A bell rings and everyone stands. The National Anthem is played. Then a strange, wild note on the *pi* — an oboe-like instrument rings out from the three-piece band. The boxers kneel and bow to each other. One of them then performs a dance to the music, as if getting himself into a trance. The boxers dance — and fight — barefoot.

The music stops and the referee appears. There is a prayer, and the mongkuns are taken off. When the music starts again, the first round begins — with a couple of playful kicks.

The band consists of a *pi*, a pair of long conga-type drums, and a pair of high-pitched cymbals. The musicians play only during the fighting.

Between rounds the contestants sit on stools to be sponged down. The stool stands on a large tin tray that protects the ring and its canvas cover from the water.

By the second and third rounds the crowd is shouting. Bets are being laid everywhere, men holding up various numbers of fingers to indicate the odds. Every blow, by knee, elbow, foot or fist, is cheered with a part-approving, part sympathetic "ooo-ah".

Suddenly it's all over. There are five bouts of three minutes each in Thai boxing matches, with two minute rests between them. Now his assistant carries one of the contestants from the center of the ring, not because he can't walk but in order to hold him on high. The fighter responds by holding his arms out like a wooden crucifix. Meanwhile the other fighter is given a vigorous massage. And then it's on to the next bout.

Backstage again, the assistant helps the boxer disrobe. But the boxer takes the tape and bandages off his hands himself, tearing at them impatiently with his teeth. There is no sense of victory or defeat, merely of a short job done. No injuries whatsoever are visible. It seems that because of all the kicking and elbowing, there is less emphasis on heavy punching, and as a result less physical injury than in the Western boxing.

After their work, the assistants backstage look at magazines featuring photos of boxers and recent bouts. The contestant, now dressed in T-shirt and jeans, with his kit in a bag slung over his shoulder, leaves as casually as a student off for a jog in Lumphini Park.

Outside the food stalls are doing a brisk business as more people arrive for the bigger fights. There are six per night, with the fifth traditionally involving the most celebrated fighters. The young contestant of the first bout takes a bowl of soup at one of the stalls.

As well as the food stalls, there are also shops selling mongkuns, shorts, embrocation — anything, in fact, associated with the sport. The trade mark on almost all the items of clothing is the same — "Windy".

Traditional Performing Arts

Sing a Song!
Traditional Thai music is a wild, energetic sound played with *pi* (a sort of oboe), *sor* and *pin* (stringed instruments), wooden xylophones as found in Indonesia, and drums. It can be difficult to get to hear, however. You hear it, of course, at the boxing matches, and sometimes you come across it in taxis or on buses. Easiest perhaps is to ask for it at the numerous cassette stalls in Bangkok.

By contrast, the music visitors hear most of the time in Thailand is astonishingly Western in style. Popular music is a thriving industry and, despite its remoteness from traditional Thai music, has a very memorable and engaging local flavor.

In addition, the Thais do love to sing — usually the current hits. "Sing a song!" is a frequent cry, and it doesn't always need a bottle of Mekong whiskey to persuade the singer, though that undoubtedly helps.

Dance
The most famous form of Thai traditional dance is the masked dance drama known as *khon*. Khon stories are derived from the Ramakien, the Thai version of the Indian Ramayana, and basically tell epic tales about the triumph of good over evil; in the old days, when khon performances were restricted to the royal palace, they could carry on for nights on end.

These days, unfortunately, only excerpts from khon are performed and what you're most likely to see — at dinner shows in Bangkok, for example — isn't usually very good since it's just put on as an extra draw for tourists. Another place where visitors often catch a glimpse of traditional dance — performed by rather tired dancers — is at the Erawan Shrine in Bangkok. Strictly speaking this dance form isn't khon but *lakhon chatri*, which is very similar to *khon* but without the use of masks. A third derivative of *khon*, called *likay*, is sometimes seen at festivals and temple fairs and is a good deal more lively, combining burlesque comedy with social satire.

If you're keen to find out more about this art form, contact TAT for details on forthcoming performances at the **National Theatre** ((02) 224-1342, or contact the **Thailand Cultural Centre** ((02) 245-7711 or **College of Dramatic Arts** ((02) 224-1391.

Even rarer these days than khon performances are shadow plays. Named after the cowhide (*nang*) from which the puppets are made, this wonderful art form was first introduced to Thailand in the early Ayutthaya period. It used to be a widely popular form of entertainment but television and video have seen it rapidly disappear. Nowadays your best chance of seeing a proper performance of *nang thalung* is in its traditional stronghold, Nakhon Si Thammarat, during festival times. But you can also call on the home and workshop of Nakhon's leading puppet maker and master, Suchart Subsin, who has been making puppets for over 40 years and is recognized as the leading puppeteer in the country. At his workshop you not only have the chance of seeing him make the puppets (or buying some) but also of seeing them in action: for 50 baht, Khun Suchart will give a short performance, complete with musical accompaniment of drums, cymbals and xylophones.

Taking a Tour

As Asia's leading tourist destination, Thailand is the focus of hundreds of different tours from Europe, America and the Asia-Pacific region. Not surprisingly, Thai International's own Royal Orchid Holidays (contact any Thai International office for details) are some of the most comprehensive and flexible, with personalized combinations of destinations and useful "Minibreaks" of two or more nights to major cities or beach resorts — perfect for those short break holidays or to combine with longer tours. Golfers also get a good deal with Royal Orchid Holidays' selection of special golfing packages in locations throughout Thailand. Or check out golfing tour specialists, **Fairway International Travel Ltd** in the United Kingdom ((44-1422) 378141 FAX (44-1442) 310716.

Other Asian airlines, such as Cathay Pacific and Singapore Airlines also offer attractive holiday packages combining Thailand with other popular destinations in Southeast Asia, such as Hong Kong, Singapore, Manila and Kuala Lumpur — definitely worth considering if you're coming all the way from Europe or America for a once-in-a-lifetime Far East trip.

But for more classic tours of Thailand, take a look at tour operators in the United Kingdom specializing in Asia such as **Travel Bag** ((44-1420) 80828, **Asia Voyages** ((44-1932) 820050 FAX (44-1932) 820633, or **Asian Affair Holidays** ((44-171) 439-2601 FAX (44-171) 287-2677. One of Asia Voyage's more unusual short tours, for instance, is aboard a traditional teak rice barge, converted into a unique floating hotel, which takes small groups on cruises along the Chao Phraya river to Bang Pa-In. **Far East Travel Centre** ((44-171) 734-9318,

offers more mainstream tours of Thailand's major cities and beaches, as does **Thomas Cook Holidays** ((44-1733) 332255, and other big-name operators.

Specialist tour operators in the United States, United Kingdom and Australia have long staked out Thailand as an ideal destination for adventure tours. **Explore Worldwide** ((44-1252) 319448 FAX (44-1252) 343170, for instance, has a select and enticing choice of tours concentrating on northern Thailand: their 21-day Northern Thai Adventure includes a seven-day trek (classified as "fairly demanding") and an unusual trip by longtail boat down the Salween River, which forms the border with Myanmar. As with most tour operators, they also offer combinations with other Asian destinations: explorers will be particularly tempted by the Mekong River Adventure where you start in Laos and then travel by longboat along the Mekong River from Luang Prabang to Chiang Khong in Thailand. Other specialist operators worth checking out are **Exodus** ((44-171) 675-5550, and in the United States, **Mountain Travel-Sobek** ((800) 227-2384 FAX (1-510) 525-7710, and **Bolder Adventures** ((800) 642-2742 FAX (303) 443-7078; the latter is particularly good at adventure activity trips such as sea canoeing.

Lastly, walkers and birdwatchers may well be interested in tours geared specifically for them. For walkers, the best of the bunch among tour operators in the United Kingdom is **Ramblers Holidays** ((44-1707) 331133, FAX (44-1707) 333-276, while bird watchers should contact **Ornitholidays** ((44-1243) 821-2301.

Bang Pa-In, near Ayutthaya, the former country residence and love-nest of Thai kings and princes; it's a curious mix of Chinese, Thai and Western style buildings.

The
Siamese
World

A VERY SPECIAL PLACE

Thailand is like nowhere else in Asia. Although for centuries its Buddhism and its social organization made it not unlike the neighboring territories of Burma, Cambodia and Vietnam, today it is unique.

Whereas Malaysia to the south is Islamic and federal, and the countries to the north and east are under the sway of variously totalitarian regimes, Thailand continues to display the traditional styles of a Buddhist monarchy. And despite or because of this, it is currently experiencing a period of unrivalled economic expansion.

Thailand is a country that's changing fast. But it remains so colorful, so easy-going, and so welcoming that there are few more attractive tourist destinations anywhere in Asia.

What, then, are the key elements of this unique and special place?

A PINK ELEPHANT

To some observers, the land of Thailand geographically resembles the head and trunk of an elephant, the animal for so long symbolic of the country and for a time featured, colored pink, on its national flag.

The country extends northward from the Malaysian border up a long, narrow isthmus before broadening out just south of Bangkok into a wide, low-lying plain. This, the delta of the Chao Phraya river, constitutes the Thai heartland. Westwards the land rises to the high hills that eventually become the border with Myanmar (Burma), while to the east a coastal plain runs down to the frontier with Cambodia. Meanwhile, in the northeast the land rises slightly to become the sandstone plain that extends to the banks of the Mekong river, and this river for a considerable distance forms part of Thailand's long border with Laos. The far north is rugged, and Chiang Mai, Thailand's second city, is situated in the only important level area. The country has no common border with China.

From south to north Thailand measures just over 1,600 km (1,000 miles), and a train journey from Hat Yai near the Malaysian border to Chiang Mai at the northern end of the country's rail system would take a good 30 hours. East to west, Thailand extends 786 km (485 miles) at its widest, just north of Bangkok.

The population of 59 million is distributed unevenly, with the greatest concentration in the central rice-growing area and the sparsest in the northern and southern hills.

A HOT CLIMATE

Thailand's climate is classically tropical, though not equatorial. The country experi-

ences three seasons — a cool, dry season from November to January, a hot and dry season from February to May, and a rainy season from June to October. The dry season winds blow out of the northeast, from China, while the rain-bearing winds ("monsoons") blow in from the Indian Ocean to the southwest.

The length, strength and constancy of the rains vary from year to year. Whereas this constitutes a nuisance in the low-lying river basins when heavy rains lead to flooding (an annual occurrence in Bangkok), the more serious problems come in the northeast which, lacking the irrigation systems of the great river valleys, is totally dependent on the annual rains. Here, if the rains are unsatisfactory, crop failure and consequent rural depopulation are an ever-present threat.

This rainfall pattern is different in the south of the country. Here the seasons begin

ABOVE: Bankok's Wat Arun, Temple of the Dawn. OPPOSITE: Popular veneration of the monarch — dried flowers adorning the picture of King Bhumipol on a float in a festival parade in a Bangkok street.

to be influenced by the more equatorial climate of the Malaysian peninsula. Rain is experienced in most months of the year, and in December and January, two of the driest months in the rest of the country, it can be particularly heavy.

Temperatures, by contrast, are remarkably constant throughout the country, rarely going above 35°C (96°F) or below 18°C (65°F). Cooler temperatures, though, are experienced in the northern hills, especially at night in December and January. What is really to the advantage of the north, however, is its lower humidity: it is the consistently high humidity of Bangkok and the south generally that makes the climate trying for many visitors from temperate regions.

ENTER THE THAIS

WHERE DO THEY COME FROM?

The Thais belong to a racial group that includes the Shans of Burma, the Lao of Laos, and Thai-speaking inhabitants of the Yunnan Province of China (the area immediately north of Vietnam and Laos, and east of Burma). Some scholars believe the Thais are a branch of the Chinese race, others that their culture existed as a separate entity before the Chinese themselves arrived in the Yunnan area.

Whichever is true, the Thais certainly established a distinctive kingdom in the seventh century in Yunnan called Nanchao, and for two hundred years competed with the Chinese for control of the territory. The Chinese eventually overcame them, and from then on, it seems, the Thais began to migrate southwards into modern Burma, modern Laos and the northern part of modern Thailand. Since then they've never looked back.

OLD SIAM

THE SUKHOTHAI PERIOD

The great power in the region at this time was the Khmer Empire, based in modern Cambodia, and in the 13th century the Thai

princelings buried their differences and challenged the Khmers in their local garrison of Sukhothai. They won, and founded their first capital on modern Thai soil on the same site in 1238.

There is little doubt that the Thais couldn't have overcome such a major power on their own. Aid almost certainly came from the Chinese who were more than willing to support anyone who might lessen the influence of the great Khmer Empire on their southern flank. As for the Burmese, who might be expected to have resisted the

establishment of a new kingdom on their borders, they were already occupied fighting off the Mongols.

The Thais found a powerful leader in these Sukhothai years in King Ramkamheng (1283–1317). Not only did he hold off the Khmers — he also extended Thai control down the valley of the Chao Phraya River (on which Bangkok stands), and commissioned scholars to create for the first time a written form for the Thai language.

Trade flourished early between the new state and its patron both by land and, once the Thais had established themselves on the coast of the Gulf of Siam, by sea. Chinese ceramicists came to Sukhothai and taught the locals the art of potting. This good relationship with China was to last nearly six hundred years.

Nations in those days were little more than areas over which families, and alliances between families, held control, and after the death of King Ramkamheng decline set in. Rival centers of strength became established in the more fertile south, and by the middle of the 14th century, Ayutthaya had established itself as the power-base of the dominant Thai faction. It wasn't long before Sukhothai was forced to accept the supremacy of the new capital.

peak when, in 1569, they surrounded Ayutthaya, beseiged it, and finally totally laid it waste.

The future King Naresuan, the Black Prince, now appears on the scene. Captured as a child during the sacking of Ayutthaya, he was taken to Burma and, following the aristocratic code of those days, not imprisoned or executed but educated alongside the Burmese princes. Little did the Burmese know the force they were nourishing. When later they sent him back to Thailand to help with the struggle in the east against the

NARESUAN THE GREAT

Over the centuries that followed, Ayutthaya became immensely powerful, extending its control into the south of modern Burma as far as the Bay of Bengal, and down into the Malay peninsula. Nevertheless, the old northern princes took the chance to re-establish a form of local independence, setting up on their own with Chiang Mai as their capital.

Burma became a more serious threat to Ayutthaya in the 16th century when its princes, who had previously been preoccupied warring among themselves, united and invaded Thailand. Their attacks reached a

Cambodians, the boy's success was so great that the Thais made him king at the age of sixteen.

Naresuan had, in the process of fighting his eastern neighbors, built up a huge Thai army, so large that the Burmese again perceived Ayutthaya as a threat, and so once again invaded, in 1581. Despite attacks at his rear by the Cambodians, who always took the opportunity of invading Thailand when the Thais were occupied fighting the Burmese, the young king repelled his erstwhile schoolmates, and then slew the heir

Stucco frieze from Sukhothai, the first Thai capital now architectural site of world importance. Buddhism arrived in Thailand from Sri Lanka during the Sukhothai period.

apparent to the Burmese throne in a one-to-one duel. It's a story known to every Thai schoolchild.

King Naresuan then went on to defeat the Cambodians, punishing their earlier opportunism by having their king beheaded in public, an act the Cambodians have to this day not forgotten. Having thus defeated his two powerful neighbors, he turned on his own independently-minded brothers to the north and suppressed the Kingdom of Chiang Mai.

Naresuan the Great never succeeded in destroying the Burmese capital of Pegu, but by the end of the 16th century Ayutthaya was once again the dominant force in the region. He died in 1605.

EARLY EUROPEAN INFLUENCES

The initial Thai contact with a European power occurred in 1518. The Portuguese had seized Malacca in 1511, and the Thais concluded a treaty with the newcomers granting them open access to the country. They also permitted them to set up a Catholic mission in Ayutthaya, and the king even donated money towards the construction of a church there.

The other European nations who followed in the footsteps of the Portuguese were at first treated with equal generosity. A treaty was concluded with the Dutch in the early 16th century, and then with the British shortly afterwards.

It wasn't long, however, before the Dutch saw fit to use strong-arm methods to secure the details of their demands. They quickly became so threatening that when King Nerai succeeded to the Thai throne in 1657 he took stern measures to limit Dutch influence in the country.

The Thais had already begun to react against foreign attempts to control them when in 1632 they massacred a number of Japanese who had been trying to influence court politics. In fact King Nerai's moves against the Dutch began what was to be a long Thai tradition of playing off one European power against another. But his attempt to persuade the British East India Company to agree to assist him in the event of further Dutch tricks failed, so Nerai turned to the French who had by now also appeared on the scene. In 1664 the Thais permitted French missionaries to establish themselves in Ayutthaya, and there was even talk of a formal alliance between Louis XIV and the Thai king.

The Thai belief, however, that some benefit could be derived one way or another from these meddlesome newcomers was short-lived. Events came to a head with the arrival of a Greek adventurer named Constantine Paulkon, originally an official with the British East India Company. Paulkon began by working in an advisory capacity with the Thai government, but soon gained the king's confidence to such an extent that he was made Minister in charge of Trade, and then Chief Minister.

Naturally the highly placed Thais were both jealous and resentful, but for the moment they had to bide their time. Paulkon was quickly instrumental in furthering the idea of a Thai-French alliance, and in 1687 six French warships carrying 636 soldiers arrived in the Thai port of Bangkok. But it wasn't long before it became clear to everyone that the French were primarily interested in converting the Thais, and especially the king, to Christianity. The disenchanted Thai nobles seized their chance when the king fell ill in 1688. They staged a coup and had Paulkon arrested and executed, along with a number of French missionaries, including the bishop. For all intents and purposes, this was the end of European influence in Thailand for 130 years.

DECLINE AND REVIVAL

During the 18th century Thailand became weak, engrossed in domestic conflicts and attacked on all sides by neighbors who saw their chance for territorial expansion. This train of events reached its climax when the Burmese, temporarily united, invaded Thailand and, in 1767, completely destroyed the glorious capital of Ayutthaya. This is seen by the Thais as their darkest hour. The country almost ceased to exist as its provinces were either annexed by foreigners or made into

Vigor and grace — detail of a carved lintel from the 12th century Khmer settlement at Pimai.

personal fiefdoms by dissident members of the Thai nobility.

The Thai resurgence began with a new king, Taksin. A military man of humble birth, he had escaped from the siege of Ayutthaya with 500 men and fled east into Cambodia. There he raised and trained a new army, and the following year marched on the ruins of Ayutthaya and easily defeated the Burmese garrison. Proclaiming himself king, he established a new capital at Thonburi, the western part of modern Bangkok. In 1771 he invaded Cambodia and proclaimed it a vassal state. Thailand was back on its feet again.

Taksin, however, was doomed to be the only king of his dynasty. In 1781 he was overthrown by a palace coup and executed. One General Chakri was proclaimed king, and took the title of Rama I.

A MODERNIZING DYNASTY

Chakri had been a successful military leader during Taksin's campaigns. He had defended Chiang Mai against the Burmese and had gone on to seize the Laotian kingdoms that had their capitals in modern-day Vientiane and Luang Prabang. They remained under Thai control until 1893.

King Chakri moved his capital over the river from Thonburi to Bangkok proper, Thailand's leading commercial center. With the colonization of Burma by the British, and the country successfully aggressive on its eastern flank, Thailand's position appeared relatively secure.

The 19th century, however, saw Thailand under its new dynasty beginning to defend itself against the fast-expanding colonial powers on its borders.

To the south, the British were extending their control in the Malay States. In 1826 Rama III signed a treaty with them recognizing their rights in Penang while in return securing Thai trading rights elsewhere in the area. And up to the death of Rama III in 1851, British, and later American, attempts to conclude treaties giving them

Seated Buddha from Mahathat, Suhkothai. Large Buddhas, similarly adorned with a yellow cloth, can be seen all over Thailand.

more extensive trading rights in Thailand were successfully resisted.

KING MONGKUT

Rama IV, King Mongkut, is one of the great Thai monarchs. He had learnt to speak and write English from American missionaries, and in addition had an enquiring mind that was fascinated by the scientific and technological developments in the West in the mid-19th century. Rama III had been his brother, and had seized power on the death of their father despite Mongkut's stronger claim. Mongkut spent his long wait for the kingship as a priest and had plenty of time to develop his mind, free from the worry of affairs of state.

It wasn't merely that Mongkut had had a Western education and was well versed in Western ideas. He also had the sobering experience of seeing the British defeat the Chinese Empire in the Opium War of 1841–42, the war which led to the ceding of Hong Kong to the British. If China, Thailand's greatest patron over the centuries, could not resist the Europeans with their iron ships, what hope of success did the relatively powerless Thais have?

Consequently, four years after his accession, Mongkut concluded a Treaty of Friendship and Commerce (known as the Bowring Treaty of 1855) with the British. This allowed opium, which the British were growing in India and selling in China, more or less free access into the country, fixed the Thai duty on English goods at a mere pittance, and allowed the British exemption from Thai laws while resident in Thailand. Similar treaties were concluded with the United States and other nations, culminating, in 1898, with one with Japan.

THE FRENCH THREAT

Meanwhile, to the east, the French were establishing themselves in the southern part of Vietnam, and laying claim to Cambodia. Following a long period of pressure, Mongkut finally concluded a treaty with them in 1867 relinquishing his claim to exercise what amounted to control over most of Cambodia.

Mongkut's son, Chulalongkorn, succeeded to the throne on his father's death in 1868 and reigned until 1910. A boy on his accession, he assumed full power in 1873.

Under Chulalongkorn, Rama V, Westernization was speeded up. The royal family were obliged to learn English, and many of the king's own sons were sent to Europe to be educated.

During the 1880s, the French extended their authority into Cambodia, and then into parts of Laos where they challenged the Thai position in the rest of the country. In 1893 France demanded that Thailand abandon its claim to all territory east of the Mekong. The Thais appealed to the British for help, but the British were reluctant to become involved with the French in Asia and counseled a policy of "moderation", one that would have doomed the Thais to defeat and eventual colonization.

What became known as the Paknam Incident occurred that July. The French sent warships up the Chao Phraya River and the Thai fortress at Paknam fired on them. The French fired back, but lost no time in sending the Thais a list of demands, including extensive territorial ones, as reparation for Thai "aggression". The British refused to do more than put in a token appearance on behalf of the Thais, and in October a treaty was signed agreeing to all the French demands.

Yet in a sense Thailand benefited from the presence of two powerful European nations in the area, for in 1896 Britain and France agreed to the continuing independence of Thailand, though stripped of its former garrisons in Laos. The matter was tied up in the early years of this century when Thai independence was again confirmed but at the expense of the surrender of four states in the north of modern-day Malaysia — Kelantan, Trengganu, Kedah and Perlis — to the British, and all of modern-day Laos to the French.

THE TWENTIETH CENTURY

At the beginning of this century, Thailand and Japan were the only truly independent states in the Far East. Both were traditional monarchies who had sought to modernize and develop their contacts with the West. But whereas Japan remained independent through its military power (it defeated the Russians in a war in 1904), Thailand probably remained independent through a combination of luck and the willingness of the British to allow the French to take territory in the east in exchange for the consolidation of a superior British trading position in an independent, though territorially reduced, Thailand.

By the time World War One broke out in Europe, Rama VI (King Wachirawut, 1910–25) was on the throne. A lover of the arts, he declared Thailand's neutrality, but opted for the Allies when the Americans joined the conflict in 1917. Twelve hundred Thais fought in France in the last months of the war.

Rama VI was succeeded by his brother Prajadhipok (Rama VII). In 1932 a bloodless coup toppled the monarchy, but invited the king back as a constitutional Head of State on the British and Scandinavian pattern. The Democracy Monument in Bangkok celebrates this event.

Rama VIII (King Ananda Mahidol) succeeded his uncle in 1935, and one of the coup leaders, Phibul Songkhram, emerged as head of the government later in the decade. He was destined to be around for some time.

When the Japanese embarked on their sweep through Asia after their attack on Pearl Harbor in 1941, Phibul, seeing that Malaya and Burma were bound to fall, allowed the Japanese into Thailand, but resistance to them was so strong he was forced to resign (in 1944).

In 1945 Britain and France demanded damaging penalties, including reparations, from the Thais for siding with the Japanese, but the Americans did not join in this demand and instead mediated on behalf of the Thais with the Europeans. This led directly to increased US influence in the country, and eventually to the establishment of American bases in the 1960s.

KING BHUMIPOL

In 1946, Rama VIII was assassinated in the palace in circumstances that have never been satisfactorily explained. His brother

Bhumipol, who succeeded him at the age of 19 as Rama IX, has proved immensely popular, and is seen by the overwhelming majority of Thais as father of the people and a man dedicated to the welfare of his subjects.

King Bhumipol's reign has, however, not been without its problems. The ideals of constitutionalism and democracy were quickly replaced in practice by variously defined versions of military rule. On October 14, 1973, 400,000 people massed at the Democracy Monument in Bangkok to demand a return to constitutional rule — as a

result over a hundred were killed by riot police. The crisis was defused by the king in person when he asked the government leaders to resign and leave the country. This they did, demonstrating the extraordinary power the monarchy once again wields in contemporary Thailand.

Later coups and coup attempts followed, most significantly in 1991 when General Suchinda seized power from the democratically elected government. Although elections were held the following year, the military decided to put Suchinda into the premier's post. Massive demonstrations followed, leading to a climax in May when scores of street demonstrators were killed by the army. As in 1973, it was the king who finally brought things under control, publicly chastising Suchinda and forcing his exile.

Indeed, it has been largely thanks to the king and his consistent support for

Buddha image regarding a *chedi* at Kampong Phet, monuments that once would have been coated in glitteringly splendid mosaics.

moderate policies that Thailand has managed to maintain relative stability and impressive economic growth in recent years.

In 1992, new elections ushered in a more promising era with Democrat Party leader, Chuan Leekpai, whose "Mr. Clean" reputation helped keep him in power for a record two years, seven months. A land reform scandal in 1995 finally brought his government down. Since then, there have been several changes of leadership, reflecting Thailand's fundamental political problem: the fact that power is still shared between the king, the military and an elected assembly, with no one of them holding, in practice, absolute and unchallenged authority. It's not democracy, but it isn't quite autocracy either.

Economically, too, some cracks have started to appear. Thailand had one of the fastest growth rates in Asia during the late eighties but in the last few years it has experienced a sharp decline in its exports to the United States and Europe. This has severely weakened its balance-of-payments position. The property sector has suffered badly and both financial and manufacturing industries have revealed serious problems. Economic growth is expected to contintue its downward trend.

THE MANY FACES OF BUDDHISM

A Land of Temples

Evidence of the religion followed by all but seven percent of Thais lies on every hand. Glitteringly ornate temples adorn even the drabbest of cities, and often apparently uninhabited parts of the countryside. Saffron-robed monks are everywhere, on the trains, the buses, or just browsing through city stalls looking over the latest pop cassettes.

Thai temples are astonishingly colorful and ornate. There is no hint of subtlety, of mellow tints and suggestive shade, as in northern Europe. A brilliance and energy that rises up to greet the sun is the Thai way. Somerset Maugham thought they were

The half-buried Buddha image in Wat Phra Thong, Phuket. The image was discovered in this state and the temple erected over it.

"like prizes in a shooting-gallery at a village fair in the country of the gods."

There are around a quarter of a million monks in Thailand. Traditionally, all Thai men enter a monastery for three months at around the age of twenty. Some spend a shorter time there, but many go much earlier, and for several years. Some enter monasteries as a means of supporting themselves while they receive an education elsewhere, others to gain merit for their parents.

Gaining merit is central to Thai Buddhism. It's a way of storing up virtue for the next life and can be done by giving money or food to monks or to the poor as well as by entering monasteries.

Buddhism is not so much a religion as a system of philosophy. Certainly the Buddha is not understood as a god, at least in the Theravada school that Thailand follows, but as a teacher. Monks are people who, for short periods or for their whole lives, enter monasteries to study Buddhist teachings and practice the disciplines that lead to successful renunciation of the world.

THE LIGHT OF ASIA

Buddhism came to Thailand from Sri Lanka during the Sukhothai period.

The Lord Buddha was born Siddhartha Gautama, son of a local prince, between 563 and 556 BC in what is now Nepal. Living at first in luxury, he had married and fathered a son before, at the age of 29, he left the palace and witnessed the suffering in the outside world. After much searching for the meaning of this suffering, he sat down under a bo tree at Uruvela, near Gaya in Bihar State, India, and achieved "enlightenment".

Gautama's answer to the problem of suffering was contained in the Four Noble Truths: that all existence involves suffering, that this suffering is caused by desire, that in order to remove suffering you must escape desire, and that the way to escape desire is to follow the Eight-fold Path. This path details the ways to become disentangled from all desire for worldly gratification.

At Benares (Varanasi) Gautama met five Brahmins who became his first disciples. Called "the Buddha", or the Enlight-

ened One, Gautama reputedly died at the age of eighty after having eaten poisoned food.

Buddhism at first flourished in India, but later died out as the older Hinduism reasserted itself. Now it is found mainly in the countries to the east, north and south of the subcontinent, in Burma, Thailand, Laos, Cambodia, Vietnam, Tibet, Nepal, China, Korea, Japan and Sri Lanka. There are virtually no Buddhists in modern India.

In the third century BC, Buddhism split. Thailand follows the Theravada, or "lesser vehicle" form, so-called because it retains only the simple elements of the religion, whereas the Mahayana school, the "greater vehicle", contains many later accretions.

The *ho rakang* is a tower with a bell, or drum, at the top.

THE LANGUAGE OF THE TEMPLES

It's useful to understand a few terms in connection with the architectural features of Thai temples.

The *boht* is the room housing the principal Buddha, a rectangular hall with elaborately painted doors and shutters surrounded by eight boundary stones. Its roof is usually decorated with a horn-shaped curl, or *chofa*, at each corner.

The *viharn* is a space used for assemblies of non-monks. A *chedi* is a tall structure shaped rather like a handbell and usually painted white. Called in India a "stupa", it generally houses a valuable relic or the ashes of an eminent (and devout) person.

OTHER ESSENCES

Brahminism

In addition to Buddhism, elements of Brahminism, adopted by the earliest Thai kings from the Khmers and itself also of Indian origin, are still evident in Thai life. It can be seen in court ritual and marriage ceremonies. What interest, after all, has Buddhism,

The ruins of Ayutthaya's Wat Phra Maha That, which was built in the 14th century. Most of Ayutthaya's temples were destroyed by the invading Burmese in the 18th century, bringing to an end the most glorious cultural period in Thai history.

a religion of renunciation, in sanctifying as natural a state as marriage? Many of the great Thai festivals, too, such as Songkran and the Ploughing Ceremony, are Brahminic in origin.

Homes for Ghosts
Similarly, the ubiquitous spirit houses seen everywhere in the country are residues from an older set of beliefs. These brightly-painted little structures standing atop posts in the grounds of houses are intended to attract the spirits that might otherwise in-

Pattani, in Yala Province, that Thailand's biggest mosque is to be found.

HOW DO THEY LIVE?

LIFE ON FOUR DOLLARS A DAY

Bangkok's teeming traffic, the deserted sandy roads between wooded hills in the north, the gorgeous beaches of the islands, the transvestite dancers, the itinerant street-sellers, the crowded buses, the monks —

habit the house itself. Little plaster figures stand around representing what the spirits will be rewarded with if they resist the temptation to molest the human inhabitants of the real house. Fruit and incense sticks are also often added.

THE MOSLEM SOUTH

There are some Catholics in Thailand, but the most visible minority religion is Islam.

Thailand's Moslems are almost all in the south, close to the border with Islamic Malaysia. Here mosques replace temples, and the call of the muezzin punctuates small town life. Not surprisingly, it's here at

Thailand can at first precipitate considerable culture shock. What, then, lies behind all this diversity and profusion? What makes these people tick?

You only have to walk down the *sois* numbered in the twenties and thirties off Bangkok's Sukhumvit Road and see the rich, and then take a look at one of the many slums (such as Klong Toey) to know you are no longer in Europe, Japan or North America. It's worth remembering that the average citizen of the USA earns seventeen times more in a year than the average Thai.

It's not a bad introduction to the fundamental realities of the country to ask one of the waiters in your hotel how much he's earning. Thais as a rule don't mind in the slightest giving this kind of information.

What you'll find is that in the average tourist-oriented restaurant on Phuket or Koh Samui he'll be earning around 100 baht (under US$4) a day, and working a seven-day week with two free days a month—just time enough to visit his family, possibly several hundred miles away. He will sleep on the premises in a room shared with several others, and receive one or two meals a day of rice with egg and vegetables (rarely meat).

are lined with billboards advertising dream houses that would look more at home in Texas than tropical Asia. And a quick look at the gleaming white Gothic apartments on Soi Suan Phlu, just down the road from Bangkok's Immigration Office, will give you some idea of the fairyland lifestyles being prepared for the country's emerging bourgeoisie.

AUTHORITARIAN WAYS

Yet old ways persist. You won't have been

Yet, despite the fact that you'll be spending more than his daily wage on every meal you take, he will almost invariably serve it up to you cheerfully and politely, and be genuinely honored that you have chosen to take your holiday in his country.

UPWARD MOBILITY

Given its historical background of absolutism and superstition, Thailand has made remarkable progress. It can't yet match the most successful countries of Asia, but it has already lifted itself a long way out of the bottom league.

Evidence of the new and burgeoning middle class is everywhere. The highways

in the country long before you see the photographs in the daily papers of accused persons in police stations, usually standing alongside some item related to their alleged offence. Few Thais see this as a violation of the rights of accused persons. Instead, such pictures are understood as proof of the continuing successes of the police in combating crime.

The position of the military, too, in Thailand is very strong. Ordinary soldiers can behave with very un-Thai arrogance in casual encounters. All male citizens are theoretically liable to military service at 21, but

OPPOSITE: Gold-leaf being placed on a Buddha image in Nakhorn Phathom. ABOVE: Gold lacquer doors at Wat Phra Singh, Chiang Mai;

the catch is that, because smaller numbers are required than are available, there's a lottery to select those who will in fact serve, and it's the poor who always seem to lose. The dire significance of this becomes clear when you consider that 41 soldiers had to have legs amputated in a Bangkok hospital after treading on landmines in the 1988 conflict with Laos over a border hill so insignificant it had no name, only a number.

The remains of Old Asia can still be seen, too, in matters of public health. You need only to look at the statistics for the incidence of leprosy, and compare them with government funding available for its treatment and prevention, to see this. It's too complex a subject to deal with in a book of this nature, but the crux is that it's a disease that strikes at the undernourished — well-fed doctors dealing with cases have never been known to contract it. The continuing incidence of leprosy in a developing country such as Thailand is an indicator that there is still some way to go on the road to genuine modernization and reform.

A BRIGHTLY LIT FUTURE

Even so, the Thais still manage to present a cheerful face to life in a way that has become legendary. In addition, perhaps because the classes are so sharply distinct, there is an absence of the endless attention to exact social status, and all the petty snobberies that go with this, observable in such long-democratic states as the United Kingdom. There is a charm about Thai life that travelers have been commenting on for centuries, and it still persists. And as economic growth continues, so Thailand will with luck move into the position of having the best of both worlds, the traditions and natural blessings that already make it such an attractive tourist destination and the comfort and sense of well-being that goes with a country emerging into the bright light of economic prosperity.

MONARCHISM

No visitor to the country can fail to be struck by the devotion of ordinary Thais to their king. Not only does Bumipol's picture hang everywhere, but also the pictures of the beloved 19th-century kings Chulalongkorn and Mongkut. Talk to a peasant in his rice paddy and he will refer, not to "the king" but to "'my king". Limestone caves all over the kingdom contain rocks signed with the royal initials to commemorate a visit. And there are few big festivals in Bangkok not graced by the presence of one of the royal family with guards with horse-hair plumes of every color of the rainbow in evidence.

There is an element of the veneration of the priest-kings of old in all this. The Thai royal family leans heavily for its legitimization on Buddhism — or rather Brahminism: pure Buddhism has no concern for affairs of state. The way the king is regarded by the average Thai is close to worship, and contains in almost all cases no element of envy or resentment. (It should be said, though, that the Thai monarchy is well protected by a strong *lese-majeste* law against any public criticism.)

Nevertheless, there is a tradition going back to Kings Mongkut and Chulalongkorn in the last century of the monarch being in the forefront of the drive for modernization, a tradition fostered by the custom of sending young Thai princes to Europe for their education. And there is no doubt whatsoever that the present ruler, King Bhumipol, stands resolutely and unambiguously in that tradition.

A MONASTIC PERSPECTIVE

Every Buddhist Thai male spends a period of his youth living in a temple, and many return for periods of varying length in later life. Given this fact, a visit to, and preferably a few days' residence in, a Thai temple can add a whole new dimension to a stay in the country.

It's relatively easy for men to arrange this, considerably more difficult for women. But in either case what you should do is approach any English-speaking monk in any temple and politely ask how such a visit might be arranged.

What you will find is a way of life that begins at four in the morning with two hours of chanting and meditation, followed by a walk through the nearby streets begging for offerings of food.

Once breakfast is over, various tasks are undertaken, and then the main meal of the day is served shortly before noon. Thai monks, following the practice of the Lord Buddha, are not permitted to eat anything after midday.

For accommodation you'll be provided with a wooden palette and a thin cloth. If you're lucky, you might get a bottle of Coca Cola with which to fight off the pangs of hunger during the long hot night.

Most people, though, will be content to visit a typical monastery rather more

a lot worse than visit Bangkok's Wat Santi-asoke where a radical abbot, Phra Pottilux, is leading his community along new paths. Situated in the untouristed Bundkapi district, it isn't easy to find. But it's a place that has seen many eminent Thais, from Bangkok's Governor Chamlong downwards, arrive to pay homage.

When I went there it was a Sunday, and most of the laymen there were dressed in the traditional plain blue smocks of the rural poor. My guide took his rings off. "Too much fashion," he said. "It isn't proper."

briefly. The big Bangkok temples are not the best choice — there are so many tourists in evidence the monks tend, not surprisingly, to be on the defensive. Choose, instead, somewhere up-country, or one of the Bangkok temples not mentioned in this, or any, guidebook. You'll soon know if you've hit on a suitable place — if you're welcome, it'll be the monks themselves who will smile first, and if you smile back, quickly approach you and begin to try out their English.

A New Direction

If, however, you're not only seriously interested in Buddhism but also eager to experience its purer manifestations, you could do

Everything at Wat Santiasoke is reasonable and well thought-out. Sunday has been adopted as a "venerable day" because that fits in with the international week–weekend routine, and temple rituals are conducted in Thai whenever possible. When the traditional Pali is used (a dead Indian language few Thais understand), there is simultaneous translation into Thai.

The temple has revived vegetarianism, an ancient Buddhist principle, even though Thai Buddhism does not formally adhere to it. The approach road is lined with

King Bhumipol takes the salute on the King's Birthday parade outside the National Assembly building in Bangkok.

vegetarian food stalls, and round the corner on the main road there are food shops so dedicated to service rather than profit that they display the prices they pay for items in brackets alongside the prices they charge the customer.

My guide took me inside the temple compound where monks sat laughing and talking to lay people about their problems. There were all classes of people there, my guide said, millionaires and farmers, doctors and factory workers. Someone was getting a very close "student" haircut —

"clean and cool, but also indicating austerity" — and other people were laying out herbs to dry in the sun.

Some monks were involved in making copies of cassettes of the Phra Pottilux's sermons, to be loaned out free of charge, while others were setting up type for printed versions. Generally the atmosphere was one of ordered, varied and meaningful work.

Wat Santiasoke is a sign of new directions in Thai Buddhism. I asked to see the main sanctuary and was shown a plain hall that bore no relation to the gaudily painted boht of a regular temple.

"We don't waste time on that sort of thing here," said the guide.

PROSTITUTION

All the world knows, however, that the Thais are not solely a devout and self-deny-

Thai monks — ABOVE: on the pre-breakfast begging round; OPPOSITE: a tattooed monk prays in Wat Maharat, Sukhothai.

ing people. Bangkok's massage parlours are celebrated the world over, and the curious male tourist won't take long to discover that they're not confined to the capital. The first-time visitor might be surprised, however, to learn that the phenomenon is not a product of foreign tourism, or of the American troop presence during the Vietnam War. Ranks of girls sitting behind a glass window with numbers round their necks can be seen in provincial hotels up and down the country, with not a foreigner in sight. For better or worse, it's a social institution that's gained a wider acceptance in Thailand than perhaps anywhere else in the world.

The reasons for this are not difficult to find. On the one hand the social, and economic, dominance of the male has a long history in Southeast Asia; on the other, Buddhism has never regarded what other religions have dubbed "the sins of the flesh" particularly seriously.

It would be foolish to try to pretend that Thailand's reputation as a land of easy sex isn't a major ingredient in its tourist appeal. Statistics show that unaccompanied males constitute a far higher proportion of visitors here than they do in most other comparable countries.

Other than that, there's little on which to comment. Some people think it's a phenomenon that sadly spoils an otherwise delightful country; others will say that the Thais involved go about their work with such ingenuous charm they are enough to give the business a good name. In a country where a man can take a "junior wife" (*mia noi*), they argue, what on earth's wrong in taking a wife just for the night. Here, rather more literally than in most other spheres, you pay your money and you take your choice.

A LIFE IN THE HILLS

By and large the Thais are a homogeneous people. Racial minorities, apart from the large Chinese presence in Bangkok and other major cities, are confined to the Malay or part-Malay Muslims in the south and the curious and much discussed hill tribes in the north.

The mysterious arrival of these hill people in Thailand is the subject of much debate.

A study of their languages shows many of the tribes originate in the Tibetan plateau. Most of them only migrated to Thailand this century.

What makes the hill tribes of northern Thailand so fascinating is that these largely migrant people will have no truck with city life. They remain essentially classless, continue to dress for the most part in traditional costume, are content to cultivate land the

Thais don't want, and stubbornly grow and smoke opium.

The Thai government is making strenuous efforts both to improve their standard of living and to encourage them to conform to more socially acceptable lifestyles. Prominent in this program is the Royal Development Project for the Hill Tribes.

There are however, considerable difficulties involved in this approach. On the one hand the opium poppy which the hill tribes are so adept at cultivating, and to which many of them are addicted, is the source of lethal heroin addiction in the cities, in Thailand and elsewhere. But on the other hand their way of life is not something that ought to be obliterated by the demands of

conformity and integration under the guise of drug control.

Furthermore, the hill tribes are a major attraction for tourists, so much so that overexposure to foreigners is fast becoming one of the biggest threats to their traditional lifestyle. There's no doubt that the hill tribes' popularity with foreigners is one of the main reasons why the Thais are likely to go easy in any attempt to coerce these colorful outsiders in their midst into a more regular mode of existence.

There's no problem at all in actually getting to see the hill people. Trekking is one of the main tourist activities up in the north, and treks out of Chiang Mai and Chiang Rai invariably advertise a night or two in hill tribe villages as among their key attractions.

And despite everything, the presence — so close to a modern society — of traditionally-dressed people living their lives very largely according to the dictates of their opium dreams cannot fail to constitute an attraction for young visitors deeply drawn to the romantic call of such an apparently carefree lifestyle.

A PASTORAL LIFE

The overwhelming majority of Thais still live and work in the countryside. There is, of course, considerable poverty and deprivation; nevertheless most of Thailand remains an immensely pleasant place.

Images of the traditional pastoral life, though, complete with elephants, and fishing from sailing boats, are nowadays rather wide of the mark. Elephants, anyway, were never used in farming — their original function in ancient Siam was ceremonial, and as instruments of war. White elephants were given to each other as presents by kings throughout Southeast Asia, and if one was stolen by an enemy, wars were waged to retrieve them.

When in the 1880s foreign nations won concessions to fell and extract timber, the British came up with the idea of training elephants specifically for the job. Though today their role has largely been taken over by machines, there are still around ten thousand of them working in the teak forests of the north, or in the far south near the Malaysian border. They are used in rough jungle terrain to bring logs to the edge of forest roads where they can be collected by trucks. An adult elephant can haul two tons, and lift 700 kg (1,500 lbs) with its tusks.

But the best places to see them are elsewhere. Treks in the north usually contain a two-hour ride on an elephant as part of the journey, and elephant shows feature in the displays of Thai country life put on at places like the Rose Garden outside Bangkok

page 187 for details) where the animals are prepared for forest work, and tourists are welcome.

FISHERMEN OF THE SOUTH

Songkhla, on the Gulf of Siam, claims to be the largest fishing port in Asia, but it's on the other side of the isthmus, in the thinly populated southwest, that fishermen's life can be seen at its most relaxed. There's also more coral here than in the southeast — coral needs abundant sunlight, and the clear

and Pattaya's Nong Nooch Village. There's also a daily show at Pattaya's Elephant Village, just outside the town. And the biggest show of all is the annual Elephant Round-Up, organized by the Tourist Authority of Thailand (TAT) at Surin every November.

There are a hundred or so wild elephants in the Khao Yai National Park, 205 km (128 miles) north of Bangkok. This is the best place in Thailand, and one of the best in Asia for observing tropical nature, including some large animals, in its natural state. Contact TAT for full details.

In addition, the government runs a Young Elephant Training Center north of Lampang (see AROUND CHAING MAI, ELEPHANT CAMPS,

water of the Andaman Sea provides ideal conditions for its growth.

But even in such a natural paradise as the coast of Krabi and Trang provinces, there are problems. Reefs have been damaged or destroyed by dynamiting for fish, and by the use of heavy anchors. And the grotesque proposal to sink old car tires covered in cement as substitute breeding grounds for fish demonstrates just how far things have gone in some areas.

Thai temples, always ornate and sometimes gorgeous, are often in addition surprising, and even on occasions odd. OPPOSITE: A rare Hindu temple, Silom Road, Bangkok; ABOVE: eyes unexpectedly regard you at Wat Yannawa, Bangkok.

Bangkok and Ayutthaya

Capitals
New and Old

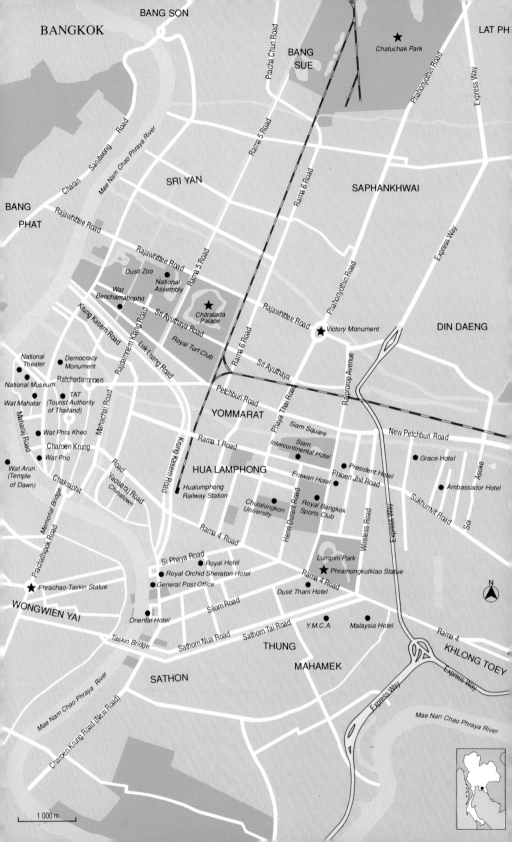

BANGKOK

"It is impossible to consider these populous modern cities of the East," wrote Somerset Maugham in 1930, contemplating Bangkok, "without a certain malaise. They are all alike, with their straight streets, their arcades, their tramways, their dust, their blinding sun, their teeming Chinese, their dense traffic, their ceaseless din. They have no history, no traditions. Painters have not painted them. No poets, transfiguring dead bricks and mortar with their divine nostalgia, have given them a tremulous melancholy not their own. They live their own lives, without associations, like a man without imagination.... They give you nothing. But when you leave them it is with a feeling that you have missed something, and you cannot help thinking that they had some secret that they have kept from you. And although you have been a trifle bored, you look back upon them wistfully; you are certain they have after all something to give you which, had you stayed longer, or under other conditions, you would have been capable of receiving."

Bangkok ("town of olives", more often called by the Thais "Krung Thep", "city of angels") no longer has trams, and the Chinese teem no more than anybody else. Few people, either, are these days bored in Bangkok. But the city nevertheless remains on first acquaintance a slightly forbidding place.

Other cities have their compensations, features such as surrounding mountains, a frontage on the sea, or an inheritance of spacious public parks, that help in some measure at least to counteract the horrors of the modern megalopolis. Bangkok has none of these. Instead, under torrid tropical skies, and with no underground or suburban railway system, it seems a city permanently held to ransom by its traffic.

Nevertheless, Bangkok is crammed with attractions. Like any capital, it exudes interest simply by virtue of the fact that it draws to it so much of the country's vital life. Its nightlife is famous — notorious if you will — all over the world. Its temples, crowded though they may be with visitors,

are anything but the lethargically picturesque structures that add such interest to the rest of the countryside. Bangkok was made into the Thai capital, almost by an act of will, in the early 19th century, and for better or worse it now exhibits all the features you'd expect from the metropolis of one of Asia's most fast-developing nations.

In addition, as the center of government and home base of the Thai royal family, Bangkok periodically lays on parades and ritual ceremonies more splendid — and photogenic — than can be found anywhere

else in the country. To watch the parade of the royal guards outside the National Assembly building on one of the royal anniversaries is to see as colorful a mix of Western and Asian, ancient and modern, as you can witness anywhere in the region.

And as for a modicum of peace and quiet, the Chao Phraya River does provide something of a respite from the noise, and even from the heat, of this tumultuous and at times oppressive conurbation.

Even so, it's as well for first-time visitors to come prepared. Bangkok does have its attractions, and they are real ones, but the transport problem is such that they do nowadays come dangerously close to being eclipsed by the mechanical onslaught.

A short time spent studying the following two sections, and referring to the map opposite, will acquaint you with the main areas and lines of communication of the city,

Roofs of Wat Saket (The Golden Mount Temple). Constructed during the reign of Rama I (1782–1809), this temple affords fine views of the capital. Its golden *chedi* contains relics of the Lord Buddha.

and stand you in good stead for coming to terms with the sometimes difficult situation on the ground.

A BIRD'S EYE VIEW

Bangkok mostly lies to the east of two bends in the Chao Phraya River.

West of the river is Thonburi, an extensive area but one that contains only one notable monument, Wat Arun (Temple of the Dawn).The modern center of Bangkok is all on the eastern side.

The Historic Center

Close to the river, and directly opposite Wat Arun, is the historic center of the city, containing the Grand Palace and Wat Pho. This is the most attractive part of Bangkok, much visited, of course, by tourists, but an area of relative peace compared with the rest of the city.

The Administrative Area

Not far to the north stands the Democracy Monument, erected in memory of Thai-

Long Live the King! ABOVE: The royal throne, Bangkok; OPPOSITE: Prince Vijiralongkorn, the Thai Crown Prince, pauses to accept a message from a young member of the public during his father's sixtieth birthday celebrations.

land's first constitution, agreed to in 1932. This marks the southern end of the administrative area of the city where most of the government offices are situated. Close to the monument itself is Khaosarn Road, the Mecca of budget travelers seeking cheap accommodation in the city. And just to the north, adjacent to the Dusit Zoo, stands the National Assembly building. The wide street leading up to its façade is the venue for major national military parades on occasions such as the King's Birthday.

Some way to the east is **Sukhumvit Road**, the major up-market residential area of the capital, and also a nightlife district. And away to the south, on the other side of Lumpini Park, is the **Silom and Surawong Road** district, the city's premier nightlife area.

MAJOR COMMUNICATIONS

Three major roads run east–west through the capital. From north to south, they are: (1) **Petchburi Road**, becoming **New Petchburi Road**, both of which can be numbered among the foulest urban highways on the planet; (2) **Rama I Road**, briefly becoming **Phloen Jhit Road**, then finally becoming **Sukhumvit Road**. Rama I Road passes Siam Square on its south side, home to several major cinemas. Phloen Jhit Road is where several big department stores are located, while Sukhumvit Road houses, in its many long sois, almost all the luxury residences and exclusive restaurants in the capital; and (3), **Rama 4 Road**, passing the Snake Farm, the Dusit Thani Hotel (and statue of Rama the Fourth himself opposite), Lumpini Park and the Lumpini Boxing Stadium — all except the hotel on the north side — before meeting Sukhumvit Road several kilometers further west.

Each of these three arterial roads runs underneath the **Express Way** which carries through-traffic north to south across the city, and without which, ugly though it is, Bangkok would certainly have ceased operating altogether some years ago.

Four important roads run north to south and link Rama I and Rama 4 in the central area. From the west, they are: (1) **Phaya Thai Road**, a major bus route which has the Mah

Boon Krong Department Store on the corner on the left where it meets Rama I Road; (2) **Henri Dunant Road**; (3) **Ratchadamri Road**, with the Erawan Shrine on the corner on the right where it meets Rama I Road, with MacDonald's and the Sogo Department Store just round the same corner; and (4) **Wireless Road**, with its many embassies.

Bordered by Ratchadamri Road, Rama 4 Road and Wireless Road is **Lumpini Park**, the only large park in the center of the city.

South of Rama 4 Road, four important roads run southwest towards the river —

Surawong and Silom roads, and **Sathorn Nua** and **Sathorn Tai** roads. Between the first two lies the world-famous nightlife area of Patphong, centered on Patphong Road. In addition, there is a tourist-oriented informal night market along the end of Silom nearest Rama 4 specializing in counterfeit-brand-name clothes, watches etc. The two Sathorn roads, both one-way, constitute an in-city throughway with few commercial premises.

Surawong and Silom intersect with **New Road** — a street running parallel with and a few hundred meters from the river. Between the river and the road is an attractive area containing the Oriental, Shangri-la and Royal Orchid Sheraton hotels (plus the much cheaper Swan Hotel), and the old Portuguese Embassy.

ABOVE: Classic elegance, focused on a seated Buddha statue, in Bangkok's marbled Sukhothai Hotel. OPPOSITE TOP: Bangkok's Royal Orchid Hotel, one of the city's many superb hotels. OPPOSITE BOTTOM: Consistently rated among the world's top five hotels, The Oriental not only boasts luxury but a century of history.

WHERE TO STAY

Now you have got some idea of the basic layout of Bangkok's central area, and before setting out to take a look at it in more detail, you'll need to decide on somewhere to stay. There are naturally a great many hotels and guesthouses in the Thai capital, and all it's feasible to do here is list a few in each price category. The main aim to is assist those arriving on their own without having accommodation booked in advance through travel or tour agents.

The **Oriental** ((02) 236-0400 FAX (02) 236-1939 (394 rooms; expensive), claims to be the best hotel in town, but the **Shangri-la** ((02) 236-7777 FAX (02) 236-8579 to 80 (700 rooms; expensive), is at least as good. These and the **Royal Orchid Sheraton** ((02) 234-5599 FAX (02) 236-8320 (775 rooms; expensive) are all on the river. Facing Lumpini Park stands the **Dusit Thani** ((02) 236-0450 to 59 FAX (02) 236 6400 (525 rooms; expensive), while the **Regent Bangkok** ((02) 251-6127 FAX (02) 253-9195 (400 rooms; expensive), is on Ratchadamri Road. The **Meridien President** ((02) 253-0444 FAX (02) 253-7565 (400 rooms; expensive) and the **Landmark** ((02) 254-0404 FAX (02) 254-4259 (415 rooms; expensive) are on Phloenjhit and Sukhumvit roads respectively, while the revamped and now extremely sumptious **Grand Hyatt Erawan** ((02) 254-1234 FAX (02) 253-5856 (400 rooms; expensive) is around the corner on Ratchadamri Road, by the popular Erawan Shrine. Increasingly popular among business travelers is the new batch of small, exclusive "boutique" hotels, such as **Mansion Kempinski** ((02) 255-7200 FAX (02) 253-2329 (127 rooms; expensive), which is on Sukhumvit Road.

Rather less expensive is the **Ambassador** ((02) 254-0444 FAX (02) 253-4123 (935 rooms; average and above) further down Sukhumvit in the middle of a restaurant and entertainment complex. On the other side of town, not far from the Grand Palace, is the old but atmospheric **Royal** ((02) 222-9111 to 26 FAX (02) 224 2083 (297 rooms; moderate).

There are a number of hotels at the river end of Suriwong and Silom roads, the **Narai** ((02) 233-3350 FAX (02) 236-7161 (480 rooms;

average and above), the **New Peninsular**
((02) 234-3910 to 17 FAX (02) 236-5526
(113 rooms; average and above) and, nearer
Patphong Road, the **Montien** (/FAX (02)
234-8060 (500 rooms; expensive).

The **Y.M.C.A. Collins International
House** ((02) 287-2727 FAX (02) 287-1996
(147 rooms; moderate) is very good value,
as is **Orchid Inn** ((02) 234-8934 FAX (02) 234-
4159 (moderate), which is close to the river,
on Sri Phraya Road. Cheaper again are the
Reno Hotel ((02) 215-0026 to 27, on Soi
Kasemsan 1, off Rama 1, the **Sukhumvit**

invasion, these are often very Thai places —
you leave your shoes at the foot of the stairs,
and the family provides you with hot water
in a vacuum flask. Rates start from around
US$4 a night for a clean room, rarely with
air-conditioning. The ambiance is congenial, with much exchanging of information
and late-night chatting in cafes. There's a
food market close by, and clothes stalls. It's
reasonably quiet, too, at least after midnight
— a rare quality in Bangkok.

It's also very easy to rent flats or rooms
for extended periods. Establishments ad-

Crown ((02) 253-8401 FAX (02) 353-5675, on
Sukhumvit Soi 8, and the **Swan** ((02) 234-
8594 FAX (02) 237-1046, close to the Oriental.

Close to the Swan is the **Executive Pent-
house** ((02) 235-2642 FAX (02) 236-1491
(moderate), where rooms can be rented by
the month or by the day.

As for the budget category, everything
you could desire can be found in **Khaosarn
Road**, close to the Democracy Monument on
Rajdamnern Klang Road. This and neighboring streets contain a mass of family-run
establishments, usually over a small restaurant. The clientele is almost exclusively
non-Thai, and the restaurants specialize in
all the things backpackers like to eat at home
or away from home. Despite this foreign

vertise every day in both the *Bangkok Post*
and *The Nation* (the latter claiming to give
up-to-the-minute occupancy levels). These
places are rarely full, and it is possible to take
accommodation for very short periods, so
there's no difficulty in changing if you feel
dissatisfied with where you've opted for.
Some differ scarcely at all from hotel rooms
with attached bathrooms; others, by contrast, have the aura of endlessly re-used
love-nests.

WHERE TO EAT

Bangkok, with its large foreign community
and huge, year-round tourist influx, has a
very wide range of restaurants, many of

them superb. The serious gourmet should invest in a copy of the *Bangkok Restaurant Guide,* published in Thailand by Asia Books in an English–Thai parallel text edition. Their claim that it could pay for itself in one meal is probably justified, depending of course on the meal.

On the River

Some of the nicest places to eat are by the river. These must begin with the world-famous, and very expensive, **Normandie** ((02) 236-0400, in the Oriental Hotel — French cuisine in a dining room imitating the restaurant car of the old *Orient Express.* Also expensive, and huge, is the **Baan Khun Luang** ((02) 241-2282, serving Thai food in several rooms. More reasonably priced is the **Tasaneeya Nava (Banya)** ((02) 437-7329, opposite the Oriental — the restaurant will send a boat for you from the Oriental's or the Shangri-la's pier. Lastly, and nicest of all, is the **Maharaj** ((02) 221-9073, situated at the stop of the same name on the regular Express Boat service. The food is Thai, not Indian as the name suggests, and there's traditional Thai music from 7 to 9 PM.

Rama I — Lumpini Park

In the central area there are several good restaurants. Along Soi Langsuan (running from almost opposite the President Hotel to Lumpini Park) **Paesano 1** ((02) 252-3592, serves good Italian food, while further down, on the other side of the road, **Whole Earth** ((02) 252-5574, serves vegetarian and other Thai food. Just past the Whole Earth, on the corner opposite the park, is the **Ngwanlee Lungsuan** ((02) 251-8366. Here cheap and excellent Chinese and Thai food is on offer in a dining room that is partly open-air (with a sliding roof for use during wet weather).

For dining in high style, the Regent Hotel on Ratchadamri Road, parallel with Soi Langsuan, has its French cuisine **La Brasserie** ((02) 251-6127, and Thai **Spice Market** ((02) 251-6603. At lunch time in the former you can enjoy a buffet of the highest order for a little over 500 baht. You'll have to dig deeper into your pockets at **Bus-saracum** ((02) 235-8915, further south off Convent Road, but it's worth it for its

unique "royal Thai cuisine", served to live Thai music.

Sukhumvit Road

The *sois* off Sukhumvit Road are thronged with classy restaurants, getting more lavish as the *soi* numbers rise. There's only room to mention three, one outstanding, and two less ambitious but deservedly popular. **Lemongrass** ((02) 258-8637, on Soi 24 is famous for serving sumptuous Thai food in authentic Old World surroundings. On Sukhumvit Road itself, on the corner of

Soi 33, and very near Elite Books, **Pan Pan** ((02) 258-5071, is a very charming Italian cafe-restaurant. Finally, further back up the road towards the center of town, **Bei Otto** ((02) 242-6836, serves traditional German food with great relish.

Equally surprising is the tongue-in-cheek humor of **Cabbages and Condoms** off Sukhumvit Road, which is run by the Population & Community Development Association to promote the family-planning message ("our food is guaranteed not to cause pregnancy").

Dining alfresco OPPOSITE by the Chao Phya river and ABOVE indoor in an equally natural setting amid typical Thai decor in the stylish restaurant of Bangkok's Royal Orchid Hotel.

Bangkok and Ayutthaya

Just off Soi 3 here is a fine Egyptian restaurant, the **Nasir Al-Masri** ((02) 253-5582 — it stays open till 3 AM. (See also under **Vegetarian**, below).

Patphong

Good French food in intimate surroundings can be found at **La Paloma** ((02) 233-3853, on Mahaesak Road, down towards New Road. The **Cafe India** ((02) 234-1720, opposite the Trocadero Hotel on Surawong Road, is close by.

Show Restaurants

For a show of Thai classical dancing along with the meal, try the **Sala Rim Nam** ((02) 437-9471, on the river (Thonburi bank) opposite the Oriental Hotel or the **Ruen Thep** ((02) 235-8760, in the Silom Village Trade Center on Silom Road. Also offering Thai dance with your dinner — but with a lot more besides — is the enormous **Tum-Nak-Thai** ((02) 276-7810, slightly out of the way on Ratchadaphisek Road. It's the largest outdoor restaurant in the world, accommodating up to 3,000 customers, with a bevy of waiters on rollerskates!

Vegetarian

Thai Buddhism is not the non-meat-eating variety, but vegetarians can find the food they require with a little trouble. Apart from the Whole Earth restaurant (see above), there is the **Mah Boon Krong** department store, near Silom Square. Here there is a wide selection of food stalls on the top floor, including one vegetarian stall (but it does close in the early evening). There are others on the ground floor of the **Mall** department store, and in the **Ram Food Center**, both inexpensive but rather out on a limb from tourists' Bangkok on Ramkhamheng Road. The one place in Bangkok to find vegetarian food in abundance is in the vicinity of **Wat Santiasoke**.

There are also a number of Indian restaurants serving vegetarian meals — the superb **Moghul Room** ((02) 253-6989, on

Soi 11, off Sukhumvit Road (opposite the Ambassador Hotel), the rather less expensive **Akbar's** ((02) 253-3479, on Sukhumvit Soi 3, and the **Shaharazade** ((02) 251-3666, on the same *soi*.

Fast Food

There is an increasing number of outlets for American fast food, concentrated in the major shopping and commercial areas. There are several **MacDonald's** (expensively smart places to the average Thai), for example on Phloen Jhit and Silom roads. There are **Dunkin' Donuts** and other scarcely distinguishable establishments on Rama 1 (between the cinemas fronting Siam Square) and at the top (Dusit Thani) end of Silom Road.

Do-It-Yourself

The supermarket where resident Westerners buy their delicacies is the **Villa Market**, close to Soi 33 on Sukhumvit Road.

GETTING TO KNOW THE CITY

Bangkok's attractions are best seen area by area. In this way, transport difficulties can be kept to a minimum. You can walk between sites, or, in the case of those accessible by water, take a delightful trip on one of the river boats.

THE GRAND PALACE AND WAT PHO

Bangkok's **Grand Palace**, and **Wat Phra Kheo**, within its grounds, were established in 1782 with the foundation of the Chakri dynasty, and the promulgation of Bangkok as the Thai capital in succession to Thonburi on the other side of the river.

Anything more like a fairy palace, a magic castle of dreams, it's difficult to imagine. It's too gorgeous, too colorful to be true — it must be a dream, a vision of true ecstasy and happiness.

It really does have the power to make you exult in its presence. Maybe that was what it was designed to do in the first place.

From time to time *son et lumiere* shows are staged here, but they tend to be rather disappointing because what this kind of architecture needs above all is the glory and

The famous Reclining Buddha in Bangkok's Wat Pho. The gigantic figure glitters in great splendor. You can walk round it and examine the revered presence from every angle. The soles of its feet are particularly noteworthy.

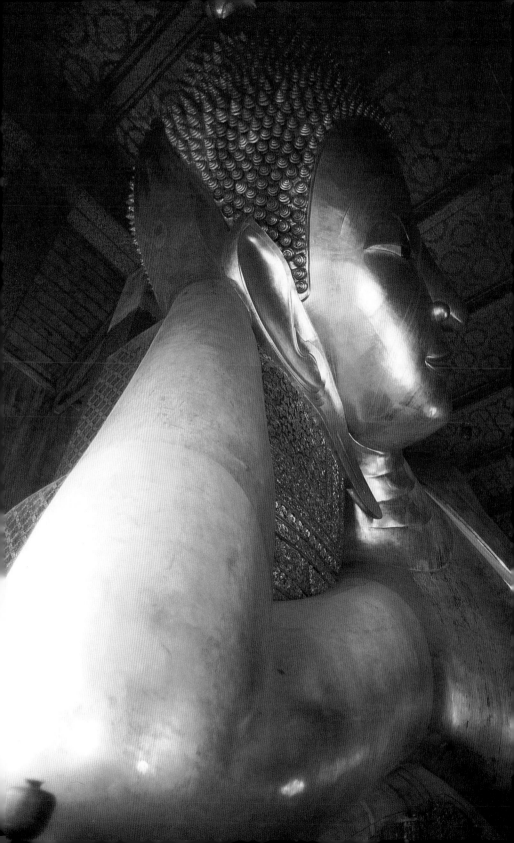

green image that it's forbidden to photo-graph and that is held to be linked to the very continuance of the Chakri dynasty itself. This is typical of the magical power attrib-uted to sacred objects worldwide, and in this case the Buddha image's supreme potency long predates the supremacy of the current Thai royal family. Its recorded history alone goes back to the 15th century, since when it has been fought over by contenders for

power of the sun. In the brilliant Thai sun-light, the multicolored mosaics and soaring gold stupas intoxicate with their sheer, unambiguous splendor.

But it isn't all show. Splendor is com-bined with serenity, and worldly display blended with spiritual confidence in an im-pregnable unity. The sumptuousness and extravagance, which seems so unrestrained to Western taste, is actually blended with an elegance that is quite as sophisticated as anything in Europe's bastions of culture, in Vienna, Paris or Venice. And in fact much of it is European — the classical courtyards and administrative buildings that flank the temple are imported 19th century state ar-chitecture in style. The Grand Palace has, combined with its magnificence, something of the quiet elegance of the colonnades of Aix en Provence or Verona.

The Emerald Buddha

Wat Phra Kheo is better known as the Tem-ple of the Emerald Buddha. It contains a

Golden Bangkok — ABOVE: the Standing Buddha of Wat Indrawihan (on Thanon Wisut Kasat in Bangkhunphrom), often called "Laung Pho To" after its builder; ABOVE RIGHT and OPPOSITE LEFT: in the Temple of the Emerald Buddha; OPPOSITE RIGHT: roofs at Wat Pho, each with its horn-shaped *chofa*.

power in many parts of Southeast Asia. To this day the Thai monarch in person ritually changes the little early-Chakri period cloaks the image wears, a different one for each of the three Thai seasons.

Admission to the complex is 125 baht. Hours are Mondays to Sundays from 8:30 AM to noon and from 1 to 3:30 PM. For-mal dress is essential — no shorts.

Wat Pho

Wat Pho is Bangkok's oldest and grandest temple, and contains Thailand's largest Re-clining Buddha which is 46 m (150 ft) long and 15 m (49 ft) high. It's also one of those monuments scattered round the world which the continual presence of masses of tourists effectively deprives of much of the atmosphere the visitors came to sample in the first place. You are yourself that which you most resent. From this paradox there is, unfortunately, no known escape.

One solution is to go early in the morning, soon after sunrise. Then, with luck, you will see this large temple more or less as it was intended to be experienced.

The temple is divided into two halves by Jetuphon Road; one half is taken up with the monks' quarters. The features you might choose to photograph in the other, public, section are the large chedis in the courtyard (either containing the ashes of or commemorating the country's first four kings of the modern dynasty), the inlaid mother-of-pearl soles of the Reclining Buddha's feet, the beautiful reliefs from Ayutthaya round the base of the main *bot* (often seen as rubbings on sale all over the city), the painted teak shutters in the hall containing the giant

Buddha, and the traditional medical practitioners who still dispense treatment daily in the main compound. Many features of the temple were extensively restored to mark the King's 60th birthday in 1988.

The Reclining Buddha itself is made of brick, covered in cement and then finally overlaid with gold leaf. It was constructed during the reign of Rama III in about 1824. Like all reclining Buddhas, it depicts the great teacher's last position before death.

You won't be admitted to the great hall containing the statue after 5 PM.

The River

The Chao Phraya River represents Bangkok's only major contact with nature, and consequently is far and away the most congenial feature of the city.

It's also an important highway, both nationally and within the capital. The Chao Phraya Express Boat Service is the most efficient means of traveling between two points on the river's course, and it's easily the pleasantest way to get about anywhere in the city.

Oriental Hotel

Begin at the **Oriental Hotel Pier**. Before embarking on a river boat, you could take a walk round the nearby area, one of the least changed in Bangkok, and perhaps take a snack on the hotel's **riverside terrace**, not cheap, but one of the most congenial places in the city. The hotel itself is worth a look, too. It's one of Bangkok's oldest, and though the newer section now dominates the scene, the old part — closest to the pier — is still in use. The hotel has many literary associations, something the management makes perhaps

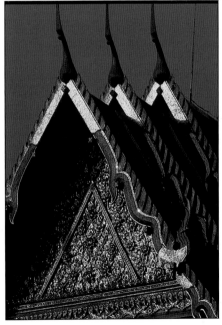

rather too much of, but at least you'll have information to hand when you're there about who stayed there when, and so on.

The Express Boat
Back at the Pier, just say "Express Boat" and you'll be shown where to wait. You want one going to the right, i.e. up-river.

Once on-board, take a seat and someone will come round and collect your fare. Charges vary according to where you're going, so you should read on and decide in advance where it is you want to get off.

For Wat Pho or Wat Arun, ask for a ticket to Tha Tien.

A Monks' Gate
You will notice that almost all the Express Boats have monks standing at the back in a group. If you ask them, they will say the reason for this is that they are not permitted by their monastic rules to sit next to or near women, but the real reason is probably that monks travel free of charge on all Bangkok

ABOVE: Detail of the finely carved and porcelain-decorated Wat Arun or Temple of the Dawn, in Bangkok. OPPOSITE: Glowing in the dark, Bangkok's huge golden *chedi*, on the grounds of the hilltop Wat Saket (familiarly called the Golden Mount Temple) is one of the city's most spectacular landmarks.
92

transport, and are in return expected not to occupy seats. At some Express Boat landing stages you are required to hand back your ticket, with a one baht fine if you can't find it. As the monks never have tickets, a special gate exists to let them out without their having to pass through the turnstile. This gate is operated at the push of a button by the attendant and is a comically elaborate mechanism to enable the continued operation of the principle of monastic poverty in modern conditions. Its essential purpose, of course, is to avoid a situation where the attendant can let people through the turnstile without paying the one baht fine at her own discretion, and hence open the way for corruption.

Tha Tien
To begin with, the Express Boat keeps to the right hand bank, and continues to do so for some way after passing under the first bridge (the Memorial Bridge). Note the plants floating down the river — they're water hyacinths and exist naturally in this state. After the bridge, look out for the Tha Tien stop, and get off there. Tha Tien is the stop for **Wat Pho**, — see under GRAND PALACE and WAT PHO above page 88, for details of this famous temple.

Before leaving the waterside, take a glance at the small **Market** immediately behind the landing stage. It seems to specialize in dried fish, and can hardly have changed since Conrad's day.

Wat Arun
Wat Arun is most conveniently reached from the Tha Tien landing stage. There's little to see (in contrast to Wat Pho), but the trip involves fresh air and gardens, and a superb lunch can be conveniently enjoyed immediately afterwards.

A ferry will take you over to the temple — enquire at Tha Tien. There is no Express Boat stop.

Named after Aruna, Indian god of the dawn, this Temple of the Dawn essentially consists of a simple *prang*, or gracefully tapering tower, in this case embedded with pieces of broken porcelain. It stands in rather attractively neglected gardens, and you can climb to half way up via some extremely

steep steps (easier to climb than descend). You get an excellent view over the city, with the river in the foreground, from the highest accessible point.

Wat Arun is a quiet place, much photographed from the river and seen as a symbol of Bangkok, but little visited. It's a good place to relax.

Maharat Restaurant

By now you'll no doubt be feeling hungry, so it's a quick trip back to Tha Tien, and then two more stops up-river on the Express Boat before getting off at the stop named **Maharat**.

Here lunch awaits you at the very fine restaurant of the same name as the landing-stage. The **Maharat Restaurant** is one of the nicest places to eat in the city. Situated right on the river, it's beautiful, charming and not particularly expensive. It is not haute cuisine, but with its flowering plants and rose tablecloths, (and Thai classical music in the evenings), it constitutes an essential ingredient of any Bangkok river-trip (see WHERE TO EAT, ON THE RIVER, page 87).

Wat Mahathat

After lunch, you'll probably feel like nothing more arduous than one last temple, and then a leisurely look at the **Royal Barges**.

Wat Mahathat stands across the street that runs past the Maharat Restaurant. This street, incidentally, is famous for its lines of stalls selling ancient amulets and other pendants. The monastery is far less touristed than Wat Pho, and is actually the premises of the Mahachulalongkorn Buddhist University so casual visitors are not encouraged. Nevertheless, you can slip in if you're discreet.

Immediately the atmosphere of quiet greets you. Pigeons flutter in the forecourt, and palm trees cast insufficient shade on orange tiles. Rows upon rows of dusty golden Buddhas line the cloisters, with memorial plaques to the recently dead, plus their photographs, at their feet. Cats and dogs pace about with a slowness that seems both deliberate and casual. Small groups of Thais chat softly round a venerated tree, the pink and yellow ribbons round its trunk fluttering in the light breeze. Some lie in the shade

asleep, stirring slightly as a bell rings high up under the eaves.

Inside in a lecture hall, the silence is absolute and only one fan in a dozen turns, like a prayer wheel. Boy monks are watching English football on television in the vestry.

You can walk through the temple compound and exit onto Phra Chan Road. At the gate you can buy a religious picture, a *memento mori* Thai-style, almost Surrealist in its iconography, depicting a pair of lovers aging, dying, and finally becoming skeletons, locked in a harsh parody of their youthful embraces.

The Royal Barges

From Wat Mahathat you can get to the **Royal Barges**, situated up a creek on the Thonburi side of the river, either by going back to Maharat landing stage and arranging water transport, or by taking a *tuk tuk* across Phrapinklao Bridge, getting off as soon as the bridge road descends to ordinary ground level.

If you do the latter, you should double back towards the river left of the bridge. The way is then well signposted in English, and leads you through a mass of wooden Thai houses, thereby giving you an insight into the lifestyle and living conditions of many Bangkok citizens it might be difficult to find otherwise.

The barges, ceremonial vessels for carrying the monarch along the river on state occasions, are housed in a large modern boathouse, looking like an aircraft hangar. There are eight of them, the longest 49 m (160 ft) long, all gorgeously decorated in red, black and gold, with rigid flags and fantastically carved prows. One old one is cut up into sections to reveal its structure. The boathouse closes at 4:30 PM. (See MORE RIVER TRIPS page 98).

OTHER TEMPLES

Wat Benchamabophit

Situated on Sri Ayuthaya Road, near Dusit Zoo, this is a very beautiful place. With its white Italian Carrara marble, orange Chinese tiles, very un-Thai stained glass (made in Florence), carved doors, embossed and gorgeously painted ceilings, this small temple encapsulates late 19th century Thai royal eclecticism. King Chulalongkorn embraced the West, and in this ornate yet oddly straightforward place, he brought all the glory of Italy to join hands with Thai piety and Thai splendor.

It was completed in 1899, and a portion of King Chulangkorn's ashes were laid to rest under the revered central Buddha image.

Wat Traimit

This temple, situated near Hualamphong Station, at the intersection of Yaowarat and

Charoen Krung roads, is without architectural or atmospheric interest but contains something difficult to believe, a statue of the Buddha made out of *five and a half tons* of solid gold.

The gold is claimed to be 18 carat, or 80 percent pure. It's assumed, on account of its style, to date from the Sukhothai period. The image was for a long time covered by plaster, and its true nature was only discovered when it was dropped by a crane while being moved in 1953. It can only have been plastered over to disguise it from enemies in time of invasion, possibly during one of the attacks on Ayutthaya by the Burmese. Why the plaster was not removed when the danger receded — unless all the

defenders in on the secret were killed — remains a mystery.

The image is about three meters (10 ft) high, and stands incongruously against a pink, gloss-painted wall.

CULTURAL ATTRACTIONS

The National Museum

To get to the **National Museum**, leave the Grand Palace by the main gate, cross the road and walk down Naphrathat Road, with the open grassy space known as Senam Luang on your right. You reach the museum entrance after passing along the front of Thammasat University.

The museum is vast, and quite varied, not only in the items it contains, but also in the standard of their presentation, and the buildings that house them. The Vejayany-Raja-Roth, a royal funeral chariot standing in a room crowded with many others, is itself worth the entrance fee. Reconstructions of scenes from Thai history (in the first pavilion you come to) are, on the other hand, less impressive.

As is often the case in Thailand, taking photos of venerable objects is not allowed for fear the resulting pictures might be used in unbecoming contexts (or take away some of the sanctity of the thing photographed).

Guided tours to the museum in English are held on Tuesday, Wednesday and Thursday mornings, a different aspect of Thai culture being covered each day. Check with TAT for the up-to-date details.

The National Museum is open from 9 AM to 4 PM daily, closed Mondays and Tuesdays. Admission is 20 baht.

The National Theater

Right next door to the museum is the **National Theater**.

This institution is not one dedicated to the best that is produced in the dramatic arts (as in some countries) so much as to regular displays of traditional dramatic forms. The theater is housed in a big, Western-style building of a kind now rather outdated in

---

Young and old monks wait with their begging bowls outside a temple in Bangkok. There are about 200,000 monks in Thailand, many committed to wearing the robes for life.

the West, with a classical front and a vast, proscenium-arch auditorium. Should you wander in through a wrong door you are likely to stumble onto dusty rooms, empty except for tribes of semi-domesticated cats.

Long historico-mythical court dramas (known as *khon*), based on stories from the Ramayana Indian epics and with instrumental and sung accompaniment, are staged in the main auditorium as follows — on the second weekend of the month: Friday at 5:30 PM, Saturday at 9:30 AM, 2 and 6 PM, and Sunday at 9:30 AM, 1 PM and 6 PM; on the fourth weekend of the month: Friday at 5:30 PM and Saturday at 1 PM only. Call ℂ (02) 224-1342 to confirm details. Entrance is 100 and 200 baht.

More to the popular taste are outdoor performances given every Saturday and Sunday at 4:30 PM. The style presented varies each week. They're very much social events, with people spreading out mats and newspapers for picnics.

Senam Luang

This open space in front of the National Theater and National Museum is the venue for interesting events at the weekends — free concerts, rallies and even demonstrations. This is where the king performs the annual Ploughing Ceremony. Kites are also flown here, and are on sale on the pavement where Phrachan Road meets the open area. In the summer months, large kites are flown, sometimes sponsored by one of the beer or soft drinks companies. Nothing could be more restful than to watch these beautiful kites while you sit down and rest your feet.

The Siam Society

This society, under royal patronage, maintains premises on the main road known as Sukhumvit Soi 21 (Soi Asoke). There are exhibitions of folk art and a reference library. Open daily (except Sundays and Mondays) from 9 AM to noon, then 1 to 5 PM.

Erawan Shrine

At the intersection of Rama I with Ratchadamri Road, you will see on one corner, diagonally opposite the site for the new World Trade Center, the Erawan Shrine, named after the sacred three-headed elephant of Buddhist iconography. This is a very important site for Thais — here requests are made, and devotional offerings promised should the request be granted. A troupe of somewhat tired-looking classical Thai dancers perform dances for a fee as part of the said offerings. The shrine stands in the

grounds of the former Erawan Hotel; the old colonial hotel's modern successor, the Grand Hyatt Erawan now stands on the same site.

Jim Thompson's House

Open every day except Sundays, from 9 AM to 5 PM, this was the home of a rich American who decided to settle in Thailand after the war and put his mind and resources to reinvigorating the Thai silk industry. His disappearance in the Cameron Highlands of Malaysia in 1967 has never been explained.

The attraction of the house — actually six fine old wooden buildings put together to make one — is that, in a country awash with Coca Cola and the Snoopy culture, it is a real

ABOVE: A glimpse of the gleaming interior of Jim Thompson's House, which houses a superb collection of Thai and Asian artifacts in a traditional teak Thai residence. OPPOSITE: A simple riverside cafe in Bangkok.

oasis of traditional Thai art. It's even worth the 100 baht entrance fee, and the often protracted wait for a guide. Most of all, it is an example of tropical luxury as it was in the old, pre-airconditioned days. It's infinitely more beautiful than anything modern day five-star Thailand can offer.

The house is full of the most wonderful objects from Burma, Cambodia, China and Thailand — the hard-working guides will tell you all you want to know about them, plus a great deal more. Thompson's silk factories were situated on the opposite bank of the *klong* (canal), and you can still see newly-dyed silk, from the few workshops that remain there, being dried in the sun.

The house stands in an idyllic setting on Soi Kasem San 2, off Rama I Road, a world away from modern Bangkok's traffic nightmare. The quiet little garden by the *klong*, empty of art objects, is almost more beautiful than the house; nature, as usual, has the last word. Entrance to this garden is free of charge.

A Bangkok *Klong*

Before you brace yourself to face the main road, turn left as you leave the garden and go down towards the *klong*. To inspect the silk factories, and see at first hand the living conditions of many of Bangkok's ordinary residents, cross the *klong* by a small punt that will come over to fetch you (fare: 5 baht). To summon this boat, just stand on the bank and wave.

SUKHUMVIT ROAD

Ploen Jhit continues under the Express Way, and over a railway track. It then becomes Sukhumvit Road. The **Regal Landmark Hotel** is on the right, and opposite are many small shops and curbside stalls dealing in craftwares, traveling bags and clothing for the tourist trade. This is also one of Bangkok's main nightlife areas — the **Grace Hotel** off to the left down Soi 3 (Soi Nana) and the **Nana Hotel** on the same *soi* to the right of the road, are central to the pleasure scene.

Next on the left is the **Ambassador Hotel**, with its attendant restaurants in the extensive forecourt between the hotel and the road. And finally, when you've passed the

wide road leading off to the left — Soi 21 (Soi Asoke) — you quickly reach the attractive sois in the thirties, and the particularly charming huddle, near Soi 33, of the **Pan Pan** cafe/restaurant, (see SUKHUMVIT ROAD under WHERE TO EAT page 87) and Bangkok's best second-hand bookstore for non-Thai volumes, **Elite Used Books**.

IN THE SNAKE PIT

The premises of the Thai Red Cross are in two parts, one on either side of Henri

Dunant Road where it joins Rama 4 Road. The part that houses the Snake Farm is on your right coming out of Henri Dunant. Alternatively, it's a short walk from Robinson's department store at the top of Silom Road, or the nearby Dusit Thani Hotel.

The public display of snake-handling and sample extraction of venom takes place daily at 2 PM with an extra display on 10:30 AM on weekends. Entry is 70 baht.

The farm was established in 1923 and its purpose is to produce anti-snakebite serum, for use at home and overseas.

The display takes place on two sides of an area of grass and water where the snakes are kept. The audience is divided into two, and two virtually identical displays take place simultaneously — presumably an arrangement to create space for the large proportion of tourists wanting to take photographs.

After a half-hour slide show, the snakes are simply held up and goaded lightly to encourage them to behave in ways that the keepers know the visitors will think photogenic. It's all very amiable, and almost unrehearsed, like so many things in Asia.

Then the small amount of venom — maybe two thirds of a gram (one fiftieth of an ounce) — is extracted from a couple of cobras, through their very large fangs into a small circular glass dish. But it's powerful stuff — enough to kill a thousand rabbits, or a significant number of human beings.

The snakes themselves are, of course, the real objects of wonder, rather than their keepers. They're immensely beautiful in their lithe, sinuous movement, as they elegantly coil themselves into spirals and then raise their proud heads to hiss.

Afterwards, a four-meter (12-ft) python is draped round the neck of anyone interested in the experience. Friends' cameras click — and for some reason it always seems to be the women who are especially anxious to volunteer.

THAI BOXING

There are two main places to see Thai boxing in central Bangkok.

On Ratchadamnoen Avenue is the **Ratchadamnoen Stadium**, the most important venue for the activity. Boxing here takes place on Mondays, Wednesdays, Thursdays and Sundays, beginning at 6 PM (5 PM on Sundays).

On the other days of the week, Tuesdays, Fridays and Saturdays, the bouts are at **Lumpini Stadium**, on Rama 4 Road, a few hundred meters west of the corner of the park at the junction of Rama 4 and Wireless roads. Lumpini Stadium is described, along with the whole business of Thai boxing, in

OPPOSITE: The Floating Market at Damnoen Saduak. This provincial early morning market is very picturesque, and somewhat less of a tourist magnet than the one in Bangkok (which is nowadays largely kept going by TAT specifically for the tourists' benefit).

SPORTS, THAI BOXING, page 49. It is the more atmospheric of the two venues and the one to attend to get the flavor of this quintessentially Thai activity.

There are three price categories — ringside at 500 baht, second class at 240 baht, and third class at 120 baht.

MORE RIVER TRIPS

In addition to the tour along the river described above, you can take a trip to the following *klongs*:

Klong Mon. Boats start from Tha Tien Pier, near Wat Pho.

Klong Bang Waek. Boats leave from the Memorial Bridge Pier.

Klong Bang Khoo Wiang and **Klong Bang Yai**. Boats leave from Tha Chang Pier, near the Grand Palace.

These trips cost only a few baht and take you to untouristed parts of the city. They're recommended.

FLOATING MARKETS

The problem with these early morning markets where vegetables and fruit are sold off boats is that the easily accessible one is nowadays extremely full of tourists, and the other one is 80 km (50 miles) out of town.

To get to the more accessible **Wat Sai** market, either join one of the very numerous coach parties heading there (any travel agent will book you onto one), or catch one of the boats going there that leave the Oriental Hotel Pier at 7 AM every morning.

To get to the slightly more authentic version at **Damnoen Saduak** in Ratchaburi Province, again either join a tour, or catch a public bus there from the Southern Bus Terminal on Charansanitwong Road any time between 5 and 8:30 AM.

WEEKEND MARKET

This is a very extensive market held every Saturday and Sunday from 7 AM to 6 PM. There are sections specializing in everything from house plants to caged birds, shirts to dinner plates. It's situated up the Phahonyothin Road, on a corner of Chatuchak Park opposite the Northern Bus terminal.

LUMPINI PARK

The only open space in the city other than the river, Lumpini is not at all a bad place, reasonably extensive and with a large lake where you can hire boats. At the end of the afternoon hundreds of joggers arrive — it's the only place in the city where they can exercise in peace.

At 6 PM the Thai national anthem strikes up from loudspeakers and everyone stands at attention. You should do the same, or at

natown. In the narrow sidestreets everything from antiques to joss sticks is for sale. The so-called Thieves' Market — ask for Woeng Nakhon Kasem — is also nearby. It specializes in antiques and objets d'art.

Out in the northern suburbs, on Soi Sukson 7, near Lard Phrao Road, is an attractive temple well-known to Chinese both in Thailand and elsewhere, the **Kuan-Im Palace.**

NIGHTLIFE

Bangkok is so much a center of nightlife,

least stand still and stop talking. Thais on the lake even try to bring their boats to a standstill. The park closes at 7 PM.

CHINATOWN

Near the intersection of Ratchawong Road and Yaowaraj Road to the west of Hualumphong Railway Station lies Bangkok's Chi-

ABOVE: The Damnoen Saduak Floating Market at dawn. OPPOSITE LEFT: Buddha images are a part of everyone's life in Thailand. Here a selection stands on sale in a Bangkok store. OPPOSITE RIGHT: The Amarin Center, Bangkok. American-style department stores are increasingly common in the Thai capital, and the introduction of non-Asian architectural styles has attracted some criticism. But "exotic" means "foreign" in Thailand, as elsewhere.

and, quite simply, sex, the subject deserves a book all on its own.

A trip out to the **Nasa Spacedrome (** (02) 314-3368, on Suapa Road, offers you the experience of what the owners claim is the biggest and most lavish disco in the world.

The three main Bangkok nightlife "strips" are: (1) **Patphong Road**, between Silom and Suriwong roads; (2) **Soi Cowboy**, between Sukhumvit Sois 21 and 23; and (3) **Nana Plaza** and adjacent area on Sukhumvit Soi 4 (Soi Nana). Between them they will provide you with enough live shows and sex by the hour to last you what's left of a lifetime.

As for **Massage Parlors**, they're all over the city. They're usually called "Turkish

Bath and Massage" in English and offer, of course, massage and more. Some are vast, multi-storied establishments staffed by hundreds of girls. To find one, simply consult the Yellow Pages classified phone book (there's an English version) under Massage. The biggest parlors in town are probably the **Atami** and the **Mona Lisa** on New Petchburi Road.

For therapeutic massage, by the way, look for the sign "Ancient Massage". This means traditional massage. This is not to imply the other sort isn't therapeutic too. It

doesn't, or at least not necessarily, mean "massage by ancient ladies" as one Thai friend assured me that it did.

SHOPPING

Many of the big department stores are situated on Rama I Road. If, beginning at Jim Thompson's House, you walk back onto Rama I, then turn left and proceed until you arrive at the first intersection, you will see, on the corner on your right, the **Mah Boon Krong** department store.

Go inside and marvel at the anomalies revealed in Thailand's headlong rush towards modernization. The building is half department store, half frenetic market, with

everything from numerous stalls competing to sell cheap cassettes to one offering very expensive cups of real coffee.

A little way further down Rama I is the **Siam Center**, on your left. It's a collection of up-market boutiques, a large number of coffee shops, some with live music and mostly on the top floor, and the American Express Clients' Mail office (in the Sea Tours agency).

On the opposite side of the road is **Siam Square**, a popular shopping and restaurant complex occupying a small grid of streets,

not expensive but nevertheless with an international, non-Thai feel about it.

Not far past the Erawan Shrine, and next to MacDonald's, is the **Amarin Center**, containing **Sogo** department store. On the opposite side of the road stands the **President Hotel**, facing sideways into a square containing many restaurants serving Western food. A little way past the President and on the same side is a large branch of the **Central** department store. Another big store is **Robinson's**, at the junction of Silom and Rama IV roads. All stores stay open till around 8 PM.

For an array of items thought to be attractive to tourists — leatherware and traveling bags especially — the top end of Sukhumvit

Road, on the opposite side to the Regal Landmark Hotel, is a good bet. (From the President Hotel, continue down Ploen Jhit Road until you pass under the Expressway — and over a railway line — and you're there).

Thai silk can be purchased in many places in the capital, either in lengths or made up into garments. Sukhimvit Road, again, has many small retailers, and **Jim Thompson's Shop**, 9 Surawong Road, is the place to go for the internationally renowned Jim Thompson Silk.

Western-style **shopping arcades** can be found attached to the Oriental, President and the Ambassador hotels.

You can find **roadside vendors** just about anywhere in the city. Of particular interest to tourists are those along one side of Silom Road, close to Patphong. They operate from late afternoon until after midnight and specialize in cotton clothes, counterfeit watches, cassette tapes and various handicrafts.

In the so-called **Thieves' Market** (Nakhon Kasem) in Chinatown look for antiques and other traditional items. Chinatown is also the place to go if you're interested in buying gold.

GETTING AROUND

Bangkok's morning rush-hour now lasts from shortly after dawn to just before lunch time. It resumes in mid-afternoon and doesn't really ease up till nine at night. At its twin heights, the times when most cities experience some problems, it's sometimes quickest simply to walk. Taxis can do little to bypass the metal log jam, and even the opportunistic *tuk tuks* cannot always escape getting bogged down in the morass.

With only the briefest of pauses in the small hours of the night, a tide of trucks, vans, motorbikes, evil-smelling *tuk tuks*, and hideously polluting buses snarl and shudder along the broad arterial highways. There is little lane discipline. *Tuk tuks* weave in and out among the larger vehicles, taxis without a fare slow down or stop on catching sight of a foreigner, government vehicles bearing a single passenger pull out from sideroads and hold up thousands of others

in the dark river of traffic. A blue-black haze rises to meet the merciless sun. The noise is appalling, and the air pollution leaves a foul taste in the mouth.

Bangkok has been trying to solve the mess for decades. Among the latest mass transit systems under consideration or construction, the one most likely to afford relief soonest is a light rail system (mostly elevated — the city's ground is too wet for a subway to be a viable option). Other elevated expressways are also supposedly in the pipeline but meanwhile you'll have to grin and bear the traffic. Your choice for getting around is simple — taxis, *tuk tuks* or buses.

Taxis and *Tuk Tuks*

Taxis and *tuk tuks* are rarely hard to come by — you're more likely to be pestered to take one when all you want to do is walk round the corner. No one walks in Asia except the very poor, and a *farang* walking can only mean he can't find a taxi.

Most taxis are now metered but for non-metered taxis and *tuk tuks* you must fix the fare before you move off. Bargain hard, but not unrealistically, with the drivers. Thais get everything cheaper, but if you want to get down to their price level you'll either have to learn some Thai or be extremely patient. And traffic conditions do count — to the driver, time is money, and it's how long it's going to take him to get you to where you want to go, rather than the simple distance, that is the relevant consideration.

A *tuk tuk* is, as a rule, quicker than a taxi, if hair-raising. It also exposes you to the full force of exhaust-pollution, its own and everyone else's. A *tuk tuk* costs the same as a metered taxi or in general around 25 per cent less than a non-metered taxi.

It's worth knowing that no Thai *tuk tuk* or taxi driver owns his vehicle. They hire them for 24-hour stints, two drivers each working 12 hours, and first have to work off the rental before they can make anything to feed themselves and their families.

Buses

There are three kinds of buses running the Bangkok streets, the long blue and cream ones without curtains and with open doors, similar vehicles with curtains and doors that are shut except at stops, and the smaller, more modern micro-buses.

The curtained and closed-in buses are the air-conditioned ones. They can be recognized in advance by the Thai lettering before the route number on the front of the bus. Fares here depend on where you're going (though it's always possible to offer six baht if you're not sure) and you stand a reasonable chance of getting a seat.

The other two operate different versions of the same thing. The flat fare is two and a

half baht, rising to three baht after around 10 PM. All types of buses only stop if someone indicates they want to get on — otherwise free-flow situations in Bangkok's traffic are too good to miss. To stop a bus, just wave.

The micro-buses are much nicer inside, though they are a bit cramping if you're tall and have to stand. And they have music. So you can sit in the inevitable Bangkok traffic jam, watching fumes pour from the vehicles pulled up beside you, and listen to pop songs.

A garland-seller; fragrant chains of jasmine hang in most taxis and some tuk tuks.

Bangkok and Ayutthaya

You will notice some of the big buses display their numbers on red or orange backgrounds in their front windows. Red means "limited stop", and orange that they take a short-cut to their ultimate destination by using the Express Way. This latter can be most alarming if you encounter it unawares. Just when you're getting near your stop, the doors are fastened shut (where they're not rusted fast in the open position) and the vehicle hurtles for 10 or so kilometers (five or so miles) at top speed along the elevated highway to an outer suburb. If you're caught in this way, the only thing is to get off at the first stop and take the next bus with the same number back in the direction from which you came.

Buses run all night on several routes. Your hotel should be able to provide you with information on how to get back late from areas where you're likely to be enjoying yourself in the small hours.

GETTING OUT OF TOWN

There are two main railway stations in Bangkok. The biggest is **Hualamphong Station** ((02) 223-3762 or 224-7788 on Rama 4. The other is over the river in Thonburi, **Bangkok Noi** ((02) 223-0341 ext. 713. Trains for Kanchanaburi and a few for the south leave from Thonburi. All others leave from Hualamphong. You must have reserved seats before you can travel, so make sure you book your tickets in advance, or get an agent or your hotel to do it for you.

For buses, there are three terminals. For Pattaya and the east coast it's **Ekamai** ((02) 391-2504, at Sukhumvit Soi 40, for the south it's in Thonburi, on **Phrapinklao Road** ((02) 434-5558 or 391-9829, and for the north and northeast the **Northern Bus Terminal** ((02) 279-4484 to 7 on Phahonyothin Road.

For transport between Bangkok and the airport, see TRAVELERS' TIPS page 224.

TOURIST INFORMATION

The national headquarters of the **Tourism Authority of Thailand** ((02) 226-0060 or 226-0072, is at 372 Bamrung Muang Road. They have an immense amount of information covering both Bangkok and the rest of the country. They're extremely efficient.

DAY TRIPS FROM BANGKOK

CROCODILES AND ROSES

Samphran Elephant Ground and Zoo
Thirty kilometers (19 miles) west of Bangkok on the road to Nakhorn Phathom, is the Samphran Elephant Ground. It's best known for its crocodiles, and is often referred to simply as the Crocodile Farm.

Richard Clayderman and "A Stranger in Paradise" blare inescapably from the loudspeaker while elephants "dance" and play football before raked stadium-style seating holding up to 500 spectators. This is followed by a "Crocodile Wrestling Show" which ends with the keeper putting his head in the crocodile's mouth — it stays open after he's walked away and has to be forcibly shut by assistants.

The elephant shows are at 1:30 PM (additional shows at 11:30 AM and 3:30 PM on holidays), the crocodile shows at 12:30, 2:30 and 4:30 PM (with extra shows on holidays at 9:45 and 11:00 AM).

Though the place is clearly popular, it's generally worth giving a miss unless you're with very young children.

The Rose Garden
A short way up the road from the Crocodile Farm is the large complex known as the **Rose Garden**. It's a good deal less dreadful, and a lot more peaceful.

The main feature is the "Thai Village" where, for an entrance fee of 220 baht, you can see various traditional crafts such as umbrella-making and pottery and then, at 2:00 and 3:00 PM daily, a Cultural Show featuring fingernail dancing, hill tribe dancing,

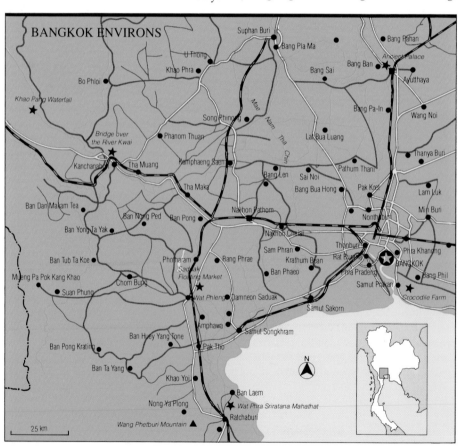

Thai boxing, swordfighting, a wedding, and elephants in procession. Short rides on the elephants are 20 baht extra. It's all packaged, of course, and consequently rather twee and unreal. But it's not bad as these things go.

A mere 10 baht will let you into the gardens themselves, laid out on the banks of the river and featuring some rose beds. The climate of the Bangkok region is not suited to rose-growing and such roses as there are here will not hold the attention of enthusiasts for long. Nevertheless, the attempt has been made, and the gardens themselves are pleasant. There's also a lake with pedalos, pony-and-trap rides are available, and you can hire bicycles (10 baht for half an hour).

Much of this area is owned by the Roman Catholic Church and referred to by some as "Thailand's Vatican City". There are several seminaries nearby.

How to Get There

The easiest way to reach both these popular tourist sites is by organized day-trip tours, available at your hotel or any major travel agency.

AYUTTHAYA AND BANG PA-IN

Ayutthaya (named after the city of Ayodhya in the ancient Indian romance, the *Ramayana*) is Thailand's main historical site, but it may, nevertheless, prove a disappointment to some visitors.

The ancient city, 72 km (45 miles) north of Bangkok, was the Thai capital from 1350 for over four hundred years. When the Burmese sacked it in 1767, the Thais established a new capital at Thonburi.

Ayutthaya was undoubtedly one of the greatest and most magnificent cities of the entire region. Today, however, it resembles a hive from which all the bees have departed. Brick ruins lean and gently crumble among carefully tended lawns, carved torsos in blackened stone lie in piles, and in the great heat gardeners hack out weeds from the tottering walls. Tourists ritually photograph the remains, locals on motorbikes putter about their business along the nearby bypass, and a low breeze wafts across the vast, muddy plain.

A ONCE GORGEOUS RUIN

A Once Gorgeous Ruin
The point about Ayutthaya is that what you are looking at is merely the stump of a previously gorgeous assembly. Whereas now you see brick, before you would have seen gold. All that remains is what the looting and pillaging Burmese didn't think worth removing. The rough inner structures whose dull surfaces are now returning slowly to nature under the humid skies were

once coated with all the dazzling richness with which the Thais have always invested their temples and palaces. Only when you picture this can you imagine the former sumptuous splendor of the place. In the long official name for Bangkok is included the title "the new Ayutthaya". Ayutthaya of old would have resembled the lavish glory of the Grand Palace in Bangkok today, but on an incomparably greater scale.

Thai serenity and languor? An Italian statue, carved in the Carrara marble Michaelangelo used, imported from Europe by 19th century King Mongkut (Rama IV). The royal summer residence at Bang Pa-In — no longer used and now open to the public.

And, as in Sukhothai, what the Burmese didn't take the museums have made off with. Most of the best pieces are in Bangkok, but the small **Chao Sam Phraya National Museum** contains some items. It's situated opposite the city walls on Rojana Road and is open every day except Mondays and Tuesdays.

For the site as a whole, notable features are **Wat Phra Sri Sanphet** within the former Royal Palace compound, the riverside **Wat Panan Choeng, Wat Phra Maha That** and **Wat Na Pramane**. It's charming to see that many of the great Buddha images are still venerated with flowers and offerings by the few remaining local inhabitants. Once these images were coated with gold which the Burmese had to melt off with the aid of fires — a procedure in which both nations were no doubt well practiced.

In marked contrast to the rest of the site is the modern **Mong Kol Bo Phit** temple. It contains a large black bronze Buddha image, and its glittering exterior provides a reminder of the brilliant color harmonies that would have characterized Ayutthaya of old.

Bang Pa-In

Almost everyone visits Ayutthaya on a day-trip from Bangkok, and almost everyone includes **Bang Pa-In** in the excursion.

Fourteen kilometers (nine miles) from Ayutthaya, the former country residence and love-nest of Thai kings and princes is a strange and evocative mixture of Oriental styles and 19th century European influences.

Bang Pa-In resembles some of the garden buildings at Versailles, though it's arguably

more beautiful. There's an Observation Tower that looks as if it should be in a novel by Thomas Love Peacock, and classical statues in Carrara marble that are wholly and unashamedly European.

But nowadays a slightly forlorn elegance characterizes the place. The Chinese palace, the towers and ornate bridges built for joy still stand in their spacious setting among lawns and waterways but their glory is beginning to fade. Topiary elephants decorate the scene, but elsewhere the paint is peeling, the shutters are all closed, and the tiles have acquired a patina of mould. Love has departed from these places especially built for it and it's as if they are resentful and in a sulk, refusing to put on their make-up any more.

How to Get There

You used to be able to take a boat trip to Ayutthaya from Bankgok. Sadly, this is no longer possible (although expensive cruises go to Bang Pa-In with bus excursions to Ayutthaya). But bus and train connections

The Chao Phraya River at Ayutthaya, with Wat Chai Wattanaram. The ancient capital was surrounded by water for defensive purposes, and today the ruins appear attractive from water-level. Once glittering with gold and mosaic ornament, they were protected by a wall rising from the "moat".

are easy: buses leave from Bangkok's northern terminal every half-hour for the two-hour trip and trains leave every hour, taking an hour and a half.

KANCHANABURI AND THE RIVER KWAI BRIDGE

A hundred and thirty kilometers (81 miles) west of Bangkok, Kanchanaburi makes a popular day-trip out from the capital. It's actually the main town of an attractive and almost wholly unspoilt province that repays a longer stay.

The road from Bangkok is a fast modern highway all the way. The only interest on the journey is the town of **Nakhorn Phathom** half way along the route. Its famous **Phra Phathom Chedi** rises above the town and can be seen from the road on your right. It's the highest Buddhist monument in the world (127 m or 417 ft) and marks the place where it is thought Buddhism was first taught in what is now Thailand. Clad in its brown tiles, it looks like a celestial handbell, waiting for a heavenly hand to reach down and clang it to mark the end of afternoon school. It was built in 1860 by King Mongkut (Rama IV) and contains inside it the smaller sixth-century *chedi* that preceded it, a replica of which stands to the south.

The River Kwai Bridge

Kanchanaburi is first and foremost famous for the nearby **Bridge over the River Kwai**, and the museum and cemeteries associated with the construction of the war-time railway.

The infamous iron bridge is situated at the north end of the town. It is black and squat and, in the event, rather small. That such a structure could have been so crucial to the outcome of a global war seems inconceivable forty years on.

It was part of the railway built by the Japanese to supply their army in Burma. This overland supply route from the east became urgently necessary when the Allies gained control of the sea routes to Burma during the latter part of the war. Most of the line ran through jungle and rolling hills and was therefore impossible to make out from the air, but the bridge was clearly visible and

so was the route's weakest point. The Allies made several attempts to bomb it, and finally, on February 13, 1945, they succeeded, using American planes based at Pandaveswar in India. The bridge was eventually reconstructed for post-war use — only the curved spans in the middle are part of the original structure.

The single track across it is still in use by trains running from Bangkok up to Nam Tok — you cross the bridge shortly after Kanchanaburi station. In addition people walk, cycle, and ride their motorbikes across

it by means of planks laid end-to-end between the rails. It presents a colorful, even a picturesque little scene, the perfect image of everyday Thai provincial life.

Between the bridge and the center of town is the **Kanchanaburi War Cemetery**, on your left coming back from the bridge.

ABOVE: Ayutthaya, a World Heritage Site of enormous cultural importance to Thailand, is an open-air museum of ruined temples, monasteries, crumbling spires and statues, with yet more treasures displayed in museums such as this one, a beautiful building in its own right. OPPOSITE: The infamous bridge over the River Kwai at Kanchanaburi. Built with materials brought from Indonesia, at immense cost in human lives, the central section was destroyed by Allied action in 1945. The new section (pictured here) allows the bridge to be used to this day, by pedestrians, cyclists and the Thai railway.

Almost seven thousand prisoners of war who died while working on the railway are buried here — mostly Dutch, British and Australian.

Jeath Museum

Close to the center of town is the **Jeath Museum** which displays information about the war-time railway in a reconstructed prison hut from the period.

As you enter the small compound on the banks of the river, a notice informs you that the name "Jeath" was used because "Death"

have died, roughly 38 for every kilometer of railway built. The deaths, among local laborers, however, were much higher. As many as 200,000 may have died on the 415 km (257 miles) of track. The camp at the Kwai bridge was only one of 42 along the length of the line.

The museum is maintained by the temple, **Wat Chaichunphon**, which stands next to it.

Over the River

If you go along the road that runs by the river from the right hand side of the museum,

sounded too horrific, and it was decided instead to take the initials of the nations whose prisoners largely built the railway, namely Japan, England, Australia, Thailand and Holland.

In a long bamboo hut, a replica of the type used in the camps, are displays of photographs and paintings of life on the "Death Railway". There's little else there — just a few objects such as boots, knives and tin plates. The photographs are for the most part less than horrific — in some the men even look quite cheerful. The paintings are more disturbing. Possibly excessive hatred guided the artist's brush. But the statistics bear out the most bitter depictions. Sixteen thousand prisoners of war are thought to

after half a kilometer (one third of a mile) you will come to a small ferry. Between the museum and the ferry are some floating restaurants; one of these is the moderately-priced **Luan Poi (** (034) 511897.

The ferry takes you over the river for three baht. There, the road leads away to the left the three kilometers (two miles) to the **Chungkai War Cemetery**. It's 1,750 graves are immaculately kept. The track to the left of the cemetery leads down to the river.

Both of these Kanchanaburi cemeteries are run by the Commonwealth War Graves Commission and they contain the remains, almost exclusively, of prisoners of European descent. Most of the Asians who died on the railway have no such memorial.

How to Get There

The most enjoyable way to reach Kanchanaburi and its Bridge over the River Kwai, 128 km west of Bangkok, is by train. Unfortunately, there are only two daily, leaving from Bangkok's Thonburi station at 7:50 AM and 1:45 PM, though there is also a special day-return tourist train from Bangkok's Hualamphong Station on weekends and public holidays, which leaves at 6:35 AM (be sure to book in advance). By air-conditioned bus from Bangkok's southern terminal, the trip takes around two to three hours.

A Slightly Special Cave

Two kilometers (one and a quarter miles) further beyond Kanchanaburi is **Khao Poon Cave**.

It's one of the nicer Thai caves, with a lot to see for very little effort. It is lit throughout by green, pink and white neon strips, and you are led by arrows along a winding passage with Buddhas, one reclining, the other cross-legged, at each end. The limestone formations are good, too, especially in and around the last cave.

Death and life beside the River Kwai. ABOVE: one of the graves kept up by the Commonwealth War Graves Commission; OPPOSITE: floating restaurants on the river on the Kanchanaburi side. The town, and the district as a whole, makes a very restful retreat from the noise and pollution of Bangkok.

Entrance is by donation, and the whole establishment is run by some jokey young monks; their pop music rising from behind the Buddha images out in the courtyard as you leave.

Hellfire Pass

When the prisoners of war were constructing the Death Railway from Thailand to Burma, they had to tackle incredibly difficult terrain in appalling conditions. One of the worst places was at Konyu, about 18 km (12 miles) from Nam Tok. Here they had to make seven mountain cuttings through solid rock, as well as embankments and trestle bridges. Working round the clock by the light of fires, the mostly Australian POWs nicknamed the worst 17-m- (56-ft)-deep section Hellfire Pass.

Today, the Pass is part of a memorial walk established by the Australian-Thai Chamber of Commerce. A circular route leads into the dense bamboo forest and down to the macabre Pass where you can see a section of the original rail track. There are plans to extend the walk even further. For now, you can just make out the embankments in the undergrowth and imagine the POWs toiling through the malarial jungle from their basecamp several kilometers away. For a fascinating guided tour of this area, contact **Punnee Bar & Cafe** in Kanchanaburi ((034) 513503.

Further Afield

Fifty and 72 km (32 and 45 miles) respectively from Kanchanaburi are the **Bor-Ploy Sapphire Mines** and the **Erawan Waterfall and National Park**. Full details are available at TAT. But these are rather far for a one-day trip. Should you want to stay in Kanchanaburi in order to explore the area, try the **Kwai Yai Garden Resort** ((02)251-5223 reservations in Bangkok (26 rooms; moderate), where accommodation is in floating, reed-roofed raft houses.

Tourist Information

The **TAT Office** ((034) 511200 is located in Kanchanaburi town where the buses from Bangkok stop on the main street. It serves as the tourist office for Kanchanaburi Province.

Pattaya and the East Coast Resorts

THE EAST COAST

The stretch of coast from Bangkok to the Cambodian border is essentially the capital's playground. Though only developed in the last couple of decades, it has successfully taken over from the longer-established places to the southwest where the nearest resort, Cha-am, is three hours' drive away. Pattaya, by contrast, is a mere two, and Bang Saen — which really is Bangkok by the sea — is just an hour and a half.

After Pattaya comes Rayong, and the popular but very small island of Koh Samet. Beyond this, the coast is still largely untouched by tourism.

HOW TO GET THERE

If you haven't got your own transport, the most convenient way to reach destinations along the eastern seaboard is by air-conditioned bus (or organized tour). From Bangkok's Ekamai station, buses leave every half-hour for Pattaya, taking two and a half hours; every 40 minutes for Si Racha (jumping off point for Koh Si Chang (two-hour ride); and every one to two hours for Trat (six-hour ride). Boats to Koh Si Chang leave at least four times a day from Si Racha, taking 40 minutes while the hop across to Koh Samet from Ban Phe is 10 minutes quicker. Hardy travelers heading for Koh Chang will first have to head for Trat, then Laem Ngop (a 20-minute *songthaew* ride away) and finally endure a two- to three-hour boat ride.

CHONBURI

Chonburi is a large town of no particular interest apart from its three temples. These are **Wat Dhamanimita** with its giant golden Buddha, **Wat Yai Intharam** with its multiple Buddhas, all facing you like imperturbable judges in a nightmare, and the tranquil **Wat Sam Yot**, looking out serenely over the coast.

Chonburi hosts street **buffalo races** every autumn, "on the 14th day of the waxing moon in the 11th lunar month". Contact TAT in Bangkok or Pattaya for details expressed in Western terms.

BANG SAEN

Ten kilometers (six miles) from Chonburi, and 100 km (61 miles) from Bangkok, is **Bang Saen**. Pattaya was developed with foreigners in mind, but Bang Saen is almost exclusively Thai. It's where hard-driven Bangkokians, with perhaps only one day's holiday a month and little spare cash, go with their children to enjoy themselves. The kilometer-long sandy beach is naturally very crowded at weekends, but its deck-

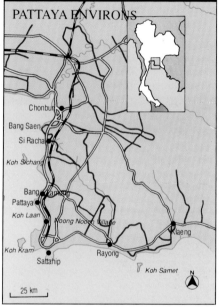

chairs, showers, inflated tire inner tubes and food stalls are exceptionally inexpensive.

It's primarily a day-trip resort, but there is some reasonable accommodation available at the **Bangsaen Beach Resort** ((038) 381675 (129 rooms; moderate; reservations in Bangkok ((02) 253-6385) and the **Bangsaen Villa** ((038) 282088 FAX (038) 383333 (70 rooms; moderate; reservations in Bangkok ((02) 253-4380 to 81).

At the north end of the beach at **Sam Muk** fishing village there's a community of wild monkeys by a local shrine, with fine views from the cliffs out to sea.

Big Buddha at Pattaya. The modern statue occupies a spectacular site overlooking the coast above Jomtien Beach.

And at Sinakarinwirot University's Bang Saen campus there's a **Marine Aquarium** with 43 tanks. Opening hours: 8:30 AM to 4:00 PM (closed Mondays). Admission is 40 baht.

Seven kilometers (four and a third miles) from the beach there's the 18-hole international championship standard **Bangphra golf course**, with accommodation and a clubhouse.

A FREE-RANGE ZOO

Further inland, 11 km (seven miles) from the golf course, is the **Khao Kheo Open Zoo**, operated by the Dusit Zoo in Bangkok. Fifty species roam freely over a 490-hectare (1,200-acre) area, and you drive round catching sight of the animals as they wander in semi-liberty. There's also Thailand's biggest aviary here, an entire hillside enclosed with netting that even covers full-sized trees. You walk around inside the net along a perimeter path and count the exotic tropical species as they flit about all round you. There's accommodation in resthouses set on a cliff — telephone the zoo in Bangkok on ((02) 281-0000 for details.

SI RACHA AND KOH SICHANG

Si Racha is a small commercial port between Bang Saen and Pattaya. It's also the embarkation point for the island so loved by former Thai kings, Koh Sichang.

Si Racha is too busy to have developed as a tourist resort, but there is a most picturesque Thai–Chinese Buddhist temple situated on a small island, **Koh Lor**, connected to the mainland by a causeway. It's a classic place to take a *samlor* (literally a three-wheeled vehicle) out to to see the sunrise.

WHERE TO STAY AND WHERE TO EAT

There is also a choice of hotels in the town, all right on the waterfront and, indeed, in some cases built right out on stilts over the sea. The most elaborate of these is the **Grand Bungalow** ((038) 312537 (13 rooms; moderate; reservations in Bangkok ((02) 392-1159). Among the others are the func-

tional but delightful **Samchai** ((038) 311134 (60 rooms; inexpensive), the **Sri Wattana** (311307 (24 rooms; inexpensive) and the **Si Wichai** ((038) 311212 (38 rooms; inexpensive).

For food — seafood is the speciality — try the good but rather expensive **Chua Lee**, or one of the garden-restaurants on the road out to Pattaya.

WHAT TO SEE AND DO

Boats to **Koh Sichang** leave every two hours from 5 AM, except for the last boat of the day which leaves at 4:30 PM. The trip takes just under an hour.

The island has a town in its center, with a Thai temple at one end, and a Chinese one raised high up at the other. Here are also the partially overgrown remains of a **Summer Palace** built by King Chulalongkorn. Begun in 1889, the palace was eventually abandoned by the king after the unpleasant experience of seeing the island occupied by the French in 1893 as they pressured the Thais into granting them territory neighboring on Cambodia. The ploy succeeded, and the shame and sorrow led to the abandonment of the royal residence.

Koh Sichang has some attractive beaches, among them **Haad Tawang**, close to the palace, and **Haad Tampang**. There's also the **Chakrapong Cave** with a chimney-like way up to the summit of a hill commanding a fine view over the island. Simple accommodation is available at the **Tew Pai Guesthouse**; either book in here or check carefully the time of the last ferry back to Si Racha — it's usually about 5 PM.

PATTAYA

It's 2 AM in the morning and in the warm night air a sun-tanned and totally naked Westerner is standing waving a beer can in the middle of the road. He's surrounded by a small crowd which includes a fully-dressed Thai girl who's clutching her handbag and pleading with him. A few feet away waves break softly on the sand, and down the road two policemen are approaching on white motorbikes.

Is it a comedy or a scandal? Your judgment of this scene will no doubt anticipate your opinion of **Pattaya** (pronounced by the Thais with the stress on the last syllable — Pat-ty-*ya*), Thailand's most outrageous and blatantly commercial (and Westernized) seaside resort.

Pattaya's potential was first realized in the Sixties by a group of luxury yachtsmen, but with the coming of the Vietnam War and the establishment of a large American base nearby, it was fast transformed into a wild and raucous R & R facility. When the Ameri-

Not that Pattaya is without its problems. One of these is water. The city has exceeded over and over again estimates made a few years ago of its probable fresh water requirements. What is certain is that unless the height of the dam at Mab Prachan reservoir is increased soon, the town will, in bad years and maybe even eventually in good ones, be faced with a problem for which there is quite simply no solution. Even more worrying has been the serious pollution caused by raw sewage being emptied into the bay. Steps have finally been taken to stop the

cans left, the sex-tourists moved in to fill the vacuum.

As it exists now, Pattaya is the ultimate test of the traditional Thai virtues of spontaneity and ingenuousness. It is good to be able to report that for the most part the population comes out with flying colors.

Perhaps one of the reasons for this is that so many of the people working here come from Esarn, the despised agricultural region of the northeast. Much of the vigor, good humor and occasional impulsive generosity of Pattaya people is rooted in this hinterland where rice farming, water buffalo-tending and periodic drought are such hard masters.

practice — there are now water treatment plants and fines for polluters — although you'd still hardly call Pattaya's bay virgin clean.

But the glittering, brash seaside town carries on, smaller than you'd expect, and almost entirely patronized by foreigners. A significant proportion actually live here, either running bars or simply retired, unable or unwilling to give up the easy life and the on-hand pleasures. The result is it's the most Westernized place in all Thailand.

Long criticized for its polluted seas and beaches, the hugely popular Pattaya resort, with its excellent water sports facilities, has recently started to clean up its act.

GETTING THERE

Air-conditioned buses for Pattaya leave Bangkok from the Eastern Bus Terminal (Ekamai) every half hour (fare: 66 baht) until mid-evening. Bangkok hotels prefer to book their guests onto private buses — which may only be 10-seaters — at a cost of around 150 baht; these leave three times a day, roughly at 9 AM, noon and 4 PM but in reality when all the passengers from the different

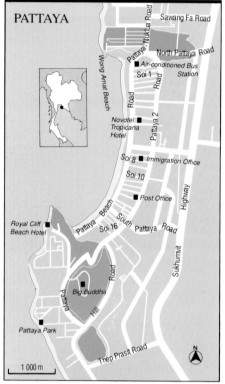

PATTAYA

Sawang Fa Road
Nukua Road
North Pattaya Road
Air-conditioned Bus Station
Soi 1
Wong Amat Beach
Road
Road
Novotel
Tropicana Hotel
Pattaya 2
Soi 8
Immigration Office
Soi 10
Post Office
Highway
Beach
Royal Cliff Beach Hotel
Pattaya
South
Soi 16
Pattaya Road
Sukhumvit
Road
Big Buddha
Pattaya Hill
Pattaya Park
Thep Prasit Road
N
1 000 m

hotels have been ferried through the traffic to the central departure point.

If you're going from Bangkok International airport direct to Pattaya you might be lucky enough to touch down at a time close to when one of the direct Don Muang–Pattaya minibuses leaves: around 9 AM, noon and 7 PM. It's worth enquiring before taking the "limousine" into Bang-

kok. Airport-bound minibuses in the other direction can be booked at the **Air-conditioned Bus Station** (meaning the station for air-conditioned buses) on North Pattaya Road.

A BIRD'S EYE VIEW

The buses from Bangkok leave the highway and enter Pattaya down the North Pattaya Road. North of here, between the Pattaya–Naklua Road and the sea, is an area that used to be quiet and rather exclusive but is currently being energetically developed. The main beach is **Wong Amat**. Pattaya proper extends for about three kilometers (two miles), from North Pattaya Road along the whole length of the bay to where the land begins to rise to the headland. The busiest part of the town lies between the road running along the seafront, Pattaya Beach Road, and the first road parallel to it inland, Pattaya 2 Road. Connecting these two roads are no fewer than 31 sidestreets; some are numbered (Soi 1 to 16), others named, and some nameless. Traffic circulates anti-clockwise on a one-way system, running from north to south along Pattaya Beach Road, and than back again the other way along Pattaya 2 Road.

This district, then, the downtown area facing out onto the bay, is divided into North and South. The distinction isn't exact, but North, extending approximately down to Soi Post Office, is Pattaya without the pavement bars, souvenirs and disco music. It's not exactly discreet, but the hotels stand back from the road in their own grounds, and the restaurants and bars appear intermittently, rather than as a continuous frontage.

South of this the real nightlife sector begins. After a few blocks the main road sweeps inland along South Pattaya Road, leaving the final section of the beach strip, now with clubs, shops and bars on both sides, mainly to pedestrians.

Behind all this is the Thai town. Try taking a look at **Watchaimongkol Market**, open daily until 7 PM, on the right of South Pattaya Road (keep straight on where the minibuses turn right to go up the hill towards Jomtien).

Pattaya's accommodation ranges from cheap guesthouses in town to deluxe seaside resorts such as the Royal Cliff Beach Resort OPPOSITE, which stretches along the southern end of Pattaya beach.

WHERE TO STAY

The **Royal Cliff Beach Resort** ((038) 428613 to 16 FAX (038) 428511 (727 rooms; expensive; reservations in Bangkok ((02) 282-0999) is situated high on the headland separating Pattaya and Jomtien, poised to make the best of Pattaya whichever way it develops.

Its large number of rooms and suites in no way implies mass tourism — instead, they are subdivided into family suites with

0021) and the **Royal Garden Resort** ((038) 428126 FAX (038) 429929 (142 rooms; average and above; reservations in Bangkok ((02) 476-0021) are both central and on Beach Road.

The classiest accommodation at Wong Amat is at the **Wong Amat Hotel** ((038) 426999 FAX (038) 428599 (207 rooms; average and above; reservations in Bangkok ((02) 541-1784 FAX (02) 541-1783).

You won't find in Pattaya the ultra-cheap accommodation available in so much of Thailand. But attractive rooms for 200 to

two bedrooms, "honeymoon" suites right down near the sea, and the ultra-luxury suites in the new Royal Wing (with its own private beach). The Royal Cliff is one of the great hotels. It has facilities for a huge range of sports, its tennis courts are "all weather", and it even has special boats for use by guests on its two private beaches.

The **Novotel Tropicana** ((038) 428645 to 8 FAX (038) 423031(186 rooms; average and above; reservations in Bangkok ((02) 234-3818) was one of the first luxury hotels in town, and its central position continues to give it a certain distinction.

The **Montien Pattaya** ((038) 428155 to 56 FAX (038) 423155 (320 rooms; average and above; reservations in Bangkok ((02) 476-

300 baht aren't difficult to find (except when the United States Navy's in town). The area around Soi Post Office is the place to start looking.

New hotels as well as tower-blocks of condominiums are going up every year at **Jomtien Beach** which runs south from Pattaya after the headland on which the Royal Cliff hotel stands.

The **Jomtien Hill Resort** ((038) 422378 FAX (038) 422378 has 64 average-and-above priced rooms. The **Marine Beach Resort** ((038) 231129; (65 rooms), the **Sea Breeze** ((038) 231056 FAX (038) 231059 (80 rooms) and the **Surf House International** ((038) 231025 to 26 FAX (038) 231029 (55 rooms) all offer accommodation at moderate rates.

And at the far southern end of the beach the gigantic **Ambassador City Jomtien** ((038) 231501 to 40 FAX (038) 231731 (average and above; reservations in Bangkok ((02) 254-0444) has an astonishing 2,600 rooms and, not surprisingly, elaborate conference facilities.

On Phra Pracha Nimit Road off the Sukhumvit Highway (the main road from Bangkok **Siam Country Club** ((038) 428002 (enquiries in Bangkok ((02) 215-0900 ext 162), offers a high-class 18-hole golf course, plus billiards, and accommodation in 30 rooms.

WHERE TO EAT

Pic Kitchen on Soi 5, North Pattaya, serves fine Thai food in a traditional setting. Excellent and moderately priced Thai food is also available at **Somsak** ((038) 428987, at the Pattaya 2 Road end of Soi 4. Meanwhile **Dolf Riks** ((038) 428269, on

ABOVE Fresh prawns, charcoal-grilled and sold as an appetizing beachside snack in Pattaya.
OPPOSITE TOP: Nighttime in downtown Pattaya where the partying never stops. BOTTOM: It's a difficult job to catch sight of a girl onstage in Pattaya. Almost all the many shows there are put on by transvestite males. Cross-dressing has a long tradition in southeast Asia, but in Thailand it has become a national specialty.

Soi 1 serves highly acclaimed Dutch and Indonesian, as well as international-style, dishes.

For Thai food served as a circus act in the manner of Phitsanulok province, hurry round to the **Flying Vegetable** on Pattaya 2 Road. Meals, flung in a wide arc from the frying-pan, are invariably caught on a plate by an imperturbable waiter some distance away, to the cheers of attendant coach-parties.

There are plenty of restaurants catering for Moslem visitors and several excellent Japanese restaurants. In the latter category, try **Akamon** at 468/19 Pattaya 2 Road.

The **Green Bottle Pub** ((038) 429675 serves European and Thai food in an English setting to the accompaniment of a three-piece band, and the prize-winning **Rim Talay Restaurant** ((038) 231683 on Soi Chaiyapruek offers fresh seafood cooked in Thai style.

AFTER DARK

Pattaya's nightlife in every way rivals Bangkok's — many prefer it on account of the more relaxed ambiance. But there's the same range, and indeed, when the United States Navy's in town, many of the same faces as well.

Discretion isn't a characteristic of Pattaya, and to walk down the southern end of Beach Road after around mid-afternoon is to see on very open display the world's so-called oldest profession. With open-fronted bars whose girls wave and call to you as you pass, Pattaya's *raison d'etre* advertises itself all too effectively. But the resort does have some other attractions after sunset.

Tiffany's ((038) 428746, was the original transvestite show in Pattaya. Thai film director Pisan Addaraserani made a feature film *Raktoraman* ("Tormented Love") based round the show, and using many of the cast, in 1987. It's still going strong, three times a night, seven days a week, as is the nearby **Alcazar Cabaret** ((038) 428746, now housed in a big new auditorium. Both shows are exceptionally — perhaps a touch too — professional, and the entrance fee includes a drink.

In the Pattaya Resort Hotel is the very popular **Disco Duck**, complete with the nowadays standard video screens.

The **Marine Bar** is vast, and as just one of its attractions shows films nightly on a full-sized cinema screen; you watch them from your table. It's open to the sea at the side and any breezes that are around help the fans with the ventilation. There's also a boxing ring, and upstairs there's the **Marine Disco**.

Enthusiasts for Japanese **karaoke** can find it at the **Sarabu Cafe**, next to the Snow White Cafe on the right of the Pattaya–Naklua Road.

GETTING AROUND TOWN

Transport in Pattaya is by converted pick-up vans. Red and white stickers inside the vehicles state the fares: En route maximum 5 baht; charter: two persons — 50 baht per trip; each additional person 5 baht per person. In many cases these figures have been scratched out — one wonders who by.

You can also get taken where you want to go by motorbike. Groups of youths wait with their machines at major intersections, and you hire them out like taxis. You say where you want to go, they name a fare and off you go.

Renting a motorbike is exceptionally popular and outlets are everywhere, especially along Beach Road. Expect to pay about 200 baht per day for a Honda Dream, more for the bigger machines.

WHAT TO SEE AND DO

Swimming and Water Sports
The main beach at Pattaya is, unfortunately, now too polluted for swimming to be without risks. Water sports still keep going and you can expect to pay the following prices for beach sports on Pattaya Beach: Water scooters, 300 baht per hour; water-skiing, 800 baht per hour; speedboats, 800 baht per hour; para-sailing, 300 baht for a five-minute flight.

If you feel like a dip you really should hop on a minibus and go over to **Jomtien**. Jomtien Beach runs south from Pattaya after the headland on which the Royal Cliff Hotel stands. The road from Pattaya arrives at the coast and then turns left. Jomtien Beach extends for about a kilometer to the right and for many kilometers leftwards along the road.

The beach is busiest on the stretch to the right. For about half its length there are continuous beach umbrellas and deck chairs, every 20 m (66 ft) or so under the eye of a different food and drink establishment. When the color of the deck-chair frames changes, you know you're in a new territory. There's no charge for the deck chairs, but you are naturally expected to order something — prices are everywhere very reasonable. Beach mats are provided free if you ask.

To the left, arrangements continue at first in the same manner. Then gradually the umbrellas peter out until, after a couple of kilometers, the new cafes stand empty (at least in mid-week), the wind hisses through the grass, women with nothing to do go through each other's hair looking for lice — or grey hairs — and the rare van lumbers over the potholed road. Occasionally someone bumps past on a water-scooter, but otherwise the blue sea breaks undisturbed on an empty shore.

Soon all this will be changed as building is going on apace, but for the moment this far end of Jomtien is very much a betwixt-and-between world.

Back under the brilliantly-colored umbrellas, Jomtien is Pattaya without some of the hassles. But these things are relative. Para-sailing, windsurfing and speedboats are all here — indeed, Jomtien is something of a windsurfer's Mecca. But for the discos and the high-pressure salesmanship of the nightlife, you must go back to Pattaya. In this respect, at least, it's quieter this side of the headland.

Minibuses run over to Jomtien from Pattaya but you have to negotiate the price. Forty baht is about normal. Coming back you can sometimes get a ride for 25 baht as the vehicles quickly fill up with passengers all going more or less the same way.

Pattaya sunset.

Tavan Beach on Koh Laan island, a 40-minute ride by public ferry from Pattaya, is an alternative beach to Pattaya's. See **Koh Laan (Coral Island)** below.

A Souvenir Portrait

In the same way that the Thais excel in counterfeit clothes and recordings, so, too, are they as painters adept at producing accurate imitations of the work of the great masters. If you want to impress your friends by exhibiting one of Rembrandt's most illustrious masterpieces in your living

room, Pattaya's the place to come in search of it. They'll even substitute your profile for that of the original sitter if you can let them have a photo for a couple of hours.

Prices are low, and the artists very skillful. They can paint a straightforward portrait of you, of course, almost with their eyes closed. The **Siam Art Shop ((038) 429045, in South Pattaya is one of several places where you can watch them at work.

Pattaya Park and Big Buddha

On the road from Pattaya to Jomtien, a side road leads off on the right for **Pattaya Park**.

Portrait artist at work in Pattaya, which is an increasingly popular destination for Arabs and South Asians.

Here there's a freshwater swimming pool complex next to the sea featuring its famous **giant slides**. It's open from 8:30 AM to 6 PM. Admission to the slides and pool is 50 baht, 30 baht for children "under 120 cm" (four feet). The park is part of the Pattaya Beach Resort.

High on a hilltop above Jomtien, with a road all the way up, stands the **Big Buddha**, its vast white torso wound round with a yellow scarf. Day-of-the-week Buddhas stand round the forecourt. The park's proximity to Pattaya is apparent in signs asking people not to climb up onto the images. Above the main Buddha's head a red light warns off low-flying aircraft.

With 24-hour access, it's a good place to visit at night. The food stalls are vacated, the tropical moon shines on the statues, and the breeze flutters the scarves, making the images seem to stir in their meditations.

The shrine was completed in 1977 and its official name is Buddha Vanothayan, or Khaoprayai. There's a good view of the coast from the approach road.

Pattaya Elephant Village

Three kilometers (two miles) from the Sukhumvit down Phra Pracha Nimit Road Pattaya Elephant Village's 12 elephants go on show daily at 2:30 PM (bookable through agents). The keepers and their beautiful animals are all from Surin, where the annual Elephant Round-Up is held (see OFF THE BEATEN TRACK, page 207). It's a congenial place, with one or two very young animals usually on show. They're not averse to taking you round at other times of day too, but then a tip — perhaps 30 baht — is in order.

Mini Siam

Back on the main road, at the intersection with North Pattaya Road, is **Mini Siam**, where miniature versions of Thailand's best known sites are on display for an entrance fee of 200 baht (100 baht for children). There's a **Cultural Center** on the same site.

Naklua

Three kilometers (two miles) north of Pattaya beyond Wong Amat, you are suddenly back in Thailand. Wooden fishermen's houses on stilts, piles of garbage, and colored scarves round sacred trees bring you back to the realities of conditions elsewhere in the country.

Nong Nooch Village

Twenty kilometers (13 miles) to the east of Pattaya there's Nong Nooch Village ((038) 429372 to 73. It's similar to Bangkok's Rose Garden. Large numbers of coach parties arrive daily to see elephant parades, traditional dances from all over Thailand, and other shows, all in a spacious 400-hectare (900-acre) garden setting featuring waterfalls and orchids.

Koh Laan (Coral Island)

Forty minutes (fare: 100 baht) from Pattaya by public ferry, this off-shore island is underdeveloped after the mainland, but it's no unspoilt paradise. The beaches are on the west side, i.e. the far side when coming from Pattaya, and the main beach is **Tavan**.

Tavan's front is entirely occupied by restaurants and souvenir stalls. The two-tier ferries from Pattaya cannot come right inshore so passengers are taken to the beach in long-tail boats. Some crazies even cross over from Pattaya on water-scooters — what happens if the engine fails doesn't bear thinking about.

Very few visitors stay on Koh Laan — almost the entire trade is of people coming over for the day. Consequently, Tavan Beach is really another alternative beach to Pattaya's, like Jomtien down the coast on the mainland.

The scene at midday is of a bay filled with the gaily-colored wooden ferries, long inshore craft, plus a bevy of water-scooters and touts for water-ski takers. Para-sailers take off and land at a platform moored out in the bay. Then, at precisely 3 PM, the entire beach population — almost all consisting of organized groups, Koreans, Kuwaitis, Germans — can be seen making for the long-tail boats, as if news had just broken of some impending global catastrophe. By 3:30 PM the beach is deserted, and the cafe women are busy washing up while the men count the day's takings.

There are other beaches on Koh Laan besides Tavan. **Tong Lang** has a couple of cafes, each with its handful of faded beach umbrellas, while **Tion Beach** is a boat trip (or a difficult walk) on the other side of Tavan. Both are very much quieter than Tavan.

Other and far less frequented off-shore islands are **Koh Sak, Koh Pai** and **Koh Khrok**. Individual deals must be done with Pattaya boatmen to arrange transport.

TOURIST INFORMATION

There are two free "what's on" magazines published in English that give an up-date on restaurants, hotels, nightlife and the like in the resort. They are *Explore Pattaya* and *Pattaya Tourist Guide*. The *Sun Advertiser* is very useful if you're interested in buying property in the town. All should be available at TAT and in hotel lobbies.

In addition, **TAT** ((038) 428750 and 427667 maintains a helpful office at 246/1 Moo 9 Beach Road.

Communications and Visa Renewal

The **Post Office** is, unsurprisingly, on Soi Post Office. For international direct dialing (IDD) phone calls, go to the **Pattaya City Telecommunications Center** on South Pattaya Road, 800 m (half a mile) from Waatchaimongkol Market.

The **Immigration Office** ((038) 429409 (for renewing visas) is on Soi 8.

RAYONG

East of Pattaya is **Rayong**, 185 km (115 miles) from Bangkok by Highway 36.

It's an ordinary Thai country town with little to see that can't be seen elsewhere. It's best known for its *nam pla,* a garlic sauce popular with Thais.

If you have half an hour to spare, you might spend it taking a look at the 12-m (39-ft) reclining Buddha in **Wat Pa Prandu**, leaning on his left side rather than the traditional right.

Six kilometers (four miles) from the town, going back in the direction of Pattaya, is **Hat Sai Thong**, a sandy beach from which boats will take you to the nearby island of **Koh Saket**. The crossing takes 20 minutes. It's a small island, but there's accommodation available at **Koh Saket Phet** ((01) 319042 (25 rooms; moderate; reservations in Bangkok ((02) 319-9929).

The coastline immediately after Rayong has recently seen a spate of development and now boasts a number of fine resort hotels, plus some others.

On the grandest scale, standing at the end of a secluded wooded peninsula, is the **Rayong Resort** ((038) 651000 FAX (038) 651007 (167 rooms; average and above; reservations in Bangkok ((02) 255-2392 FAX (02) 255-2391). Just as nice, though, and with a better beach, is the **Novotel Rim Pae Rayong** (/FAX (038) 614678 (109 rooms; average and above; reservations in Bangkok ((02) 247-0247 FAX (02) 246-9974), some 10 km (six miles) further along the coast.

Close to the Novotel are the comfortable **Palmeraie** ((01) 211-7763 (65 rooms; average and above; reservations in Bangkok ((02) 213-1162 FAX (02) 213-1163) and the much less sophisticated **Ban Phe Resort** (118 rooms; rates:moderate; reservations in Bangkok ((02) 250-0928 FAX (02) 280-3648). Back towards Ban Phe, the **Ban Phe Cabana** ((01) 211-4888 (33 rooms; average and above; reservations in Bangkok ((02) 280-1820 FAX (02) 280-3648) occupies a less-than-satisfactory situation, while in Ban Phe itself the **Pines Beach Hotel** ((035) 651636 FAX (038) 651641(150 rooms; moderate; reservations in Bangkok (/FAX (02) 332-0805) is an excellent, modern hostelry.

KOH SAMET

This attractive and popular holiday island is nowadays crowded with small hotels, all relatively inexpensive and all of the beach-bungalow type. There are only a handful of rooms with air-conditioning, and there is an increasingly serious water shortage in the latter part of every dry season (April and May). But if what you want is a simple, relaxed holiday, yet with plenty of others

Sit back and relax: a typical beachside scene on Koh Samet, only three hours or so from Bangkok.

like yourself around, Koh Samet could well provide the answer.

Several travel agencies operate mini-buses from Bangkok, but it's an expensive, cramped and often time-consuming service — far better to take the public air-conditioned bus from Bangkok's Eastern Bus Station (Ekamai) on Sukumvit Road to **Ban Phe**, the small port 200 km (125 miles) away from which the boats to the island depart. Highway 36, bypasses Rayong and allows the journey to be done in under three hours. The fare is 90 baht, and buses leave hourly from 5 AM to 10 PM.

The crossing from Ban Phe is six and a half kilometers (four miles) and takes half an hour. The boats are colorfully painted, wooden, and accommodate around 50 people. There is no timetable and craft leave when it's judged there are enough passengers to make a profitable journey. The fare is 30 baht, though more is asked if there are only a few of you and you're impatient to be off.

ARRIVING AT NADAAN

The scene at the simple wooden jetty where you arrive is like something out of the eastern novels of Joseph Conrad. The hamlet — known as **Nadaan** — is merely a cluster of grass-roofed huts in a clearing in the trees. Boats moor alongside each other and it is necessary to clamber across the adjacent decks to reach the jetty. The few simple restaurants and food stalls will not detain you, and minibuses wait to take you the short distance to the long line of sandy beaches on the other side of the island.

If your destination is the first, and in many ways best, beach, **Hat Sai Kaeo**, it's actually just as easy to walk. Follow the broad sandy road past the **Health Center** on your left, and in five minutes you will be at the gate into the **National Park** where an entrance fee of 50 baht is exacted. The office of the National Park is here too but has no information to offer other than a small duplicated map which doesn't contain the names of the hotels.

The minibuses turn right, but if, at the sandy crossroads immediately past the

National Park entrance, you continue straight ahead you will almost at once find yourself by the sea, half way along Hat Sai Kaeo beach.

Passengers on the minibus should note it first reaches the coast at **Ao Phai** beach, and then continues south, turning inland to skirt a rocky outcrop, until it arrives at **Ao Wongduan**. After Ao Wongduan the road is effectively for pedestrians only. The fare ranges from 10 to 30 baht.

If your destination is Wongduan — or Ao Cho — you can take the boat all the way, though this will take you longer than if you get off at Nadaan and take the bus. Only boats wholly filled with Wongduan-bound passengers go directly there without stopping at Nadaan first.

WHERE TO STAY

Accommodation on Koh Samet is all relatively simple, ranging from two-room bungalows with air-conditioning in the evenings renting out at around 1,000 baht a day to very basic huts, containing little more than a mattress and a mosquito net, for as little as 80 baht. All prices go up at weekends and during public holidays, and all are negotiable if you plan a stay of more than a few days.

Koh Samet is a very different place mid-week than at weekends. It is common not to be able to find a room on a Saturday night — this is when the island fills up with Thais from Bangkok seeking a well-earned rest. They frequently come in large groups, and on arrival set up in the shade of the palm trees (Thais have a horror of darkening their skin with sunlight) and, opening the first bottle of Mekong of the trip, prepare to serenade the rising moon with the latest chart successes. Some of the classier places claim to vet locals arriving in large groups with the aim of excluding raucous elements "and gigolos". But most visitors will agree they provide welcome relief from the rows of *farangs* reading novels and perfecting their suntans.

Most of the places now have electricity and running water though electricity may be limited to the evenings-only in some places.

SAI KAEW

Beginning at Sai Kaew beach in the north, **Diamond ℂ** (01) 321-0814 (inexpensive) has an ever-increasing number of bungalows, and a restaurant offering very friendly service and reasonable food. It's a successful family establishment in a prime position at the top end of the island's best beach. The swimming is excellent, and if you feel like being alone you can walk round onto the rocks of the nearby headland and gaze at the expanse of blue sea and the islands to the east.

A short way down the beach, **Toy ℂ** (01) 321-0975 (inexpensive) has only a few bungalows, but boasts an excellent restaurant that attracts many visitors from neighboring establishments. **Sai Kaew Villas ℂ** (01) 321-0975 (moderate to expensive) offers good quality bungalows and cocktails. **White Sand ℂ** (038) 321734 (inexpensive), is large and with a good restaurant. The last place on this beach is **Sun Sand**, close to the concrete mermaid that separates Hat Sai Kaew from Ao Phai beach. It's very cheap, and a popular late-night partying venue.

AO PHAI

The top end of this beach is dominated by **Naga ℂ** (01) 321-0732 (inexpensive), an inspired establishment where Mozart flute concertos accompany breakfast and there is a good library of Western books. It's situated on a rocky hillside, and flowering plants frame the view so that you may imagine you are in Capri. The bungalows are elegant but basic, but the food is excellent and served in large portions. Not surprisingly, it tends to get crowded at dinnertime. Naga is perhaps most celebrated for its cakes and varieties of bread, all made on the premises daily to the exacting standards of the English owner.

Next door is **Nui's** (inexpensive), a smaller place with ten bungalows and excellent ice cream. Lastly on this bay is **Ao Phai Inn** or **Nop's Kitchen ℂ** (01) 211-2968 (inexpensive) a shady but slightly dusty place with a large number of bungalows.

Continuing south, you arrive next at **Sea Breeze ℂ** (01) 321-1397 (inexpensive), a

straightforward place with thirty bungalows. Very inexpensive accommodation can be found at **Tub Tong**, while **Samet Villas** (inexpensive) has a mere eight bungalows, each with fans and shower.

Ao Phai beach is divided into several coves, and the last of these contains **Pudsa Beach** (inexpensive) with 23 bungalows, and **Tub Tim** (inexpensive), a friendly establishment attractively situated behind palm trees and with a small cocktail bar.

AO CHO

The coastal footpath now rises to cross a rocky section — when it descends again you're at **Ao Cho**. This is a tranquil little bay with exceptionally clear water and a small wooden jetty where the boats of the "White Shark" line depart for Ban Phe four or five times a day. Here, **Tantawan ℂ** (01) 321-0682 (inexpensive) serves simple local dishes in an idyllic setting. After fried fish and rice and a bottle of Kloster, you feel you could stay here for ever. Additional accommodation is available at a very slightly higher price at the next place, **Tarn Tawon**.

WONGDUAN

A minute's walk takes you over to the next bay which is crowded with resorts. You are now approaching Koh Samet's up-market sector, but the first place, **Samet Resort** (inexpensive) is unassuming. However, the **Malibu Garden Resort ℂ** (038) 651292 (30 rooms; moderate; reservations in Pattaya ℂ (038) 423180) marks the beginning of the **Wongduan** group of establishments catering for a clientele interested in mini-golf (on a concrete course), *petanque* and a Saturday-night discotheque. All these delights are to be had at **Wongduan Villa ℂ** (01) 321-0789 and 211-0509 (reservations in Bangkok ℂ (02) 525-0220; moderate). The **Wongduan Resort ℂ** (038) 651777 (moderate; reservations in Bangkok ℂ (02) 250-0423 to 26) offers quiet, large bungalows, while **Sea Horse ℂ** (01) 323-0049 (70 rooms; inexpensive) has a large number of less ostentatious places.

OVERLEAF: a Thai truck makes for the end of the road.

Whether Wongduan is really worth the extra cost depends on your tastes. But most people will find it preferable to the beaches further south.

A VIEWING POINT

After Wongduan the beaches become rockier and the accommodation rather rough and ready. More bungalows, however, are going up all the time, and given that there is little room for development further north, this area is bound to change in character before very long.

Immediately before Bungalow Lung Dam a sign "Sunset 200 m" points to the right, and a narrow path leads up into the trees. The island here is very narrow, and this is an excellent place to cross over to its largely uninhabited west side.

Once across, you arrive at a viewing point of great beauty. Before you is a vast expanse of ocean, dotted with fishing boats with their arms outstretched. To the right lie the hills of the mainland, beautifully arranged as an attendant vista. Ban Phe is clearly visible; the rocks of this inhospitable side of the island slope away below you. It's a wonderful place at any time of day, and an easy walk from Wongduan to see the sunset.

AO PHRAO

There is one bay on the west side of the island, **Ao Phrao** ("Paradise Beach"). It's quiet, backed by wooded cliffs and, of course, it faces the sunset. Ferries will take you there direct from Ban Phe for a minimum of 100 baht. Otherwise boats and taxis go from Nadaan, or you can walk (15 minutes) from Sea Breeze bungalows.

There are four bungalow establishments at Ao Phrao. **S.K.Hut** (22 rooms; inexpensive) is at the south end by the wooden jetty. Next comes **Dhom** ((01) 321-0786 (17 rooms; inexpensive), probably the best bet of all. Then there is the rather basic **Ratana's** (10 rooms; inexpensive). And at the northernmost end of the bay is **Ao Phrae Resort** (inexpensive).

Ao Phrao is probably too quiet for most people. There is coral at the jetty end, said to be the best on Koh Samet, though there are better examples round the outlying islets. The coral generally, though, doesn't compare with that in the clearer Andaman Sea off Thailand's southwest coast.

Note: Malaria is present on Koh Samet and visitors should be sure they are taking the necessary precautions.

CHANTABURI

Two hundred and eighty kilometers (174 miles) from Bangkok by Highway 36,

Chantaburi town is famous as a center for the mining and cutting of gems. Sapphires and rubies are found nearby and you can buy them in this town as cheaply as you'll find them anywhere.

Chantaburi's other claim to fame is Thailand's biggest Roman Catholic church, the **Church of the Immaculate Conception**. It was built by Catholic refugees from Vietnam between 1905 and 1909.

Outside town is the **Khao Sar Bab National Park**. Its **Pliew Waterfall** is a popular local beauty spot, and minibuses leave for there from outside Chantaburi's Municipal Market. Reasonable accommodation is provided at the **Hotel Eastern** ((039) 312218 to 20 (142 rooms; moderate).

The new **Chantaburi Riverside Hotel and Resort (** (039) 311726 FAX (02) 512-5726 (expensive) is very exclusive.

TRAT PROVINCE

Close up against the Cambodian border, Trat Province is the easternmost part of Thailand. **Trat** is an attractive small town. Simple but good accommodation can be found at the **Hotel Muang Trat (** (039) 511091 (123 rooms; inexpensive), overlook-

track to the northern village of Ao Khlong Son and another two hours to Hat Sai Khao. It's easy enough to walk between any of the west coast beaches, too, though you can also pick up motorbike taxis almost everywhere.

For upmarket accommodation on Koh Chang there's the **Rooks Koh Chang Resort (** (01) 329-0434 (reservations in Bangkok **(** (02) 277-0482 FAX (02) 276-1233). For inexpensive and basic huts, but with a reliable restaurant, try the **Kaibae Hut** on Hat Kaibae.

ing the night market. Western food is served in the Coffee Shop.

It also contains several virtually untouched islands, including the large **Koh Chang**, which is increasingly popular and has many places to stay.

Boats to Koh Chang, as well as to **Koh Koot, Koh Kradat** and **Koh Rad,** leave from **Laem Ngob** cape, 20 km (12 miles) south of Trat .

As Koh Chang's best beaches and most of its accommodation is on the west coast, you should choose boats heading directly there (**Hat Sai Khao**, White Sand Beach, is the most popular destination). If you get a boat to the east coast village of Sai Thong, it's a two-hour walk along a dirt

The smaller islands are currently being actively developed — TAT in Bangkok or Pattaya should be able to provide you with up-to-date details.

Lastly, note that the islands are malarial; make sure you're taking prophylactic tablets while — and after — visiting the region. See under HEALTH in TRAVELERS' TIPS, page 225 for details.

Monks on a beach on the Gulf of Siam. All Thai boys enter a monastery for a time during adolescence, and even in adult life often return for periods of retreat. Being a monk is in no way necessarily an "all-or-nothing", life-time calling in Thailand.

The
South
and
Phuket

HUA HIN

Hua Hin, just over 200 km (125 miles) south of Bangkok, is Thailand's traditional royal resort, and its lifeline has always been the railway.

Today the country's main north-south road runs right through the middle of the town, but in the 1920s it was the construction of the single-track railway down from Bangkok that first put Hua Hin on the map.

At last the wealthy could escape the suffocating heat of the capital in April and in three hours be in their villas along the sands, cooled by the breezes off the Gulf of Siam. Foreigners arrived to inspect the exotic new resort, and Hua Hin became the Nice of Asia. People played golf — that newly fashionable game popularized in Asia by the young heir to the English throne — on a picturesque and intriguing **18-hole golf course** opposite the quaint wooden station, rode horses along the sand, and socialized in the celebrated Hua Hin Railway Hotel.

Elsewhere in the world railway hotels tend to be rather down-market affairs catering for commercial travelers who arrive late and have to be away on the first train of the morning. Not so Hua Hin's. In its heyday this colonial-style hotel on the sea was every bit the equal of the Oriental in Bangkok and the Raffles in Singapore.

Then, as suddenly as it had come, fashion abandoned Hua Hin. Created by the railway, it was killed by the road — the road east from Bangkok, to Bang Saen and Pattaya. For twenty years from the mid-Sixties, Hua Hin's charms came to seem decidedly frowzy.

WHERE TO STAY

Nowadays, however, things are looking up. The Railway Hotel, not so long ago a place with only a handful of spider-filled rooms from which to watch the few remaining horses sheltering from the sun beneath faded beach umbrellas, has been extensively and beautifully renovated by the French Sofitel group. Renamed the **Sofitel Central** ((032) 512021 FAX (032) 511014 (207 rooms;

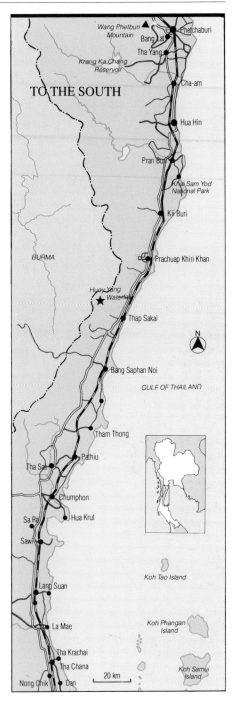

Fishing boats OPPOSITE at Hua Hin. Attractive old-world wooden buildings cluster round the harbor — many of them have been converted into restaurants offering the freshest seafood. It's a busy area at night in an otherwise quiet town.

expensive; reservations in Bangkok ((02) 541-1463 FAX (02) 541-1464), it has retained all the style of its past while gaining the comforts and conveniences of the modern era. Afternoon tea is now served in the old lobby, a period jazz band serenades you at cocktail time, and soon vintage cars will transport you the short distance from the station. The topiary garden and its much-photographed elephant (with painted wooden tusks) remains.

Of course this sort of thing is not to everybody's taste, and if you prefer a more lively ambiance then there is the **Royal Garden Resort** ((032) 511881 to 84 FAX (032) 520259 (220 rooms; expensive; reservations in Bangkok ((02) 251-6859 or 252-4638 or 252-8252) with its **Jungle Disco** half a kilometer (one third of a mile) to the south down the beach.

For more or less budget accommodation, the **Jed Pee Nong Hotel** ((032) 512381 (35 rooms; moderate) on Damneonkasem Road is very popular — clean and good value.

WHERE TO EAT

Many fine seafood restaurants are to be found by the Harbor. Of these, the **Meeka-runa Restaurant** ((032) 511932 (moderate) and the **Saeng Thai Restaurant** ((032) 512144 (moderate), are especially recommended.

A small way from the center of town is the **Bann Tappikaew** ((032) 512210, 7 Naeb-khehat, a very attractive restaurant based round a beautiful wooden house. Most of the tables are in the garden which fronts onto the sea. It's very popular with the better-off local Thais, and the cuisine is classical Thai.

Foreign food isn't hard to find in Hua Hin either. A stylish little French restaurant is **Le Chablis** ((032) 531499 (moderate) at 88 Naresdamri, while on the same road the Italian-run **Euro Seafood and Steak Garden** ((032) 922-0154 (moderate), serves a variety of European dishes. German food can be found at the **Thai-German Restaurant** ((032) 512536 (moderate) 22/32 Petchkasem Road, and the **Sailom Hotel** ((032) 511890 to 01 (average and above), offers Japanese food as well as Thai.

Further Information

Many of the facilities you're likely to need in Hua Hin are concentrated in the broad road running directly down to the beach from the station, Damneonkasem Road. The **Tourist Information Service Center** ((032) 512120, is there, as is the **Post Office**, and a clutch of tourist-oriented restaurants, souvenir stalls, tour agents, together with a variety of budget, and other, hotels.

The **bus station** isn't far away from this complex, though in fact there is no station as such — buses wait at the four corners of a

large crossroads, where Descharnuchit Road crosses Srasong Road. It's a 10-minute walk, or a 10-baht pedi-cab ride, from the station.

AFTER DARK

Everything in Hua Hin has the appearance of being prosperous and up-to-date. Even the **night market**, in many places attractive because of its very sleaziness, is here clean and brightly-lit. It's adjacent to the bus station.

More attractive place to go at night, and a colorful place at any time, is the **harbor**. Here, old wooden houses back onto the water, and many of them have been made into restaurants. As you might expect, seafood is their speciality (see under WHERE TO EAT, above).

THE BEACH

Hua Hin's long sandy beach extends both north and south of the harbor. There is no road running along the front — instead, large houses, a few hotels and one palace back directly onto the shore. Commercial development along the shoreline is as a result almost entirely nonexistent, and the is an access lane from the main road through Hua Hin, but from there you can see comparatively little.) When members of the royal family are in residence, however, sentries seal off this portion of the beach. His Majesty prefers to wind-surf — a sport which he is said to enjoy particularly — in peace.

KHAO TAKIAB

South of Damneonkasem Road the beach sweeps uninterrupted to **Khao Takiab**

exclusive quiet sought by the original visitors is effectively maintained.

Access to the beach for the rest of us is by Damneonkasem Road, running direct from the station and passing the Sofitel Central on the right.

Where this road reaches the sea there are some rocks, but for the rest the beach is sand and, according to the authorities, safe for children. North of this point is the harbor, then, a kilometer further on, the royal **Summer Palace**, situated on the sea, with formal steps leading down onto the sand. It is possible to walk right past the palace for most of the year, and this is the best place to get a glimpse of the buildings — relatively modern and set in spacious grounds. (There ("Chopstick Hills"), four kilometers away. If walking in the heat seems too hard, you can get a bus from the bus station — they leave every half hour and the trip takes 15 minutes.

Khao Takiab is a rocky outcrop on the sea's edge. There's a tall white Buddha close to sealevel, a monastery higher up, and various shrines and outhouses sited in scenic positions. The monastery's regimen

Hua Hin — the quiet beach ABOVE with private villas backing directly onto the extensive sands and the famous Sofitel Central hotel OPPOSITE. This famous hostelry used to be known as the Railway Hotel and saw in its heyday much high living. It was renovated and considerably enlarged in 1987.

appears relaxed. Monkeys live in the trees in the first part you come to, and food for them — bananas and peanuts — is on sale at the entrance. They won't bother you if they see you haven't bought anything.

Eight kilometers (five miles) further south is **Khao Tao** hill with its twin peaks, and the very quiet **Suan Son** beach backed by pine trees. Fishermen will also take you from here (or from Khao Takiab) to the off-shore island of **Sing Toh**.

PHETCHABURI

Sixty-six kilometers (41 miles) to the north of Hua Hin, Petchaburi is easily accessible by road or rail. Approaching the town by either means you can see its two main attractions, a palace and a temple, perched on their twin hilltops ahead of you.

Rama IV's Summer Palace known as **Khao Wang**, and the **Museum** inside it, are open from 9 AM to 4 PM Wednesdays to Sundays (closed Mondays and Tuesdays). To get there you can either walk from the town center, up a once-paved road that was clearly meant for horse-drawn traffic, take a *samlor* ride or the cable car up the hill. The palace features an observatory — astronomy was one of old King Mongkut's enthusiasms — and you get an excellent view from the top.

You can easily walk from the Summer Palace across the hill pass to **Wat Tra Keow**, five minutes away on the neighboring hilltop. This has just been extensively renovated and is now a sparkling jewel in a magnificent location.

The large *chedi* that you pass on the way there is at the time of writing in a dilapidated condition, but it's interesting to go inside it, and to come out via some steps onto a ledge at a higher level.

From the temple you can go down to the road without going back to the Palace, by a track leading through monastery buildings.

Phetchaburi is rich in temples, and **Wat Khao Bandai It** with its leaning *stupa* (said to show the original patron's preference for one of his two wives), together with **Wat Yai** and the several other *wats* close to it in the center of the town, are all well worth a visit.

A Buddha Cave

Khao Luang Cave is five kilometers or three miles out of town and contains an underground shrine. A minibus will take you there for 50 baht, will require the same again to bring you back, and may ask for something more for waiting for you.

You arrive at a little group of wooden houses and the cave entrance is 50 m (55 yards) ahead up a paved track. The cavern is full of old Buddha images, which have been here for decades. There's no admission fee, but a donation is always gratefully received.

OTHER TRIPS FROM HUA HIN

Cha-am

Hua Hin's less than regal sister resort is nothing more than a four-kilometer (two-and-a-half miles) long sandy beach backed with casuarina trees along which, over the years, a variety of hotels and guesthouses have established themselves. Whereas Hua Hin is dominated by its palace, colonial-style hotel and second homes of the very rich, Cha-am is pleasantly democratic and easy-going. Few Westerners stay there, but it's very popular with Thais.

Cha-am gets very full at weekends as it is one of the closest resorts to Bangkok, but on weekdays, even in high season, you can have the beach almost to yourself. It's a pleasant, unassuming place unspoilt by the international invasion that is the bane of so many other resorts in Thailand.

Getting to Cha-am is no problem. It's on the railway, slightly disguised as Ban Chaam, and on the country's main north–south road. Most foreigners visit Cha-am, if at all, as a sidetrip from Hua Hin, and from here too you can take either the train or a bus. Going by road is probably easier as there are plenty of buses, at least until 6 PM, after which there are none at all. The fare is 15 baht. The main road from Bangkok to the south passes within a kilometer of the beach, and if you arrive by bus you'll be put down

Roof decoration at Phetchaburi. The small country town was a favorite of King Mongkut (Rama IV) and is rich in temples, both on the hill overlooking the town and in the central area near the railway station.

where motorbikes are waiting to transport you to the seaside (fare: 10 baht).

Small restaurants and hotels extend for about a kilometer both to the left and right of the point where you arrive on the front. There are many budget and near-budget places, and three five-star places including the **Regent Cha-am Beach Hotel** ((032) 471480 FAX (032) 471491 (420 rooms; expensive; reservations in Bangkok ((02) 251-0305) and the **Dusit Resort and Polo Club** ((032) 520009 FAX (032) 520296 (expensive) which features excellent sports facilities.

several days there — in which case you'll need a guide as well as a great deal of mosquito repellent — you have little choice but to pay your 600 baht and join an organized tour. All the agents in Hua Hin run these, but according to demand, not every day.

KHAO SAM ROI YOD NATIONAL PARK

As you drive south from Hua Hin, after passing extensive pineapple plantations

There are in addition several other more or less grand establishments along the beach between Cha-am and Hua Hin.

Pa La-u

This waterfall lies 63 km (39 miles) inland, near the Burmese border. It's a series of cascades in jungle settings, and there are Karen villages and a reservoir nearby. If you don't have your own transport, the only feasible way to get there is by taking a day trip. Public transport is timetabled for the benefit of the local villagers, and buses consequently leave the up-country areas early in the morning and return from Hua Hin in the afternoon. This is the reverse of what the tourist requires, so unless you plan to spend

(recognizable by the bluish sheen of the leaves of the cactus-like plant) you come to the small market town of **Pranburi**. There is nothing to detain you here, but as you continue south an extraordinary spectacle begins to appear on the horizon to the left. The turrets and pinnacles you are seeing are the summits of the sheer limestone hills known as Khao Sam Roi Yod ("300 peaks"), and the National Park that has been created around them is one of the most attractive places for naturalists in all Thailand.

Without a hired car, transport into the Park used to be difficult. Now, however, there is a minibus service between Pranburi's town center and the Park Headquarters. You'll have to ask your hotel staff for the times of this new service, and they may conceivably be reluctant to give them to you as most hotels in Hua Hin run their own private tours (in conjunction with a local agent) when demand is sufficient. Public bus services to Pranburi from Hua Hin bus station are frequent during daylight hours.

A WILDLIFE PARADISE

The Park consists of spectacular limestone hills that rise sheer out of salt and semi-salt marshes. The marshes form the habitat for

numerous bird species, and this is the best of the Thai National Parks for observing waders. Other birds to be seen here are herons, blue crab-eaters, bee-eaters, egrets, white-breasted kingfishers and white-bellied sea-eagles. Most of these birds are migratory and spend the summer in China, Siberia or Northern Europe — the best time to see them here is between November and January.

For the most part the birds occupy the saltwater and semi-saltwater mudflats. Up on the hills are found serow (a goat-like antelope whose habitat is inaccessible crags), porcupines, crab-eating and dusky leaf-eating monkeys, and the very rare, fish tiger.

The South and Phuket

The 98 km (61 miles) square Park isn't without its problems. Much of the mudflat area is outside its jurisdiction and prawn-farming has become popular with the local fishermen. This involves increasing the amount of seawater in the creeks, but the increased salinity is killing the mangrove trees, home to the insects that bring the birds to the area. The Park authorities are responding by planting new mangroves in areas under their control, but the basic conflict of interests persists.

UNCROWDED PLEASURES

The National Park in general has many attractions, but most notable are its rugged interior and its caves.

Phraya Nakhon Cave is the most popular. It's situated 500 m (550 yards) from **Haad Laem Sala Beach**, and as it's a long, rough trek from Bang Pu (the nearest village), most people get there by boat. Its oddest and most astonishing feature is that it contains a royal pavilion, put there to receive King Rama V in 1896. Recently redecorated, it makes an impressive spectacle, lit by the shafts of sunshine that strike the cave floor from two large holes in the cave roof.

Kaeo Cave is also close to Bang Pu and is noted for its brilliant white limestone formations (*kaeo* means "shining" in Thai). A guide is essential as the cave has hidden ledges that are very dangerous.

Sai in Thai means "ficus", and these trees surround **Sai Cave**'s wide opening. It's a 15 minute walk up from the beach — there are steps all the way but it's steepish. The entrance is 300 m (980 ft) above sea level. Check on the beach that there's someone up at the cave to operate the lamps (the fee for the lamps and guide is 30 baht). It's a moderately interesting limestone cave, but with no special features.

Pine-backed Sam Phraya Beach is a short drive from Park Headquarters (on the coast in the far south of the Park). You can camp there, and there is one food and drink stall.

Sign at Khao Sam Roi Yod National Park. Thailand's National Parks are excellently maintained, and this is the country's oldest, containing a number of animals, most notably elephants.

You can also stay at Haad Laem Sala Beach (see above) where there are four bungalows; there are another four at Headquarters.

The best way to see the interior of the park on a short visit is to take a boat trip up the creek. At 150 baht per boatload per hour, this is excellent value, and the views of the high pinnacles, which fall sheer down to the river in places, are spectacular. For these trips, enquire at Headquarters, or at Khao Daeng Village. Early morning and late afternoon are the best times to see wildlife, as well as for taking photos.

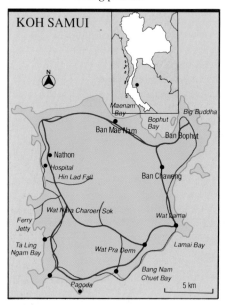

KOH SAMUI

Koh Samui has been a popular tourist destination since the late 1960s when it was "discovered" by hippies. Now everyone is getting in on the act, and there are many quite classy beach hotels and restaurants. The present situation is that the more popular beaches have a wide range of facilities, while the less frequented places still retain something of their earlier, drug-culture atmosphere.

GETTING THERE

You can fly direct from Bangkok's Don Muang airport with Bangkok Airways. They depart five times a day and the round-trip fare is 4,160 baht. Ferries run to Samui from Thatong pier, six kilometers (three-and-a-half miles) northeast of Surat Thani, as well as from Surat Thani's Ban Don Pier and from **Donsak**, an hour's drive to the south. Boats leave Donsak at 6:50 AM, 8 AM, 10 AM, noon, 2 PM and 5 PM; the trip lasts one hour, and the fare is 40 baht. For the slightly longer (two-hour) trip from Thatong, boats depart at 7:15 AM, 11:30 AM and 2:30 PM in the dry season (November to May) and at 7:15 AM and 12:30 PM only during the rainy season (June to October). The fare is 105 baht. There is also a faster (one-and-a-half-hour) jet boat service which leaves Thatong at 8 AM and costs 130 baht. The slow (six-hour) night boat from Ban Don is not recommended.

KOH SAMUI ISLAND

There is nothing really worth seeing in Surat Thani, 885 km (549 miles) from Bangkok, the domestic airport and mainline rail link for Koh Samui, though there is an interesting monastery, **Wat Suanmoke**, in the forest close to the nearby town of **Chaiya**. Most people head straight on for **Koh Samui**, a rather large, hilly island 35 km (22 miles) from the mainland south of Surat Thani.

NATHON

All ferries arrive at **Nathon**, the only town on the island. It's a busy little place with a post office, an immigration office, a Catholic church (masses on Sundays at 8:30 AM and weekdays at 6:30 PM) and travel agents. The biggest of these is the semi-official **Songserm Travel Center** ((077) 421228 or 421316 to 19, just to the left of the pier; **Paradise Seagull Tours** a few doors further on is also recommended. But nobody stays in Nathon.

Koh Samui — Coconut palms OPPOSITE TOP surround a comfortably furnished jungle-style hideout at the Resort Hotel which also offers more traditional rooms BOTTOM.

A BIRD'S EYE VIEW

Transport on Samui is well-developed, with a modern concrete road extending round the

58 km (36 miles) of the island's periphery. Buses leave in droves from Nathon from first light till sunset for the beaches on the north and east sides of the island (fare 20 to 25 baht), and even after dark they can be privately hired as "taxis", but at a much higher rate, for the thirty minute trip.

Essentially, there are two "big" beaches, Chaweng and Lamai. More isolated clusters of bungalows are sited south of these, and this southern strip is where the cheapest accommodation can be found. North of Chaweng and Lamai, on the beaches of **Maenam** and **Bophut**, the rates are somewhere between the two, and some very attractive places, neither too developed nor too remote, can be found on this north coast of the island. For Bophut beach, take a bus that advertises its destination as "Big Buddha".

Some agents will try to interest you in bungalows they are in contact with while you are still on the boat crossing over from the mainland. They will probably tell you the island is overrun with tourists and finding a room is difficult. This may well be the case in the high season, despite recent newspaper reports suggesting that Samui has over-anticipated demand for accommodation by as much as 40 percent. But not all the touts' stories are true: agents can only book you into places they can contact by telephone, and many beach hotels in Samui don't have phone service.

An outstandingly informative map, showing all the hotels and clusters of beach huts, is the *Guide Map of Koh Samui, Koh Pha-Ngan and Koh Tao*, usually on sale on the ferries for 35 baht. Nowhere else in Thailand has such a detailed tourist map.

CHAWENG BEACH

The island's premier strip is **Chaweng Beach**, and it really is very beautiful, coconuts palms leaning out over white sand, and a coral reef offshore. The beach slopes gradually, so quite a lot of sand — more than at Lamai — is exposed at low tide. Chaweng extends for three kilometers (two miles), with Chaweng Noi, ("Little Chaweng") adding another kilometer to the south.

Walking the length of the beach, the island's recent history is laid out before

you. At several points fishermen sit under the coconut palms, watching their boats and waiting for the evening's fishing. They are the original Samui. Elsewhere are low-price bungalows offering "magic mushroom soup", representing the first influx of Westerners who disturbed the primordial quiet of the island. Then there are the upmarket establishments with striped deckchairs and advertisements for cocktails. These represent the yuppies, the latest arrivals.

The nicest part of Chaweng Beach is the quiet north end, where friendly and unassuming, and in some cases even rather chic, clusters of bungalows overlook the islet known as **Koh Matlang** (or Mudlung). Here the **Matlang Resort** (/FAX (077) 421171 (45 rooms; moderate) is smartish and has a garden, yet is very reasonable. Moving south, **Moon Bungalows** (45 rooms; inexpensive) is relaxed and charming. **O.P. Bungalow** (34 rooms; moderate) is notably clean and specializes in Chinese food.

After an undeveloped gap you come to the **Samui Cabana** (57 rooms; moderate), an impressive place with sophisticated food and drinks. Close by is the friendly if basic **Montien** (12 rooms; inexpensive). Among the smarter resorts, the **Blue Lagoon Hotel** ((077) 422037 FAX (077) 422401 (61 rooms; expensive) has attractive rooms.

The **J.R. Palace** ((077) 421402 (70 rooms; inexpensive) offers a range of a accommodation and pleasant service.

In the central and southern stretches of the beach several establishments attempt to go upmarket. Notable among these are the **Chaweng Cabana** ((077) 421377 to 79; FAX (077) 421377; 26 rooms; average and above) and, especially, the **Pansea** ((077) 422384; FAX (077) 422385 (50 rooms; expensive; reservations in Bangkok ((01) 235-6075 to 56). But the natural conditions on the beach are so idyllic it's difficult to see what else, over and above what everyone offers, is really needed.

This tendency to go upmarket reaches its peak at the southern end of the beach where the buses from Nathon first hit the coast. Here the **First Bungalow** ((077) 423444 (60 rooms; moderate), is smart, has a shop and a pricey restaurant, while round the corner on Chaweng Noi, the **Imperial Samui**

Hotel ((077) 422020 FAX (077) 421397 (expensive) offers luxury accommodation.

LAMAI BEACH

Lamai faces southeast and is separated from Chaweng by a rocky headland where a couple of coves offer do-as-you-please seclusion. **Coral Cove Resort** (20 rooms, inexpensive) is casual and friendly — ask the bus to put you down at the Brown Sugar "reggae" cafe.

Lamai basks in the tropical sun in sleepy languor, but its mass of coconut trees in fact hides an extensive network of sandy roads linking up not only numerous bungalow hotels but also some rather trendy ice cream parlors, discotheques and bars. Even so, Lamai remains less developed than Chaweng, though the difference is unlikely to last long. If Chaweng's beach has the edge, Lamai's the place for laid-back indulgence and dreamy ease.

Fishing boats moor at Lamai's northern end, and the beach proper doesn't really begin until you've passed the little river and the sign announcing "Ban Lamai". At this northern end, **Rose Garden Bungalows** ((077) 421410 (18 rooms; moderate), has a quiet, half forgotten air that might appeal to some people.

You can take your pick of the bungalow hotels on the main stretch of the beach. They almost all fall into the inexpensive category, and in some of them you could easily imagine you'd taken a time-trip back twenty years. The **Lamai Inn Bungalows** (/FAX (077) 421427 (40 rooms; inexpensive) is just one of many. Only a few such as the **Best Resort** (30 rooms; moderate) aim to cater for a very slightly more affluent clientele. At the luxurious end of the maket is the **Aloha Resort** ((077) 421418 FAX (077) 421419 (expensive).

At the south end of the beach, where the buses emerge from the sandy Lamai lanes onto the hard road, is **Cafe Roma** (moderate) offering Italian food (including pizza), ice cream and cocktails.

The **Nightlife** on Chaweng and Lamai consists of bars, video parlors and several discos, including the **Flamingo** on Lamai, and the **Arabian, Madonna** and huge high-tech **Reggae Pub** at Chaweng.

TONGSAI, BOPHUT

Luxury rooms are available at the **Imperial Tongsai Bay Hotel and Cottages** ((077) 425015 FAX (077) 421462 (expensive) while on **Bophut Beach,** the **Samui Palm Beach Resort** ((077) 421358 FAX (077) 422358 (50 rooms; expensive) is both comfortable and relaxed.

KOH PHA-NGAN ISLAND

All in all, Koh Samui is an up-and-coming resort paradise that is very well patronized by those it aims to please. Simpler and more natural places than those on the main beaches can still be found, but if you're convinced that Samui is already just too popular for anyone seeking the true Blue Lagoon life, then you should head north for the second largest island in the group, **Koh Pha-Ngan.**

The ferry from Nathon to Koh Pha-Ngan leaves twice a day, at 10:30 AM and 4:30 PM (returning from Pha-Ngan to Samui at 6:15 AM and 12:30 PM). The 25-km (16-miles) trip takes 50 minutes; the fare is 50 baht. The morning boat connects with the ferry from the mainland to Samui; it always waits for it, so you can be sure of making the trip from the mainland to Koh Pha-Ngan direct, without having to spend any time at all on Samui if that's what you want.

Boats also run to Koh Pha-Ngan from Bophut Beach. They're sturdy fishing boats with an enclosed section under the square superstructure and they carry around 20 people. They put you down at Haad Rin Beach. Departures are at 10:30 AM and 3:30 PM; the return boats from Pha-Ngan leave at 9:30 AM and 2:30 PM. The fare is 60 baht each way.

THONG SALA

Koh Pha-Ngan is a great contrast to Koh Samui. This is clear the moment you arrive at the harbor and one-street port, **Thong Sala.** Whereas in Nathon on Samui it's all travel agents booking trips to Bangkok, Kuala Lumpur and Singapore, in Thong Sala the typical shopkeeper is asleep under a straw hat, and his wares are medicines for humans, medicines for animals and sea shells.

A proportion of the visitors arriving on the morning boat immediately take the connecting fishing boat for Haad Rin, the island's most popular beach and inaccessible (except on foot) by land. A few opt to stay in town, perhaps at **Pha-Ngan Central Hotel** ((077) 377068 FAX (077) 377032 (moderate). Most, though, settle down to a welcome second breakfast in one of the simple cafes situated where the road reaches the beach, and then make off by minibus "taxi" or newly rented motorbike for one of the bungalow establishments along the island's southern coast between Thong Sala and Baan Khaay.

SOUTH COAST

The bus for Baan Khay (fare 30 baht) bumps over the sand road loaded with crates of soft drinks and tourists' rucksacks. Signs with names like "Liberty" and "Green Peace" point down narrow tracks to where the sea glitters blue between palm trees.

Each of these clutches of bungalows has a whole stretch of the long sandy beach to itself. Some, such as **Laemthong** (20 rooms; inexpensive) are on rocky outcrops commanding extra-beautiful views, and rooms cost as little as one or two US dollars.

At **Baan Khay** the road ends, and as a result the places immediately after there do a good trade. The first of them, **Thong Yang** (20 rooms, inexpensive), with some of its bungalows perched on rocks washed by the waves, is the nicest.

HAAD RIN

This is Koh Pha-Ngan's most popular beach. It lies at the far southeastern corner, and is actually two beaches, one on either side of a narrow isthmus. It's a three-minute walk from one beach to the other.

The east-facing beach usually has some small waves, welcome to some people, but it's the west-facing one that has the nicer bungalows and restaurants. Of these, **Rin Beach Resort Kitchen and Bakery** does excellent cakes and is a pleasant place to sit and gaze at the sea. By and large, though, Haad Rin is something of a betwixt-and-between

place, aiming for a degree of sophistication but with none of the advantages — or the quality of beach — of the best places on Koh Samui.

WEST COAST

The west coast of the island is generally low-lying and life in its holiday bungalows is very quiet. Pines line the beach, crickets chirr in the night, birds twitter in the bright mornings. At **Laem Son** (10 rooms; inexpensive) the food's good, though the beach isn't special. There are fishing boats and solitude. Further along, at **See Thanu** (30 rooms; inexpensive) the beach is better.

The roads on the island are mostly dirt track. Much of the transport is by motorbike — riders will take you anywhere for roughly the same price as the buses (which may only run every couple of hours).

KOH TAO

There are many other islands in the Koh Samui group. An irregular service connects Thong Sala with Koh Tao, 47 km (29 miles) away to the north. If the weather is clement the boat owner will undertake the three-hour trip daily around noon. The fare is 150 baht.

There are plenty of cheap and simple places to stay on Koh Tao. It's mainly known for an offshore islet, Koh Nangyuan, where three beaches, each facing a different way, have become joined back-to-back. It's claimed to be a unique phenomenon.

A MARINE PARK

Very spectacular is the **Ang Thong National Marine Park**, which consists of 40 steep and forested islands 31 km (19 miles) west of Samui. They are uninhabited except for a National Park staff of 30 on Ta Lap ("Sleeping Cow Island"). There are simple bungalows to rent on this island, but almost everyone visits on day trips from Samui, and the Park authorities are no doubt happy to keep things this way.

Attractions are snorkeling, diving, and clambering up a steep track on **Mae Koh** ("Mother Island") to see a brilliant green saltwater lake surrounded by cliffs called Talai Nai.

Trips from Samui are organized daily in high season by several tour operators including **Highway Travel** ((077) 421290 or 421285. You leave at 8:30 AM and are back by 5 PM (300 baht; lunch included).

PHUKET

Over the last couple of decades Phuket has become Thailand's premier tourist destination. It has its own airport, and several foreign airlines — in addition to Thai International — have acquired rights to fly there direct. The road from Surat Thani across the isthmus to Phuket on the western coast (four and a half hours by minibus) passes through spectacular lime-stone mountains on an excellent modern highway.

Phuket is big, 810 sq km (312 sq miles), and actually hardly a true island — it's connected to the mainland by a causeway. It's hilly, and its name derives from the Malay word *bukit* meaning "mountain". It was an important and prosperous province long before the first foreigner thought of lying on any of its numerous beaches, and undersea tin mining has always been important.

A BIRD'S EYE VIEW

Basically, it's the indented west coast that has all the finest beaches, while the lower-lying east coast is more involved with

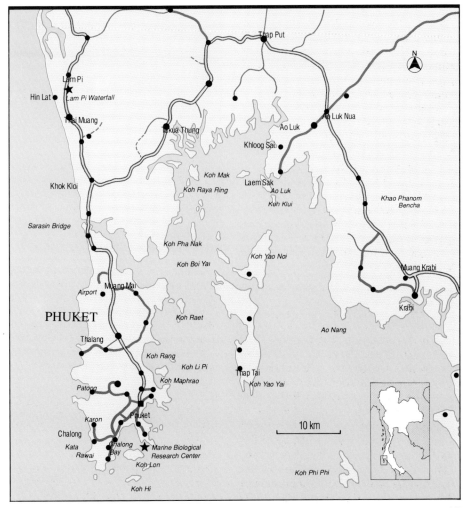

commerce and industry. Phuket Town, also often referred to simply as "Phuket", lies on the island's eastern side, two thirds of the way down from the causeway.

Since tourist development has tended to be on the western beaches, the town remains relatively untouched by the massive foreign influx.

From Promthep Cape in the south to the Sarasin Bridge in the north, then, Phuket's major beaches are Nai Harn, Kata Noi, Kata, Karon, Patong, Kamala, Surin, Bang Tao, Nai Yang and Mai Khao. Details of **accommodation** will be given on a beach-by-beach basis.

BEACH BY BEACH

Rawai

Before looking at these western beaches, mention must be made of **Rawai Beach**, east of Promthep Cape. Popular with local people, it has no upmarket developments and remains an unassuming place with good sea food — at, for instance, the **Salaloy Restaurant** ((076) 381297 (inexpensive). Nearby there is a **gypsy settlement** similar to the one at Pang Nga. **Promthep Cape** itself is a classic place to go to see the sunset — at the weekend in the company of coachloads of other enthusiasts.

Close to Rawai is the **Phuket Island Resort** ((076) 381010 FAX (076) 381018 (300 rooms; expensive; reservations in Bangkok ((01) 252-5320 to 21), a large hotel attractively spread over a hillside sloping down to the sea and commanding superb views to the south. One of the many islands you can see, Koh Bon, is owned by the hotel, and during the daytime a boat ferries hotel guests across to a private beach and barbeque restaurant.

This spacious hotel also features Thai, Japanese and European restaurants, a discotheque, and a wide variety of sports and sea-sports facilities.

Nai Harn

This beautiful beach is unspoilt and enclosed by well-wooded headlands. At the northern end stands one of the island's very best hotels, the **Phuket Yacht Club** ((076) 381156; FAX (076) 381164 (108 rooms; expensive; reservations in Bangkok ((02) 251-4707).

Kata and Kata Noi

The coast road that connects Nai Harn and Kata affords the most spectacular view on the island at its summit. Looking north, Phuket's sequence of magnificent sandy beaches, each separated by a rocky headland, is spread out before you. The road arrives back at sea level at a point where Kata Beach lies to your right and Kata Noi to your left.

Kata Noi ("Little Kata") is dominated at the north end by the **Kata Thani Hotel** ((076) 381417 FAX (076) 381426 (183 rooms; expensive; reservations in Bangkok ((02) 235-5120

FAX (02) 235-9529). All other accommodation in the area is much more basic, but generally the fishermen's huts — some of which offer lodging and food — are nowadays kept away from the actual beach front, at least at the showy north end.

Kata is a fine bay, a deep bite into the land with a picturesque island plumb in the middle. At the southern end is the comfortable **Kata Beach Resort** ((076) 330530 FAX (076) 330128 (202 rooms; average and above). Thailand's only **Club Med** ((076) 381455 FAX (076) 330461 (300 rooms; expensive; reservations in Bangkok ((01) 253-9780)

ABOVE: The Chedi Phuket. The hotel consists of luxury bungalows overlooking a private beach. The pattern is typical of many Thai beach hotels.

is also situated on this beach, very attractively built in traditional Thai styles and with the usual wide variety of facilities. The **Boat House Inn and Restaurant** ((076) 381557 FAX (076) 381561 (36 rooms; expensive) offers genuine comfort and elegance without ostentation.

Karon

Between Kata and Karon are situated a number of shops selling souvenirs, a branch of the Thai Farmers' Bank, and several important diving centers (See DIVING, page 156).

Karon to Patong

Take the new coast road connecting Karon and Patong and on the way you will pass the deluxe **Meridien Phuket** ((076) 321480 to 85 FAX (076) 321479 (470 rooms; expensive; reservations in Bangkok ((02) 254-8147 to 50). It stands on its own bay and specializes in, among other things, sports facilities.

Out on the headland south of Patong proper half a mile out of town, the **Coral Beach Hotel** ((076) 340106 FAX (076) 321114 (200 rooms; expensive; reservations in Bangkok ((02) 252-6118) has its own small beach.

Karon Beach itself is open, long, and has few trees. The beach is backed by low dunes behind which there's a brackish creek; behind this runs the road, and on that, facing the sea, are the hotels.

Karon has only recently been developed and lacks the comfortable appearance of longer-established places. There are already many hotels, however. The 11-story **Phuket Arcadia Hotel** ((076) 381038 FAX (076) 381136 (255 rooms; expensive) is large and modern. The four-story **Thavorn Palm Beach** ((076) 381034 FAX (076) 381555 (210 rooms; expensive) is also modern, while the **Phuket Island View** ((076) 381919 FAX (076) 381632 (51 rooms; average and above) offers accommodation in solid bungalows.

Patong

Patong Beach is everything opponents of mass tourism dislike and fear most. A vast coconut grove fills a basin of flat land backed by hills and fronting onto the sea, and not so very long ago all there was was a narrow road running parallel with the water and linking up a few idyllically-sited huts and a monastery. Today there are restaurants and shopping centers, hotels and bars, along the entire strip as well as some way inland; motorbikes roar off into the morning and local girls call out at foreign men just as if they were in Hat Yai or Pattaya.

Patong in other words has become Phuket's fun center: young, slightly raucous, and increasingly showing signs of Pattaya's air of polluted seediness. It had to happen somewhere, and if Patong can avoid Pattaya's mistakes it will probably remain for some time some people's number one choice.

Discos, bars and European-style restaurants aren't only found along the sea front. More of them line a recently-developed street in mock-European classical style running at right angles to the sea in the center of town, while to the north the castellated yet strangely anonymous **Paradise Complex** manages to be simultaneously reminiscent of Rotterdam and something out of Tolkien's *Lord of the Rings*.

Patong offers a big choice of places to stay. The **Club Andaman** ((076) 340530 FAX (076) 340527 (128 rooms; expensive; reservations in Bangkok ((02) 270-1627), with its bungalow rooms set in spacious grounds, still survives, though nowadays increasingly hedged around by high-rise development, while the **Patong Beach** ((076) 340611 FAX (076) 321541 (245 rooms; average and above; reservations in Bangkok ((02) 233-0420) is a traditional hotel right in the center of town. The **Patong Merlin** ((076) 321070 to 04 FAX (076) 321394 (297 rooms; expensive; reservations in Bangkok ((02) 253-2641), the **Holiday Inn Phuket** ((076) 340608 FAX (076) 321435 (280 rooms; expensive; reservations in Bangkok ((02) 254-2614) and the **Holiday Resort** ((076) 340119 FAX (076) 321101 (105 rooms; moderate) are just three among the many other places offering international-standard accommodation.

Meanwhile, towering in pink and pale green over the Paradise Complex's 200 shops, cafes and a gay bar, stands the glitzy **Royal Paradise Hotel** ((076) 340566 to 70 FAX (076) 321565 (250 rooms; expensive; reservations in Bangkok ((02) 260-3254 to 55) which, with its sunken poolside chin-level bar, pastel tapestries and general air of metropolitan chic, aims to be a pleasure complex in its own right.

The Sheraton Grande Laguna Beach is one of the four luxury hotels built in Bangtao. Pretty lagoons complete with watersports facilities, a series of canals, freeform swimming pools, lush tropical gardens and an 18-hole golf course have all been created out of what was once a wasteland of open-cast tin mining.

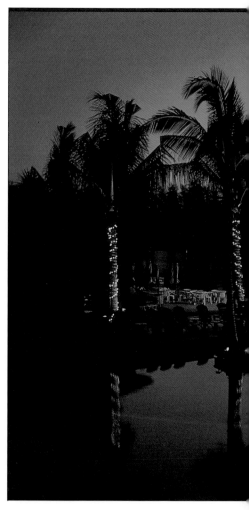

You can eat in a wide variety of cuisines in Patong, Italian, German — and even Indian, at the **Shalimar** ((01) 723-0488.

Kamala and Surin

North of Patong, **Kamala** and **Surin** beaches are best reached from Phuket Town — head north and turn left at the Heroine's Monument. Surin, with its rough waves, is magnificent to look at and has a **9-hole golf course**, but you *cannot* swim there as off-shore dredging in search of tin has created a lethal undertow.

Surin and Kamala are relatively undeveloped, but just to the north of Surin are two top-class hotels. The **Chedi Phuket** ((076) 324017 FAX (076) 324252 (110 rooms; expensive) offers traditional-style but luxu-

rious bungalows scattered over a steep slope running down to a private bay, while nearby the ultra-exclusive **Amanpuri** ((076) 311394 FAX (076) 311000 (40 "pavilion suites"; reservations in Bangkok ((02) 250-0746) would probably be more than happy to agree it is the most expensive place on the island.

Nai Yang
To reach **Nai Yang**, take the road towards the airport and you'll find the beach some four kilometers (two and a half miles) south. It is for the most part deserted What facilities there are are all at the southern tip. There's one hotel, the giant **Pearl Village** ((076) 327006 FAX (076) 327338 (163 rooms; expensive; reservations in Bangkok ((02) 260-1022).

Bangtao
Just north of Surin, in an area that was once known for its tin mining, you'll reach Bangtao.

Backed by whispering casuarina trees and beautifully sculpted lagoons, Bangtao is a fine sandy beach boasting five luxury hotels, an 18-hole golf course, a shopping center and excellent watersports facilities. The best hotels are the **Sheraton Grande Laguna Beach**, **Dusit Laguna Resort** and the **Banyan Tree Club** (with its associated golf course).

Nai Yang merges into **Mai Khao** (Airport Beach), the lonely extent of sand where between October and February the big sea turtles lumber ashore at night to lay and then bury their eggs.

Finally, if you take the road south of Nai Yang, you will eventually come to the small beach known as **Nai Thorn**. It's a really delightful ride over pastoral hills and through agricultural villages that could be a hundred miles away from Kata or Patong. Nai Thorn has fishing boats, but there's no accommodation available at the time of writing.

PHUKET TOWN

Not many people stay in the town, but it's an attractive enough place nevertheless, prosperous by Thai standards, with a touch of Portuguese influence in the architecture, some simple shops, and generally considered a nice place in which to work in or retire.

Take a taxi up **Khao Rang** hill and you'll find a pleasant restaurant and cafe that catches the breezes off the sea and has a fine view over the town and surrounding country.

Transport inside the town is by little pick-up taxis, and the fare is a standard 10 baht. Transport out of town is by open-backed buses holding 20 or so passengers, also referred to as "taxis". These depart from outside the market in Jawaraj Road or, in the case of Rawai bound buses, from beside the roundabout a short distance away.

Phuket Town has a **post office** on Montri Road, an **immigration office** (for renewing visas) on Phuket Road, near the **Boxing Stadium**, and a **TAT Office** ((076) 212213, for a wide range of information and help.

Superior accommodation in Phuket Town can be found at the **Pearl Hotel** ((076) 211044 FAX (076) 212911 (250 rooms; average and above; reservations in Bangkok ((02) 260-1022 to 27 FAX (02) 260-1027), the **Metropole** ((076) 214020 FAX (076) 215099, and at the **Phuket Merlin** ((076) 212866 to 70 (180 rooms; average and above; reservations in Bangkok ((02) 253-2641 to 42 FAX (02) 254-2663). Considerably cheaper rooms are available at the **Thavorn Hotel** ((076) 211333 to 35 (200 rooms; inexpensive to moderate).

Laundry can be very expensive in the larger hotels. A good, cheap and fast service

is provided in town by the **Bay Laundry** on Phuket Road.

AWAY FROM THE BEACHES

With a selection of four 18-hole international standard golf courses, enthusiasts are spoiled for choice. The top three are the luxurious **Blue Canyon Country Club** (located near the airport) the **Phuket Country Club**, just east of Patong Hill and the prestigious **Banyan Tree Club**, in Bangtao.

Phuket has two major aquariums for visitors who would like to come face to face with the beauties of the Andaman Sea, but who prefer not to get wet. The first is the **Marine Biological Research Center,** seven kilometers (four miles) south of Phuket

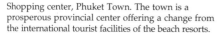

Shopping center, Phuket Town. The town is a prosperous provincial center offering a change from the international tourist facilities of the beach resorts.

Town, and the second is the **Phuket Aquarium and Butterfly Farm**, just on the northern outskirts of Phuket Town. Here the aquatic fauna and flora are matched by a wonderful, enclosed walk-through butterfly garden.

Further north on the road to the airport stands **Wat Phra Thong** with its half-buried golden Buddha. On your way there, you will pass the **Heroines' Monument** commemorating the two women who led Phuket to victory against the encroaching Burmese in 1785.

Ton Yai Waterfall is located off the main road at Thalang, down a side road running between rubber plantations. Three kilometers on there is a large clearing in the forest, with a small lake where a river reaches the plain from the hills. You can walk up half a kilometer or so into the jungle where your'll reach the falls. Despite the lack of water, it is a pleasant spot.

The **Gibbon Rehabilitation Project**, up at Bang Pae Waterfall is a project that teaches once-captive gibbons to readapt to life in the wilds, and is a worthwhile and interesting place to visit. Dare-devils can have their fill of fun bungy jumping at **Tarzan's Bungy Jump**, in Kathu, near Patong. The site was once part of Phuket's tin mining industry but has been attractively landscaped into pools and gardens. A restaurant affords prime viewing for those not taking the plunge. And, lastly, don't miss the glittering and gleaming **Wat Chalong**, in the southern part of the island. It's a gem.

DIVING

Phuket is Thailand's major diving center. It offers varied inshore exploration round the many nearby islands, notably **Koh Racha** (pronounced *raya*), **Shark Point**, and **Koh Doc Mai**, plus longer trips out to the Phi Phi Islands. Further away still, **Surin Island**, on the border of Thailand and Burma, also provides exceptionally fine diving opportunities.

But it is the celebrated **Similan Islands** that are the for the divers the finest jewels in the Andaman Sea's crown. They are 110 km (68 miles) north of Phuket and are a Marine National Park. They are uninhabited except for the Park Headquarters staff on one of the islands.

Here the diving is world-class, with clear water up to 40 m (130 ft), excellent underwater growth, and large marine creatures (such as reef sharks, rays and barracuda) due to the proximity of the edge of the continental shelf.

Phuket's diving centers for the most part congregate round Patong and Kata beaches. **Santana** has two premises, one between Kata and Karon beaches ((076) 381598, the other at Patong (/FAX (076) 340360. Also between Kata and Karon are the **Siam Diving Centre** — with another office on Phi Phi Don — and **Marina Divers** ((076) 381625 FAX (076) 213604 (attn Marina). At Patong there are the **South East Asia Yacht Charter Co.** ((076) 340406 FAX (076) 340586, and the **Holiday Diving Club** ((076) 321166. All companies offer one-day initial instruction plus trial dives for beginners.

For non-diving trips out to the Similans, contact **Songserm Travel** ((076) 222570 FAX (076) 214301.

PHUKET'S CHINESE VEGETARIAN FESTIVAL

A Personal Memory
(Dates for the Vegetarian Festival vary from year to year as it's fixed according to the lunar calendar. But it's always at the end of September or in early October — TAT will inform you in advance of the dates for any particular year).

The man with the javelin protruding equidistantly from each cheek stops, turns towards me, and waits for me to press the shutter. I do so, though by this time almost resignedly. He gives me a little bow, which causes the flesh to sag away from his eyes, and then rejoins the procession with what looks like a skip of pleasure.

It is Phuket's annual Chinese Vegetarian Festival, the nine days' autumn orgy of skewered cheeks, pierced tongues, ladders of knives and walking on fire.

As evening approaches I join a crowd making its way to one of the temples. The sky burns with a sultry tropical sunset as the sun sinks unhurriedly behind purple and crimson clouds.

During this period, many Thais join with the large local Chinese population in abstaining from meat, dressing in white, and paying daily visits to the various Chinese temples in Phuket town where the main ceremonies are staged.

In the temple forecourt boys are raking the coals in preparation to a broad rectangular bank and coaxing them into a dull glow with electric fans. Drums are being beaten, and there rises from the dense crowd an expectant hubbub.

As I walk up the steps an old man comes up to me and points his finger at my black T-shirt. "Black not so good," he says. Then "Black very bad!" Dismayed, I go down into the street and quickly buy a fancifully decorated white shirt for a few dollars. I put it on, and as I walk up the temple steps I'm greeted on all sides by the incomparable smiles of Thai approval.

The men who are going to walk on the coals are striding about indiscriminately in the inner temple, naked except for elaborately wound loincloths. They are down the steps towards the fire, shaking and juddering as they go, I know that this is "possession by spirits" as travelers and anthropologists have described it in many parts of the world.

Then they begin. As the crowd presses forward and the photographers adjust their lenses, the thirty or so men begin to cross the now grey but gently smoking coals.

The older men stride across with a resolution bred of past experience, but the teenagers run across, and then stop to dance wildly for a moment, kicking the

flexing their muscles, as if summoning up strength for the ordeal.

"Soon they will become into the monk," says my Thai friend. He keeps on saying it and I can't work out what he means.

Then the drums, gongs and bells increase in intensity to announce the beginning of the ceremony. I notice that the men are going in turn to a place at the back of the temple from which they return shaking their heads and with their eyes raised to the roof. Suddenly I realize what my friend had been trying to say. "They will become into the monk" means "The spirit will enter into them", in other words they will become "possessed". And as I watch the men crowd normally hostile element in disdain before jumping off and running round to join the queue for another crossing.

It is soon over. The drumming stops, the lights go on in the open-air theater set up in a corner of the forecourt, and the peddlers and hawkers begin to jig their toy monkeys and plastic windmills for renewed business.

Over the last decade the Similan Islands have emerged as one of Asia's favorite dive destinations, In clear, warm waters, divers can sight rays and sharks, swim through unusual underwater formations, laze on dazzling white beaches and discover the colorful world of coral fish.
OVERLEAF: A mosque dominates the simple Muslim fishing village of Koh Panyi, one of the many little islands in Phang-Nga Bay.

SOUTH FROM PHUKET

PHANG-NGA

This is a most spectacular bay 75 km (47 miles) from Phuket town. To get there you cross back onto the mainland and turn right. It's almost invariably visited as part of a conducted day trip.

What is special about Phang-Nga is what is also special about the coast south of Phuket — towering limestone formations rising dramatically straight out of the sea. At Phang-Nga there's an impressive group of them contained in a largely untouched bay.

Travel round the bay is in low-lying long-tailed boats powered by outboard motors. Each seats about 14 people, two abreast. Pineapples and eggs for delivery offshore are piled aft. The boats leave the muddy creeks that wind their way through mangrove swamps, and enter the bay itself at considerable speed, throwing up coils of spray on either side.

The spectacular islands rise sheer to several hundreds of meters, like high-rise buildings in the sea. On the tops, tufts of trees flourish incongruously. Sometimes the summits are in cloud.

Most trips pass under the craggy arch known as **Tam Lod Cave** where huge stalactites hang from the roof halfway to sealevel. A stop is usually made at **Khoa Ping Gun**, "James Bond Island" to the Thais because one of the scenes of *The Man with the Golden Gun* was filmed here. Nowadays disconsolate locals wait to sell you shell jewelry, and there's really not a great deal to see.

Far more interesting is the Muslim village of **Pan Yee**. This is the regular lunch stop. The villagers do look rather jaded at having had their lives so changed by this daily tourist invasion — even so, it's a curious and marvelous place. The entire village is built on stilts stuck into the seabed. The only settlement in this part of the wild and spectacular bay, the village is an extraordi-

nary and impressive sight. But if you want a beer with your lunch you'll have to bring your own.

Superior accommodation is available at the **Phang-Nga Bay Resort Hotel (** (076) 412067 to 70 FAX (076) 412057 (average and above; reservations in Bangkok **(** (02) 216-2882 FAX (02) 215-7910).

A Buddha Cave

Between Phuket and Phang-Nga are the caves at **Suwan Ku Ha**, and many of the day tours stop there. They're well worth seeing.

The first impression you get on entering the caves is of the squeaking of innumerable bats. From the opening at the foot of a cliff, the caves rise in a series, and a current of air ventilates them from lower to upper (the top cave is open to the sky).

Consequently it isn't until you are past the first cave, full of Buddhas and incense-sellers, that you encounter the foul smell of the guano. It's therefore as well to buy incense sticks and light them when the need arises.

Incised steps in the rock lead up to the last and narrowest cave, glistening white and lit by a shaft of sunlight.

This final, bat-less cave is a real treasure. Its shining rock formations are like swirling organ pipes, or, where they are flat and smoothed by aeons of water action, like perfectly arranged drapery. It's a natural temple, and, perhaps in recognition of this, the Thais have made no attempt to add any further, pious decoration.

KRABI PROVINCE

Phi Phi Island

Phi Phi is a very attractive island group one and a quarter hours, 45 km (28 miles) south of Phuket by the express boats. It's visually striking because it is largely made up of the kind of limestone seen most dramatically at Phang-Nga.

A Bird's Eye View

What is usually referred to as Phi Phi Island is actually Phi Phi Don. This is the island where everyone stays. Its sister island, Phi Phi Lay, is uninhabited, but incomparably more interesting.

OPPOSITE: Tourism has arrived very recently at Phi Phi Don, usually known simply as Phi Phi Island but in fact one of a pair of islands. The other, Phi Phi Lay, is uninhabited but magnificent.

Phi Phi Don village stands on a sandy strip between high limestone hills. It has two beaches, back to back: it's only a three-minute walk from the one to the other. Imagine a capital letter "H" and that's Phi Phi Don. The horizontal bar in the middle is the village, the two uprights the limestone hills, and the space between them the island's two beautiful bays.

Almost all the boats berth at the southeast side where there's a jetty and a small fishing fleet, but some of the boats bound for Krabi anchor out in the other, shallow bay

and you may have to wade out with your bags under your arms even to get to the open boats that are going to take you out to the ferry itself.

If you arrive from Phuket you will certainly land at the jetty, and this is the place to take a general look at the island. Facing out to sea, the village proper, with its shops, is behind you. On your right are some of the better restaurants and bungalow hotels backed by high cliffs, while the coast stretches away to **Long Beach** to your left.

Where to Stay

There are several places on Phi Phi Island where you can stay. The **PP Island Cabana** ℓ/FAX (075) 612132 (moderate for bungalows; expensive for hotel), for example, is on the right in the first bay and has a good restaurant. Or, if you find you prefer the peaceful northwest facing side, the **Krabi Pee Pee Resort** ℓ (075) 612188 (inexpensive) offers clean and quite comfortable rooms at half the price. The most luxurious hotel at the northern end of the island is the **PP International Resort**

ℓ (01) 214297 (120 rooms; expensive; reservations in Bangkok ℓ (02) 255- 8790 to 98).

Long Beach is where most of the best budget accommodation is, the **PP Paradise Pearl** ℓ (01) 723-0484 (inexpensive to moderate), for instance. These places, however, can be quite basic. On the other hand, the snorkeling is close inshore here, and there are new bungalows going up all the time. Boats will take you to Long Beach from the harbor for 10 baht.

A Peaceful Place

Tourism has only very recently reached Phi Phi Don, but there's already concern that there has been too much developemnt campared to Phuket of Koh Samui, however, the island nevertheless provides a restful ambiance.

But the real attraction of this pair of islands is Phi Phi Lay.

Homage to Phi Phi Lay

The uninhabited island of Phi Phi Lay stands next to Phi Phi Don and is one of the world's major sources of birds' nests of the kind used to make the celebrated Chinese delicacy, bird's nest soup. One company has the concession to harvest the immensely lucrative nests from the caves there, and no commercial development is allowed on the island that might disturb the birds and cause them to nest elsewhere. Nevertheless, the snorkeling nearby is unparalleled, and day or half-day trips can be arranged, with landing permitted on the one beach on the island's north side. The so-called "Viking" drawings on the cave walls are of unknown origin, but Viking they are certainly not.

From the sea, Phi Phi Lay presents a striking outline. Its sombre peaks rise up sheer from the water, and as you approach you feel in harmony with the poets who have written that the sea is death, vast, formless and engulfing.

Soon you see the ropes and long bamboos used to get at the precious nests. The boatman pulls the long boat with difficulty up against the cliff, next to a rough landing stage projecting from the cave's mouth. You clamber up and walk along planks into the cave. It's like entering a pirate's lair.

The cave is like a cathedral, and the high bamboo structures appear like religious totems, or items from a bizarre construction-ist theater set. These structures reach into the upper dark and are really just bundles of very long bamboos tied together with string, the string providing the footholds for the harvesters. The only light is what comes from the cave mouth.

The overall impression is that of Piranesi's *Carcieri* engravings, of a place both forbidding and awesome, and symbolic of a great and impenetrable mystery.

In corners stand petrified limestone cascades, resembling side-altars where a

And indeed it is Number One. You enter between high cliffs, as if into the jaws of death. The water is an unreal green. Limestone turrets and pinnacles topped with dwarf shrubs form the skyline. It's a site for a performance of a Wagner ring cycle opera, or for a private audience with the immortals.

Great stacks of land follow. Now the rock's color begins to come on display — orange smudges on ochre cliffs. Then, as you come into the shadow of the north side of the island, more strips of bamboo structure

myriad candles have been burned for centuries, their wax falling to make elaborate formal structures.

At first you don't see the birds. But you hear them, and smell their droppings. They nest high up, like bats, in the dark vault of the cave. The invisible seemingly secret nature of the work in the cave makes it appear eerie as well as impressive. Lone plum-colored insects crawl on the guano. From outside comes the sound of the sea endlessly washing against the cave's mouth.

Number One

After the cave, a tour round the island will take you into an enclosed bay, almost a womb. "Number one!" announces the boatman.

begin to appear high above you aimed at darkly stained, remote cave mouths, caves like bubbles in a block of ice that has been shattered open with a knife.

The sides of the island are everywhere wholly inhospitable and sheer, with the exception of the very occasional minute beach at the foot of the cliffs. But, inside another, less forbidding enclave, there is the island's one beach of any size, sandy, and with a couple of thatched huts backed up against

ABOVE: The so-called "Viking Cave" on Phi Phi Lay, a major source of birds' nests for the soup so loved and valued throughout the Chinese world. The cave is a 20-minute boat trip from Phi Phi Don, the main island. OPPOSITE: Fishing boats in the Gulf of Siam.

the cliff. This is where snorkelers make their base, and by midday it's usually crowded with day-trippers, an unwelcome violation of the island's solemnity.

Moving on, the formations of the limestone itself are staggering. Stalactites hang from every protuberance, stained black underneath as in a sooty Victorian railway station. Here and there trees, locked into rocky clefts, flourish with a strange delicacy of leaf and branch. In one place a column has crashed into the sea, and its spiny roots of rock stand exposed and ruddy in the dark shadows.

Then you pull away into the open sea, the boatman hauling on the long motor handle to keep the craft on course. And you cross over back to Phi Phi Don. But the coastline is at first very like Phi Phi Lay's and more nests became visible, almost glutinous now, like threads of solidified toffee hanging off a spoon.

Here on Phi Phi Don there is yet another enclosed amphitheater, smaller than those on Phi Phi Lay and less formidable. At the head of this bay there is another cave. This one goes in long and deep. Oil lamps generally stand in the entrance, but you need to bring your own matches.

Boat Hire

Boats can be hired on Phi Phi Don — the standard rate is 600 baht a day, 400 baht a half day, per boatload. But deals can sometimes be struck for less.

Boats leave Phi Phi Don for Krabi several times a day. You can either take the "express" boat (one and a half hours) for 125 baht, or the regular one (two hours) for 100 baht.

Bookings for this, as for other excursions, can be made with the very reliable **Friendship Tours** at the harbor.

PHI PHI TO KRABI

This trip passes further magnificent limestone stacks — forested turrets and wholly inaccessible fortresses of sheer stone. They're forms the imagination can easily populate — the lairs of beasts elsewhere long extinct, or the haunts where terrorized souls at last find their beleaguered rest. As you enter the Krabi estuary, they become if

anything even more wonderful, jutting tigerishly out over the sea, walls of rock stained only with their own natural coloration, isolated stumps like beached mines — but 200 m (660 ft) high.

And these stalactited culinary bird's nest sites — found here too — look as if some haggard witch has retreated into an elevated cave and hung out her tattered lace curtains to dry — only in reality it's all of stone.

The fast boat goes to Krabi, but the regular one puts its passengers ashore at Ao Nang, a beach half an hour's dusty bus journey from the town.

Ao Nang

This is a fine beach with spectacular marine views, a much nicer place to stay than

Krabi itself. There's accommodation on the seafront at **Ao Nang Villa** ((075) 612431 (average and above), or a little way inland at **Krabi Seaview Resort** ((075) 611648 (moderate). The **Krabi Resort** ((075) 612160 FAX (075) 612421 (80 rooms; average and above; reservations in Bangkok ((02) 208-9165) offers luxury accommodation.

And bagging the best spot on Krabi's spectacular **Laem Phra Nang** headland is the discreet but deluxe **Dusit Rayavadee** with its towering limestone formations dominating the three gorgeous sandy beaches.

A Shell Cemetery

Between Ao Nang and Krabi, at the foot of a small headland, is the unspectacular **Shell Cemetery**, so called because the scattering of broken paving-stone-like slabs of rock on the shore resembled fallen gravestones. These pieces of horizontal strata — compacted sea shells some 75 million years old — catch the imagination of the tour organizers, and the flat top of the headland is a mass of foodstalls and souvenir shops (selling, incidentally, some very beautiful shells). Though frequently visited by tours, the "cemetery" is rather difficult to get to by public transport. It's about 17 km (11 miles) from Krabi, but six kilometers (four miles) or so from the main road where the buses run. Boatmen will bring you from Ao Nang (100 baht maximum), or you can arrange to be go by motorbike from Krabi, or charter a minibus.

A remote cove on Phi Phi Don.

The whole coastline north of Krabi is a magnificent assembly of untouched sandy beaches, backed by forest and the ubiquitous partially-wooded limestone stacks. Many of these beaches are only easily accessible by boat and while this remains the case it's unlikely that commercial tourism will establish a foothold. But you can't be sure — its tentacles are ever-expanding.

KRABI TOWN

Krabi Province may be grand and untouched, but the town itself has little to recommend it.

To look at, Krabi Town is just four blocks of concrete, two-story offices and shops, with a cinema, a post office, a few travel agents and hotels. The town fronts onto the river estuary where there's a pier from which boats leave for Phi Phi Island.

There's also a night market of sorts (largely daytime shops that stay open late), and a couple of massage parlours recognizable by the exceptionally dimly-lit coffee-shops which form their lobbies and the fairy-lights that festoon their doors.

Comfortable accommodation is available at the **Vieng Thong Hotel** ((075) 611188 FAX (075) 612525 (153 rooms; moderate), and there is also the plain but satisfactory **Riverside Hotel** ((075) 612128 (51 rooms; inexpensive). There are also several very unprepossessing but inexpensive guest-houses.

The helpful **PP Family Co.** ((075) 611717, at 35 Prachachoen Road, or **Chan Phen Travel** on Utarakit Road, will book travel to Trang, Had Yai, Bangkok, Malaysia or Singapore, as well as to Phi Phi Island, and other nearby attractions.

Krabi is the capital of Krabi Province. For more information on the three southwestern provinces of Krabi, Trang and Satun, see section OFF THE BEATEN TRACK, page 209.

ABOVE: One of the great culinary delights of Thailand is its mouth-watering choice of succulent fruits. OPPOSITE: They cost a small fortune but birds' nest soup and shark's fin soup are still widely popular in Thailand's Chinese restaurants such as this one in Hat Yai.

KRABI TO HAT YAI

By bus, this journey takes four and a half to five hours and the fare is 78 baht. The buses come from Phuket and don't go into Krabi itself — you have to go five kilometers (three miles) out of Krabi Town to the main road (minibuses leave from near the Thai Hotel for the main road every 15 minutes — (5 baht). The last bus of the day along the main road for Hat Yai goes at 2 PM.

If you decide to stop overnight at Trang (see page 209), you can get a non air-conditioned bus from Trang to Hat Yai the next day from outside the Thumrin Hotel on the hour — fare 30 baht.

HAT YAI

Twenty years ago an insignificant frontier market, Hat Yai is today a remarkably vigorous and even sophisticated place. The reason for this is the prosperity of neighboring Malaysia and Singapore. Thailand is the prime holiday destination for these countries, and Hat Yai is quite simply the first town they come to. If what they are looking for is primarily sex and secondarily cheap shopping, they have no need to venture any further.

If they do find time for other pleasures, then there is the coastal resort of Songkhla, 30 km (19 miles) down the road. Songkhla by day and Hat Yai at night is a common weekend visitors' formula in these parts.

GETTING THERE

Hat Yai is 947 km (593 miles) south of Bangkok. Flying time is one and a quarter hours and there are two flights a day, with additional flights at weekends. The airport is 11 km (seven miles) from the town. When in Hat Yai, contact **Thai Airways** ((074) 245851 to 52, for details.

By rail, Hat Yai is 16 hours from the capital. Comfortable overnight trains leave in the late afternoon in each direction. The line also continues south into Malaysia, through Butterworth (for Penang), Kuala Lumpur, and ends up in Singapore. **Hat Yai Railway Station** ((074) 244362, is on Ratakarn Road.

Bus services cover just about everywhere, including south to Singapore and Malaysia. For details phone **Hat Yai Bus Station** ((074) 232789, or contact any travel agent.

WHERE TO STAY

Accommodation in Hat Yai begins with the fine **Dusit JB Hotel** ((074) 234300 to 08 FAX (074) 243499 (209 rooms; expensive; reservations in Bangkok ((02) 258-2663). Situated a two-minute drive from the town center, it's the best hotel in town with a wide range of facilities including a swimming pool and tennis court.

Among the many others are the **Grand Plaza** ((074) 234340 FAX (074) 234428 (145 rooms; moderate), comfortable and particularly good value; **The Regency** ((074) 245454 to 09 (189 rooms; moderate); the **President** ((074) 244477 (110 rooms; moderate); the **Montien** ((074) 245593 FAX (074) 230043 (180 rooms; moderate) and the rather more basic **Laem Thong Hotel** ((074) 244433 (133 rooms; inexpensive).

WHERE TO EAT

There are many places to eat in Hat Yai — try the **Sukhontha Bakery and Coffee Shop** (real coffee) on Saneh Anusorn Road, and **Krua Luang** round the corner on Pracha Thipat Road. There are excellent restaurants in major hotels such as the Dusit JB.

For cheap late-night eating, Hat Yai has four **night markets**. They're situated as follows: (1) close to the President Hotel and the nearby Bus Station (the biggest); (2) near

Wat Chu Chan on Supphasan Rangsan Road; (3) at Chee Uthit Road; (4) at the intersection of Sri Poowanat Road and Tan Ratanakorn Road.

WAT HAT YAI NAI

There are few tourist sights of the traditional kind in Hat Yai. Wat Hat Yai Nai is distinguished by its gimmicks. It's a short distance from the town center, on Petch Kasem Road, and for the most part follows the usual Thai arrangement of food stalls, monks' living quarters and a gigantic Buddha image. This last is here reclining, and is claimed to be the third largest in this position in the world. It's 35 m (115 ft) long and 15 m (49 ft) high, and at the time of writing is being given a glittering new roof.

But what you shouldn't miss is the aerial cableway that, with whirring claxon, and originally, and perhaps soon once again, flashing lights, conveys tiles paid for by devotees' donations up to the roof. The celestial chariot is drawn by two plastic horses. It only takes a small donation for the attendant to be persuaded to give it a whirl.

You can alternatively place your offering in one — or all — of the bowls of ten life-size model monks, clasping their begging bowls and rotating in a circle propelled by electric motor. They alone make a visit essential.

GOLF

Four kilometers (three miles) out of town there's the 18-hole **Kho Hong Army Camp Golf Course** ((074) 243605. Green fees are: Mondays to Fridays 150 baht; Saturdays, Sundays and public holidays 200 baht. Phone for more information. It seems you cannot hire clubs there.

ATTRACTIONS

Shopping and Nightlife
The shopping is centered on the three parallel roads, Niphat Uthit 1, Niphat Uthit 2 and Niphat Uthit 3, and there's a night bazaar on Saneh Anusorn Road. Clothes and imported electronic goods are the attractions.

There's an immense variety of nightlife in Hat Yai, from hotel lounges and coffee shops with live music, to discos and massage parlors. The Dusit JB Hotel (see page 167) has its **Palm Court** restaurant with constant music, Thai and Western, as well as its own **Metropolis Disco Club**. The Emperor Hotel has its **Disco Palace**, the Montien Hotel has its **Cetus Night Club**, and the International Hotel its popular **Inter Disco Club**. The Sukhontha Hotel's large **Zodiac Disco** offers a gay night on Thursdays.

The best-known massage parlor is probably the **Pink Lady Massage and Coffee Shop** ((076) 244095 (behind the Sukhontha Hotel) and beauty centers, Turkish baths, "ancient massage" and health centers are not difficult to find.

Bullfights
Southern Thai bullfighting, a test of strength between two bulls and not a Spanish-style ritual slaughter, can be seen at one of two arenas — near the Nora Hotel on Tamnon Vithi Road on the first Saturday of the month, and out near the Hat Yai airport on the second Saturday.

GETTING ABOUT

Transport within Hat Yai is by open-back pick-ups. In effect they're shared taxis on the Malaysian pattern. Get in one that already has other passengers in it and you'll get where you want to go, but not necessarily by the shortest route, for 5 baht; get in an

empty one and you'll be deemed to have "chartered" it — you'll get directly to your destination, and the fare will be 10 baht.

The system for taking a taxi out of town is as follows. Go to the President Hotel, a couple of minutes' walk north of the bus terminus. Opposite the hotel entrance is a car park, and a wooden cafe where the drivers wait. Tell a driver where you want to go — preferably have it written down in Thai beforehand — and you'll be shown to a car which you'll eventually share with other passengers.

Fares are very reasonable — the 60 km (37 miles), for instance, to the Waterbird Sanctuary at Thale Luang (Khu Khut) is 30 baht (see page 170). You pay before you leave. Drivers will try to extract a higher fare from foreigners, but if you show you know the approximate rate (ask at your hotel, or TAT) they'll be keen to take it from you. Transport is by saloon cars as opposed to open-backed city taxis. It's not a bad idea to take a quick look at the tires before you set off.

Ton Nga Chang

A popular excursion from Hat Yai is to **Ton Nga Chang Waterfall**, 26 km (16 miles) southwest of the town. A direct minibus

SONGKHLA

Before going to Songkhla, it's a good idea to take a look at the map. The town is situated on a spur, but rather than jutting out to sea, this serves to divide a large lake to the west from the open sea on the east. Furthermore, although the town appears to come to an end at the rocky point marked by a statue of a mermaid, this is not in fact the tip of the spur, as might be expected; instead, it extends again to end in a sandy spit some way

leaves from close to the Plaza Shopping Mall.

A river descends via seven cascades through a large upland area that is also a wildlife sanctuary. It's a short walk from the parking area to the first three falls, and it's at the third, where the river divides into two streams, fancifully compared to an elephant's tusks, that most people stop. Above here the track becomes more difficult. The time to see the falls at their best is, naturally, in the rainy season.

TOURIST INFORMATION

There's a helpful **TAT office** ((076) 243747 at 1/1 Soi 2 Niphat Uthit 3.

further to the north. For views of Songkhla's intriguing location, climb the rough path past the monkeys up **Khao Noi**, not far from the mermaid.

Yet despite its interesting situation, there's little to see in the town. The best positioned hotel is **Lake Inn Hotel** ((074) 314240 FAX (074) 321044 (moderate), which gazes over the lake. Overlooking the gulf are some undistinguished sea-food restaurants. And nearby, on Hat Samila beach, there's the bronze mermaid fixed to the rocks so it can be photographed with off-shore islands

OPPOSITE and ABOVE: Highly-decorated fishing boats such as these can be seen in many places in the Muslim south, from Songkhla's Kao Seng village down into Yala Province.

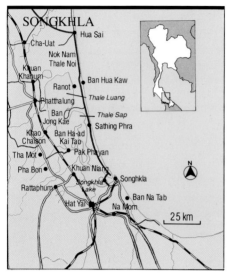

Maew and Nu ("cat" and "mouse") in the background.

SAMILA BEACH

Extending for a few kilometers and backed by pines, this is extensive and sandy, and some overworked ponies provide fuel for the professional beach photographers' ever-ready cameras. Samila itself merges into the long spit of **Son On Cape**, with its deck chairs and seafood restaurants.

KAO SENG

If you get on a *songthaew* down the long beach running south from the mermaid, you will eventually come to a small Muslim fishing village, **Kao Seng**, on the left. Here elaborately painted fishing boats are worth seeing, and though most are well-weathered there are usually one or two newly refurbished ones that will tempt anyone's camera.

THE HARBOR

The large-scale modern fishing, though, gets done at the **harbor** on the other side of town. To see the barrels of fish and the colorful scene that surrounds them, take a

Fishing nets in the south — suspended from bamboos, they're raised and lowered at will.

"taxi" (5 baht) to Wichianchom Road and walk down one of the *sois*, for instance Soi 5. Near here, too, is the ferry over to **Koh Yoh** where handwoven cotton goods are produced and can, of course, be bought. Also worth visiting on Koh Yoh is the **Folklore Museum**, which is open 8:30 AM to 4:30 PM, Mondays to Fridays, and is full of fascinating folk crafts from the region.

SONGKHLA NATIONAL MUSEUM

The Songkhla National Museum is situated on the campus of the Srinakharinvirot University, four kilometers (three miles) out of town. There are 11 rooms displaying objects from the region's rich past. One wing houses a collection of ceramics from archaeological sites from all over Thailand. The building itself is interesting as an example of 19th-century southern Thai–Chinese architecture. Opening hours are 9 AM to noon, and 1 PM to 4 PM, Wednesdays to Sundays (closed Mondays and Tuesdays).

THALE LUANG WATERBIRD SANCTUARY

The water Songkhla's main harbor fronts onto is the seaward end of **Thale Luang**, Thailand's biggest lake. It extends womb-like up into the land, and is the breeding ground for a huge bird population. A vast area — 364 sq km (142 sq miles) — has been declared a waterbirds' sanctuary, Asia's largest. It contains 219 recorded bird species, including purple herons, purple gellinules, teals, grebes, egrets, cormorants and black-winged stilts. The headquarters is a 60 km (37 miles) drive from Hat Yai, but the sanctuary is well worth the effort of getting there.

The sky reflects in the shallow water, birds bat across towards the reedbeds, white egrets rise, dragonflies hover and moorhens hurry away in the languorous heat. In the distance are the high cow-horn gables of temples. From headquarters you purr off in a long-tailed boat across the brilliant reflective surface of the lake.

The water is only inches deep. Isolated trees stand like sculptures above the surface. Colors are pale green, pale blue and the yellow of the reeds. With colors so delicate

and reminiscent of northern pellucidities, it's very un-Thai.

The heat is intense. Pairs of ducks skid-land, and boys in straw hats pole punts, shadowy behind reeds. The guides meander their way along the channels, and occasionally accelerate and surge across a reedy barrier with a cheer. Dawn and sunset, of course, are the times to see any birds; even so, there's plenty to see in the middle of the day as well.

Back at headquarters, the boys pole the punt silently under the stilted house. Inland, a cock crows, a radio launches into a sweet Thai pop tune, you walk on wooden slats to a simple restaurant, and the impression everywhere is of a perfect tranquility and contentment.

More birds can be seen at the head of Songkhla Great Lake, at **Thale Noi Nok Nam** near Phatthalung (on the railway, north from Hat Yai).

YALA PROVINCE

Hat Yai is close to the Malaysian frontier on the western coast, but here in the east Thailand extends south another 200 km (134 miles) into **Yala Province**, famous for the **town mosque** at **Pattani**, the painted fishing boats of **Panare Beach**, and, last of all, the border town of **Sungei Golok**, sensuously welcoming whether you're coming from the north, or, like most of its patrons, from the south.

Muslim schoolgirls in the far southeast.

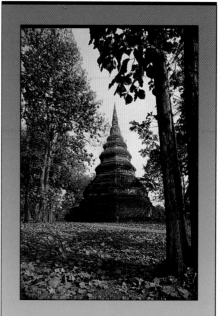

Chiang Mai and the North

HILL TERRITORY

The north of Thailand has an immense amount to recommend it.

To begin with, the climate is less humid than anywhere else in the country, and, after prolonged exposure to the clammy south, to step out of the night train from Bangkok into the cool morning air of Chiang Mai is a joy with few equals.

Chiang Mai, too, is a very attractive place. Though it's Thailand's second city, it's far smaller than Bangkok, and with few of the capital's horrors, environmental and otherwise. The atmosphere is relaxed, prices are reasonable, and the people particularly friendly and informal.

The north, too, contains some wonderful countryside. It's hill territory, and thinly populated except in the major valleys. The Thais themselves have for the most part kept to the fertile lowlands, and the hills are inhabited by the famous non-Thai hill tribes.

The area is not without its problems. Opium poppies are still being grown here and this, together with the fact that the Burmese government does not exercise full control over its territory adjacent to the frontier implies that the area as a whole is not quite as settled in its ways as the central Thai provinces.

Nevertheless, tourism flourishes, and though there have been incidents of attacks on river boats carrying foreigners, the Thai government, with the high priority it puts on maintaining international tourism to the country, is determined to do all it can to prevent recurrences. It's a wonderful part of the country, and not to be missed, but it's wise to take care, and try not to be too conspicuous, particularly conspicuously affluent, in the remoter places.

PHITSANULOK

Not many people visit **Phitsanulok**, 390 km (244 miles) north of Bangkok. But it's half way between Bangkok and Chiang Mai, it's on the railway, and so makes a reasonable

stopping-off point if you feel you don't want to rush the journey north. It's an important provincial capital, and has an airport with a daily flight from Bangkok. But the real attraction is neighboring Sukhothai, 58 km (36 miles) away.

Thais know Phitsanulok for the Buddha image in **Wat Phra Si Rattana Mahathat**. Cast in 1357 in the reign of King Mahatammaracha of Sukhothai, it's considered the most beautiful Buddha image in Thailand and copies of it can be seen just about everywhere.

Otherwise, the town has nothing remarkable besides the custom of cooks flinging food from the cooking pan up into the air, to be caught by a waiter standing with a plate some distance away. This bizarre habit can be observed at some of the restaurants at the riverside night bazaar.

All rooms at the **Amarin Nakhon Hotel** ((055) 258588 (124 rooms; moderate) are air-conditioned.

There is a **TAT office** (055) 252743 FAX (055) 252742 in Phitsanulok at 209/7-8 Surasi Trade Center, Boromtrailokan Road, Amphoe Muang, Phitsanulok 65000.

The life of the countryside penetrates everywhere in the north. OPPOSITE: newly-planted rice fields reflect the sky; ABOVE: home from work.

SUKHOTHAI

Sukhothai was Thailand's first capital. The Thais are thought to have come south from China (see OLD SIAM page 58) and so it isn't surprising their capital was first in the north, and only later moved south to Ayutthaya, and finally Bangkok.

Modern Sukhothai is a pleasant country town — the extensive remains of the old capital, now declared a historical park, are situated 12 km (eight miles) to the north. Neither is on the railway and the usual way to get there is by bus from Phitsanulok. If you want to stay overnight in the area, the **Northern Palace (Wang Neua)** ((055) 611193 FAX (055) 612038 (moderate) in the modern town has air-conditioned rooms.

Old Sukhothai is like Ayutthaya — ruined and semi-ruined monuments standing forlornly, but still with traces of magnificence, in dry grassland crisscrossed nowadays only with footpaths. There is a central headquarters, housing administrative offices both of the Thai government Fine Arts Department and of UNESCO who are helping in the work of reconstruction and preservation. Sukhothai is considered a site of world significance.

The remains extend over a wide area, but there are fine things to see close to the headquarters building if you decide to allocate only a small amount of your time to the site.

THE SUKHOTHAI ERA

The period during which Sukhothai was the Thai capital was 1238 to 1365. Originally the Thais formed small principalities in what is now northern Thailand, but in the early 13th century two of these combined to fight the powerful Khmer Empire to their south. They won, and established a combined capital in the former Khmer frontier post of Sukhothai. The event is now taken as marking the establishment of the first Thai kingdom, and essentially the foundation of the state of Thailand.

Austere and august — the extensive and large-scale ruins of Wat Mahathat in ancient Sukhothai.

The third Sukhothai ruler, King Ramkamheng, extended the power of the new kingdom even beyond the country's modern borders in this northern region. He established trade relations with China and visited the country twice, the first time to negotiate with the great Kubla Kahn. Chinese artists came back to Sukhothai with him and established the **Sawankalok School** of Thai pottery.

King Ramkamheng also oversaw the creation of the modern Thai alphabet from various old Khmer scripts. A famous inscription of the period carved in stone reads: "This City of Sukhothai is good. There are fish in the water, there is rice in the fields. The king does not tax people who ride the road to market, leading their oxen and their horses. Whoever wants to trade in elephants does so, whoever wants to trade in silver and gold does so." The fact that it was discovered inside the Royal Palace, though, might indicate it was a piece of self-promotion by the illustrious monarch himself.

Sukhothai's time of glory passed when, after 127 years, it became subject to the new

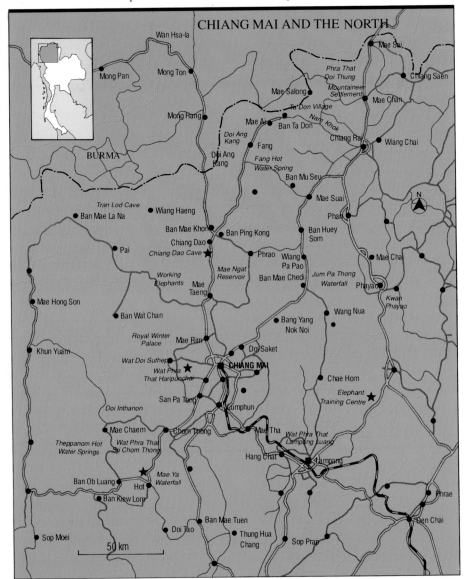

and more powerful kingdom of Ayutthaya in the south.

THE RUINS

The remains at Sukhothai are spread over a wide area. Many of the main ones are concentrated within the square central "walled city", with others scattered at some distance in all four directions.

Inside the walled area, the **Royal Palace and Wat Mahathat** is surrounded by a moat. There isn't much left of the palace, but

original state. This is true, and the reasons are that the city was sacked when it fell in 1365, that the tropical climate is not ideal for the preservation of anything, and that what valuable items remained have for the most part been removed and put in museums.

LAMPANG

Mention Lampang to the average Thai and he'll think of horse-drawn carriages. Mention it to most tourists and, if they think of

the huge *wat* contains many semi-ruined *chedis* in the lotus-bud shape characteristic of the Sukhothai style. Other temple remains in this central compound are **Wat Traphang-Thong**, **Wat Sa-Si**, and **Wat Traphang-Ngoen**.

One place that can help you orient yourself is the **Ramkamheng National Museum**. It's in the central area and is open 9 AM to noon and 1 to 4 PM; closed Mondays, Tuesdays and official holidays.

Other sites are difficult to get to—it's best to get advice from the headquarters before attempting a trip out to them. You can rent bicycles near the park entrance.

It may seem that ancient Sukhothai has little to offer in anything approaching its

anything at all, they'll probably think of baby elephants.

Horses still provide a regular means of transport round the small town, but you'll need something more powerful to get you to the **Young Elephant Training Center**. It's situated 25 km (14 miles) to the northwest, off the road to Chiang Mai.

The small elephants, only as big as a medium-sized dog at birth, are taught like children. Their "school" has summer holidays (from March to May), is closed on religious festivals, subjects its pupils to

Dreaming of ages long past — a Buddha silhouetted against the evening sky at Sukhothai's Wat Mahathat.

primary education between the years of three and five, and secondary between six and ten.

They then begin their working lives at 11, doing apprentice work until they are 16, by which time they are considered adult members of the community. Their official retirement age is 61.

Demonstrations — of assembly, communal bathing, log-rolling and carrying, and piling logs — are given every morning (though not on festival days, or during the two month summer vacation). Hotels and

congenial though the city center is increasingly congested with traffic. Still, there has been little high-rise development; temples and wooden houses stand alongside modern hotels in the central area, and an escape into the nearby hills is a short *songthaew* ride away.

A BIRD'S EYE VIEW

The city is sited on the broad plain of the Mae Ping River. Some 30 km (18 miles) wide, this plain is the major level area in what is

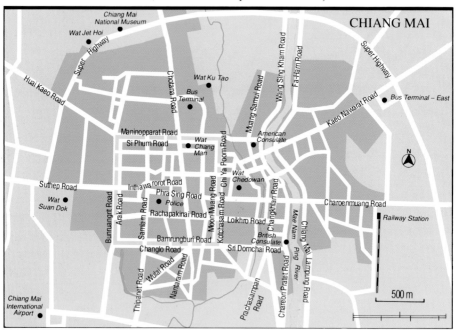

tour agents in Lampang will make all the arrangements necessary to get you up there.

There are several unassuming hotels in Lampang. The **Tip Chang Garnet Lampang** ((054) 224273 FAX (054) 225362 (125 rooms; moderate to average and above) provides air-conditioned accommodation.

Lampang is on the main Bangkok–Chiang Mai railway, and can also be reached by bus from Chiang Mai.

CHIANG MAI

Thailand's second city, 761 km (472 miles) by train north of Bangkok, is much smaller than the capital and very much more

otherwise rough hill country. Prominent in all views from the city is the dramatically-located temple of Doi Suthep, perched high in the hills overlooking the town. Chiang Mai has a domestic and international airport, and its station is the northern terminus of the rail system.

The original walled and moated city was completed in 1296 as the capital of the then independent Lannathai kingdom. The Burmese seized it in due course, along with most of what is now northern Thailand, but it has been Thai territory continuously since 1774.

Over the centuries the city has shifted eastwards, and what is remarkable is how comparatively uninteresting the area enclosed by the old walls now is. The heart of modern Chiang Mai is the area that lies between the east wall and the river. This is not just a recent development — several old temples are to be found here.

The walls of the old city have recently been rebuilt. Antiquarians may grumble, but throughout Thai history things that have been valued have been maintained, and few will complain when the result is as magnificent as it is in the vicinity of Tha Phae Gate (at the top end of Tha Phae Road).

Chiang Mai is celebrated for the friendliness and beauty of its people, for its rich cultural heritage, and as the center from which to organize treks out to the rivers and hills that surround it.

WHERE TO STAY

The premier Chiang Mai hotel, traditionally used by the government for putting up heads of state, is the **Chiang Mai Orchid** ((053) 222099 FAX (053) 221625 (265 rooms; expensive). Newer and flashier is the **Westin Chiang Mai** ((053) 275300 FAX (053) 275299 (526 rooms; expensive). The **Rincome** ((053) 221044 FAX (053) 221915 (158 rooms; average and above to expensive) is even nicer, tranquil and exquisitely decorated. The **Dusit Inn** ((053) 281033 FAX (053) 281044 (200 rooms; average and above) and the **Chiang Inn** ((053) 270070 FAX (053) 274299 (170 rooms; average and above) are also in the luxury class, as is the **Chiang Mai Plaza** ((053) 270040 FAX (053) 272230 (444 rooms; average and above to expensive). Note that prices are everywhere noticeably lower here than in Bangkok.

The **Pornping** ((053) 270100 to 07 FAX (053) 270119 (328 rooms; moderate to average and above) is also very comfortable. The **River View Lodge** ((053) 271110 FAX (053) 279019 (36 rooms; moderate) is a family hotel with a beautiful setting on the banks of the Mae Ping, while a good bet for the visitor wanting something simple but central, clean and air-conditioned, would be the **Montri** ((053) 211070 FAX (053) 217416 (80 rooms; inexpensive to moderate).

In the budget-price category there is a wide choice. The area to look is essentially around Tha Phae Gate. The **New Chiang Mai Hotel** ((053) 236561 (43 rooms; inexpensive) on Chiyapoom Road is a basic Thai-style place with few foreigners in evidence. **Happy House** ((053) 252619, also changes money at all hours. Other guesthouses in this area are the **Top North** ((053) 213900, the **Sumit** (/FAX (053) 214014 and the **Kent Guest House** (053) 217578.

There are more budget-category hotels attractively sited on the river bank. Cross the river from the downtown area by the Nakornping Bridge and take the first road on your left. Among these are the **Je T'Aime**

((053) 241912, the **Hollanda-Montri** ((053) 242450 and the **Gold River Side** ((053) 244550.

Visitors should not expect too much from these very inexpensive places where the overnight charge can be as low as US$4.

WHERE TO EAT

The **Chalet** ((053) 236310, on Chareon Pratet Road offers quality French cuisine in a Northern-style teak house.

The **Whole Earth** ((053) 232463, a Thai food and vegetarian restaurant, is on

Wat Phra Singh, Chiang Mai. Begun in the 14th century, the temple is famous for the ancient Buddha image kept there.

Sridonchai Road. It's in the middle-bracket as far as prices go and serves ten types of real coffee.

Just out of town, the **Baan Suan (** (053) 242116, has tables on lawns under the trees and tends to cater to the more upmarket coach parties. Birds sing, sprinklers hiss and corks pop. Look for the knife and fork sign on the right, 500 m after the first silk factory on the road out to Borsang.

Traditional *khantok* dinners (eaten with the hands to the accompaniment of local dances) can be had at, among other places, the **Khumkaeo Palace (** (053) 214315. Also out of town is the **Chiangmai Lakeside Ville (** (01) 510-0258, where you can eat, and stay, in a Thai ambiance beside a small artificial lake. Japanese food is on offer at the **Musashi Restaurant (** (053) 210944, and Arabic at **The Cafeteria (** (053) 235276, near the Night Bazaar. There's live music — folk and blues — at the **Riverside (** (053) 243239, opposite the Chinda Hospital, and a congenial atmosphere at **Bier Stube (** (053) 210869, on Moon Muang Road, with reasonably priced cocktails, beer and substantial German and Thai food. **Daret's House (** (053) 235440, is an excellent, cheap and deservedly popular outdoor eating place close to the Tha Phae Gate. (They also run a guesthouse and motorbike rental service). Nowadays, however, they are experiencing severe competition from the Montien Hotel's smarter, air-conditioned **JJ Bakery** opposite.

A City Tour

The town itself can easily be explored on your own. It's quite small enough, and flat enough, to hire a bicycle and just pedal round. If this seems too much like hard work, there are motorbike hire establishments on every street corner, though the traffic can be just a touch too heavy for absolute beginners.

A day's sightseeing should take in at least some of the following. First **Wat Phra Singh**, with its fine grounds. Then **Wat Je Dee Luang**, with its large 15th-century *chedi* (Je Dee = chedi), and **Wat Chiang Man** with its tiny Crystal Buddha, all in the walled district.

Then there's the seven-spired **Wat Jet Yot**, built to an Indian model to the northwest, close to the Superhighway. Nearby is the **Chiang Mai National Museum**, open daily from 9 AM to noon, 1 to 4 PM, except Mondays and Tuesdays.

Finally, **Wat Suan Dok** off Suthep Road to the west has some striking wall-paintings, and the **Night Bazaar**, close to the Chiang Inn and Suriwongse hotels, serves to round off the day. Near the bazaar, the mural across the front of the Sang Tawan Cinema on Sri Dornchai Road (by the Whole Earth restaurant) is worth a few minutes' admiring gaze.

SHOPPING

Northern Thailand is famous for its crafts, and almost all the craft shopping in Chiang Mai — for silk, silver, lacquerware, woodcarvings and hill tribe crafts — is out on the Borsang road. The village of Borsang itself is where painted umbrellas are made and sold. See SHOPPING FOR CRAFTS, page 188 and BORSANG — UMBRELLA VILLAGE, page 189 for details.

The two biggest bookshops in Chiang Mai are the **Suriwong Book Center** on Sri Dornchai Road and **D.K.Books** on Tha Phae Road.

The **Library Service (** 053) 210518, on Ratchamankha Soi 2, off Moon Muang Road, has a selection of second-hand English, German and other books for sale. They can be sold back later at half-price.

NIGHTLIFE

Chiang Mai is rather well known among Thais for its night life as it's a popular destination for long weekends out of Bangkok.

Discos in the big hotels include **Crystal Cave** in the Empress, **Club 77** in the Chiang Mai Orchid, **Bubbles** in the Pornping, and the **Plaza Disco** in the Chiang Mai Plaza.

Honey Massage, situated on the Superhighway, near the Rincome Hotel, and **Vanda Massage and Coffee Shop** on the

Chiang Mai's Wat Jet Yot. The temple is celebrated for its "Indian style", but all southeast Asian culture is deeply influenced by India, both its religions and its resulting artistic forms.

seventh floor of the Muang Mai Hotel offer Thai massage of the world-famous variety.

GOLF

Enthusiasts can enjoy the fresh northern air on the 18-hole **Lanna Golf Course**, north of town on the Chotana Road, or on a nine-hole course at the **Gymkhana Club**.

EXPLORING BY MOTORBIKE

Motorbikes can be rented from many places, including **Pop's** ((053) 276014, at 53 Kotcha-sarn Road, and **Daret's** ((053) 235440. The best place for motorbike information is the **Chiang Mai Motorcycle Touring Club** ((053) 210518.

TREKKING

For trekking, there are many organizations competing for your custom. We can recommend two, though this in no way implies that others are not as good or even better. The two following companies, though, are long-established and both insure their customers against mishaps. They are **Singha Travel Ltd** ((053) 233198 (in Bangkok ((02) 258-0160 to 65) and **Summit Tours and Trekking** ((053) 233351. Both are on the Tha Phae Road.

More locally, **Ox Cart Tours** ((053) 222019 will rumble you for the day beside paddy fields for 200 baht a person.

FESTIVALS

Chiang Mai has one special festival of its own, the **Flower Festival** which features floral floats and parades and lasts for three days from the first Friday in February.

In addition, Yee Peng and Songkran are observed, as elsewhere in the country. (See FESTIVE FLINGS page 43 for details).

TOURIST INFORMATION

The Chiang Mai **TAT office** ((053) 248604 to 05, faces the river on the Chiang Mai — Lamphun Road (turn right immediately after crossing the Nawarat Bridge when coming from the Tha Phae Gate).

Mail

The Post Office is just by the railway station — look out for sign "Chiangmai Satellite Earth Station Office". It's open 8:30 AM to 4:30 PM weekdays (closed 12 noon to 1 PM for lunch) and 9 AM to 12 noon Saturdays and Sundays. Overseas phone, fax and telex services are open 24 hours.

GETTING THERE

Thai Airways fly to Chiang Mai seven times a day from Bangkok. Economy class costs 1,650 baht at the time of writing. Call ((053) 211541 for return reservations, or flights onwards to Chiang Rai or Mae Hong Son.

Chiang Mai is the terminus of the country's northern railway line. Two daytime and four overnight trains make the 14-hour trip from Bangkok. They're comfortable, and there's a good restaurant car.

It's a long way to go by coach, but there are overnight coaches, from Bangkok's Northern Bus Station.

AROUND CHIANG MAI

Many of the most popular attractions are a few kilometers out of Chiang Mai.

On the road out to Doi Suthep the **zoo** and the nearby **arboretum** are small-scale but attractive. And, at the foot of the hill, the **Khru Ba Siwichai Statue**, erected in 1935 and commemorating the monk who initiated the scheme to build the road up to Doi Suthep in 1934, is rarely without its devotees. The 11-km (seven-mile) road was built by voluntary labor without any mechanical assistance. It was completed in an astonishing five months and 22 days, each village that contributed labor being responsible for no more than five meters (18 ft).

DOI SUTHEP

But it's **Wat Doi Suthep** itself that is the real attraction.

The temple (its official name is Wat Phra That Doi Suthep) was built in the 14th century to house a relic of the Buddha discovered near Sukhothai. The relic was brought to Chiang Mai and what is now known as

Wat Suan Dok was built to house it. But one day it mysteriously divided in two, and so a new home had to be found for the new half. So a sacred white elephant was released. Followed by a band of eager monks, it made its way up onto the mountain, turned round three times and lay down. This was clearly the correct site for the new temple.

The startling position of the temple testifies to the perspicacity of elephants. Accompanied by numerous Thais, you climb over 300 steps, past musicians and blind beggars, from the car-park to the sacred

A ROYAL PALACE

Ten kilometers (six miles) further up the road, the grounds of the **Royal Winter Palace** are open Fridays, weekends and public holidays except when members of the royal family are in residence (traditionally in January).

The gardens exude an almost English air. The benign and dignified Chiang Mai citizens move through the misty, rose-scented coolness, with pines above and cloudlets below, in a double trance, posing for photos

precinct. Below you lies all of Chiang Mai, its airport almost at your feet. Wispy clouds threaten to interrupt the view, while behind you children run the length of ranks of holy bells, pushing each as they pass till it emits its sonorous tone into the still air. "Don't shake the bells" requests a sign.

The Buddha relic is contained in the golden *chedi* at the rear. The central part of the small space is occupied by the main temple building — you're not allowed into this wearing shorts.

Down in the car-park area again, hollyhocks bloom in the dry season and strawberries are on sale, both reminders of the temperate climates emulated by this part of the country.

holding on to particularly gorgeous blooms, excelling even themselves in docility and dignified languor.

Four kilometers (three miles) further on again lies a **Meo village**, unfortunately much visited by tourists. But a few meters from the souvenir stalls there is a striking viewing point with vistas towards Burma out over hills covered with teak forests.

ELEPHANT CAMPS

North of the city lie the elephant kraals. You can watch the magnificent creatures

Chiang Mai — LEFT: Wat Phra Singh; RIGHT: Doi Suthep.

washing in a small river, rolling and piling logs and taking visitors for short rides any morning at 9 AM at the **Mae Sa Elephant Camp**, 10 km (six miles) from town on Route 1096. Commercial and contrived it may sound, but the elephants at least are doing it for real. And with their huge, butterfly-wing ears and massive toenails, their penetrating eyes and cumbrous grace as they indulgently wallow in the stream or ingest whole hands of bananas, plastic string included, they are true objects of wonder.

drive from Chiang Mai, and on the way there you can visit the partially reconstructed remains of the ancient city of **Wieng Goomgarn**.

SHOPPING FOR CRAFTS

For some reason, all the **craft centers** are out along the road to Borsang, running straight out of Chiang Mai to the east.

The pattern is usually the same. What you see is a small workshop where you can inspect the processes by which the

The same sort of thing can be seen on a rather larger scale at the **Chiang Dao Young Elephant Training Center**, 65 km (40 miles) north on Route 107. Here you can in addition take a look at the large **Chiang Dao Cave**, a few kilometers further on, in the same excursion. And on either trip, the **Sai Nam Phung Orchid Nursery** can also be included.

LAMPHUN

Tumphun is reputed to be the oldest in Thailand, and its **Wat Jamathevi** and **Wat Prathard Haripoonchai**, both little visited by Western tourists, each claim a thousand years of history. Lamphun is a half-hour's

product is created, and next to it is a far larger show-room where a wide variety of produce is on sale. So long as you don't believe all the material in the showrooms was made in the workshops you are shown, you should find it an interesting experience.

There are several establishments dealing in the various crafts, silverware, silk, woodcarving and lacquerware. Near to the Superhighway, on your left leaving Chiang Mai, is **Lanna Thai** ((053) 331426, where the various stages of working silver are on show. You see the metal heated, hammered into shape, and then decorated with innumerable blows using sharp-pointed nails.

A little further, on your right, is the **Shinawatra Thai Silk Factory** ((053) 331959. Here girls work handlooms with hand-operated flying shuttles as in the early days of the textile industry in Europe. Boys dye the silk by hand, and there are a few specimen silkworms and an explanation of their lifecycle. What you learn here is that the worms are boiled to death when in the chrysalis stage to release the silk hair with which they sought to protect themselves — a feature of the process that might put off some prospective customers.

of paper or cloth, are famous round the world.

One of the smaller workshops is **Suwan House** where carved teak furniture is also made. The heavy tables, with scenes of rustic life deeply cut into the tabletops, and every available inch decorated in some way, are very beautiful. Each table, together with its eight chairs, takes two men six months to make. The prices are reasonable, but the cost of shipping these bulky items to Europe or America more than doubles the sum would-be exporters have to reckon on.

Further on, down a lane to your left, is **Lanna Lacquerware** ((053) 331606, a small family business where the wooden ducks, bowls and plates could easily have all been made on the premises.

Woodcarving, as well as various kinds of weaving, can be seen at the **Hilltribe Handicrafts Center** ((053) 331977.

BORSANG — UMBRELLA VILLAGE

All of this commercial activity comes to a head in the village of **Borsang** itself where the main street consists entirely of shops aimed at the tourist. The speciality here, though, is umbrella-making, and Borsang's handpainted umbrellas, whether made

When in Borsang, no one should miss **Wat Bauk Pet**, a kilometer further along the sideroad that constitutes the village's main street. A new temple has been constructed next to the older building, with a striking mural of massed monks on the wall facing the road. Inside, the ceiling is on object lesson in the deceptive arts of *trompe l'oeil*, while celestial elephants, pink and emerald lotuses, reclining matrons and green-bodied gods crowd the walls.

This kind of Indian-inspired Thai art perfectly exemplifies the national belief in

Northern crafts — LEFT: Silk umbrellas from the "umbrella village" of Borsang; ABOVE: hill tribe products — dolls made by the Meo tribe on sale in Chiang Mai.

the virtue of brilliance and intensity, and the general Asian preference for the gorgeous and the new as opposed to the faded and old, however venerable.

MAE HONG SON

The best way to get to the remote hill town of Mae Hong Son is by the half-hour flight from Chiang Mai. The alternative is an eight-hour coach journey by Highway 108 via Mae Sariang or via Pai in the north.

A BIRD'S EYE VIEW

The flight from Chiang Mai shows how un-inhabited vast tracts of upland northern Thailand are. Wooded hills succeed each other as far as the eye can see, with a very occasional tiny patch of cultivation visible in the river valleys.

Mae Hong Son is a delightful place. As soon as you get out of the little plane, you are aware of the quiet, the dry air and the pastoral relaxation.

OPPOSITE: Novice monks clean their begging bowls at the Wat Phra That Doi Kong Mu, whose golden towers ABOVE, crown the Doi Kong Mu hilltop west of Mae Hong Son.

The town occupies a rare flat area in the valley of the River Pai. It's small and for the most part built of wooden houses. The population is only six thousand or so, plus the few dozen hill tribe people who come down in the cold early mornings to the market. Hondas and the occasional pick-up truck try to give the place a touch of bustle, but they don't succeed. Boys play football on the airport runway after the last flight of the day has left, and a couple of miles out of town you're in a world of buffalo carts trundling along empty roads that wind through undramatic but most attractive hill scenery.

Tourism has in fact only recently arrived here. As recently as the early Eighties the high level of Communist guerilla activity led to an official policy of discouraging foreigners from visiting the district. Now the only danger is from the occasional bandit — something visitors should be aware of, but not allow to spoil their stay in this very special landscape.

WHERE TO STAY

The **Maetee Hotel** ((053) 611141 (39 rooms; inexpensive) is a typical provincial small-town hotel, simple but clean, conveniently situated right in the center of town, and with the advantage of being patronized mostly by Thais. The **Siam Hotel** ((053) 612148 (14 rooms; inexpensive) is similar. A third hotel but more upmarket is the **Baiyoke Chalet Hotel** ((053) 611486 (moderate), near the post office. For the top end in town, there's the **Holiday Inn Mae Hong Son** ((053) 611390 FAX (053) 611524 (114 rooms; average and above). There are in addition a number of extremely cheap guest-houses off the main street and down by the lake.

For more upmarket accommodation you have to go a few kilometers out of town. The **Rim Nam Klang Doi Resort** ((053) 612142 FAX (053) 612086 (16 rooms; moderate) is a very attractive place. There's a restaurant and bungalows dotted about on the banks of the Pai. Campers are welcome (tents are provided), and there's also inexpensive accommodation available in a dormitory.

The **Mae Hong Son Resort** ((053) 611504 (27 rooms; moderate) is similar in arrange-

ment, but the rooms are rather more luxurious, and the place makes further gestures towards being the top people's choice by providing a cocktail lounge and a souvenir shop. Even so, it too offers cheap dormitory accommodation. Again, it's right on the bank of the river.

AROUND TOWN

After Dark

There isn't a lot to do after sunset, and people generally go to bed early. The **Bai-Fern**

Restaurant ((053) 611374 has an excellent menu and pleasant surroundings while the **Bua Tong Restaurant (** (053) 611187, is the best in a town; and it's impossible to spend more than US$4 on a meal. It serves good local food in an attractive atmosphere. Mae Hong Son's nightlife, such as it is, is centered at the Holiday Inn and its disco.

Two Temples

The town itself has two main attractions — a small and picturesque lake, overlooked by a temple with a corrugated-iron roof, and a second and more substantial temple spectacularly situated on top of a hill.

Turn left at the post office to get to the lakeside **Wat Chong Klang**. It's brilliantly

colored, like all Thai temples, and houses paintings on glass brought from Burma in the last century.

To reach the hill-top **Wat Phra That Doi Kong Mu**, from the crossroads outside the Maetee Hotel take the road opposite the hotel entrance, past the red post box. This will lead you to a colorful roadside monastery, **Wat Phra Non**. The road goes up just to the left of the monastery and is a 20 minute walk. An alternative for the sturdy is to walk up through the monastery, pass between two stone lions, and scramble up the steep track directly to the summit temple complex. There were once steps here but they have been for the most part buried in mud (baked earth in the dry season). This route will get you to the top, hot and very thirsty, in little more than 10 minutes.

The view over Mae Hong Son and the surrounding hills is wonderful. The smallness of the town and the vast silence of the countryside is very beautiful.

TREKKING

There are a number of advertisements for treks and one-day outings displayed outside establishments along the length of the main street, but they're almost all for the same tours. Bamboo rafts (or boats) will transport you down-river, just as they will in the more frequented country around Chiang Mai. The difference is that there are fewer tourists in this region, and that Mae Hong Son itself is such a delightfully restful place in which to be based.

Of the agents themselves, **Don Enterprises (** (053) 612236 FAX (053) 611682 appears reliable, as do the owners of the Bua Tong Restaurant (see above) who operate two- and three-day tours under the name **Central Tour**.

The trips themselves are the usual mix — expeditions by truck, boat and on foot taking in a number of hill tribe villages. Most include a short section riding on an elephant — this, though, is expensive and can double the price of a one-day trip. Only the visit to the "long-necked women" (Karens) south of the town is unlikely to be enjoyable — there are only a few of them, and they are virtual, if not actual, prisoners,

192

held specifically to be "exhibited " — for a price — to tourists.

OUT OF TOWN

The country around Mae Hong Son consists of wooded, steep-sided hills between which vigorous rivers run. It is wholly unspoilt, either by tourism or industry. Houses are almost invariably built of wood, and many are roofed with large leaves.

One of the nicest things to do is to hire a motorbike and head off into the coun-

The Fish Cave

Called in Thai "Tham Pla", this small recreation area is clearly marked on the left of the road. It isn't, on the surface, much to write home about, yet it has a touch of true innocence, and a lot of genuine charm.

Its name derives from a place where a stream emerges from under a cliff and large blue carp can be seen down through a hole in the rock, circling in wait for visitors' tidbits.

In itself it's unspectacular, but the adjacent area has been turned into an attractive

tryside. Anyone renting you out a bike will give you a sketch-map of the district and suggest routes that take in points of interest and keep to the more reasonable roads. A sturdy little Honda Dream will take you to many of the places you will want to visit.

There's only the one modern road, and it follows the valley without staying close to the river. Both north and south of the town are fascinating.

To the north, the road winds easily beneath cliffs until, after seven kilometers (four miles), it crosses the Pai by a solid modern bridge. It then rises to give some fine views, descending again after another 11 km (seven miles) to the valley floor of a tributary of the main river.

waterside garden with lilies, a large waterwheel, and tables and chairs set out under the trees. It's the work of a National Park — not surprisingly, as they're responsible for the excellent management of beauty spots all over the country. Food and drink are available near the entrance.

A Forest Park

A few yards back up the road before the Fish Cave, an unpaved road leads off left —

ABOVE: Highly-wrought gilded metalwork in Chiang Mai temples. Although increasingly popular with trekkers and tour groups, the mountain town of Mae Hong Son OPPOSITE, on the edge of the border with Myanmar (Burma), still feels wonderfully remote.

coming from Mae Hong Son — towards a waterfall (seven kilometers or four miles) in a Forest Park. The road is good for the first three kilometers (two miles), as far as a village, but then deteriorates as it begins to climb. Motorcyclists have found the way difficult — organized trips from Mae Hong Son in four-wheel drive vehicles go there most days.

Southwards
The countryside is less striking to begin with south of the town, though there's an attractive road that runs past the Rim Nam Klang Doi and Mae Hong Son resorts, between the main road and the river.

After 12 km (seven miles) you come to the **Hot Springs** at **Pha Bong**. These are not worth visiting. It looks as if an attempt has been made to landscape the area around where the very hot and foul-smelling sulphurous water emerges, but clearly enthusiasm quickly waned.

After Pha Bong you can either follow the road where it climbs a long and rather steep hill, or you can turn off to the left down a track, almost immediately after the village, and visit the **dam** across the Mae Ra Mat River.

If you stay on the main road, after a few kilometers you'll come, at the top of first long hill, to a clearly marked **scenic area** on the left. This has an excellent view of the valley below, and of the dam across a side-valley a couple of kilometers away straight ahead, with distant mountains behind it.

THE FAR NORTH

CHIANG RAI

Situated on the banks of the Kok River, Chiang Rai is the gateway to the far north. It has sometimes been denigrated as a place with little to recommend it, but with its wide main street and good hotels, its very pleasant Thai restaurants and fresh climate, Chiang Rai is no bad place to spend a day at

The Kok River runs down to Chiang Rai from wild border country close to the Burmese frontier. Treks upriver from Chiang Rai tend to appeal to the more daring traveler.

Chiang Mai and the North

the beginning and end of any tour of this border region, or to use as a base for day-long excursions.

Getting There

You can fly to Chiang Rai from Chiang Mai — the three daily flights connect with the ones coming up to Chiang Mai from Bangkok. Flight time is 30 minutes.

Most people, though, take the bus. The three and a half hour trip up Highway 1019 is relatively painless, with a short stop for refreshments at Ban Mae Kachan.

turn of phrase — "We welcome to service you" — it's centrally situated on the Banparrakarn Road. A branch of the popular restaurant **Cabbages & Condoms** ((053) 719167, is at 620 Thanalai Road, serving excellent Thai food with tongue-in-cheek humor ("our food is guaranteed not to cause pregnancy") to promote the family planning message. German food is available at the open-air **Bierstube** on Phahonyothin Road, close to the Wangcome.

Chiang Rai's nightlife centers on the Wangcome's **Music Room**; there is also a

Where to Stay

The best hotel in town used to be the **Wangcome** ((053) 711800 FAX 713844 (221 rooms; moderate), a luxury hotel with remarkably reasonable room rates. Now there is another top-class establishment — but it's also top-priced. This is the **Dusit Island Resort** ((053) 715777 to 79 FAX (053) 715801 (expensive), situated on a small island in the Kok River. The **Wiang Inn** ((053) 711533 FAX (053) 711877 (260 rooms; moderate) is also both comfortable and reasonable.

Restaurants and Nightlife

Apart from the hotels, a reasonable place to eat is the moderately-priced **Hownaliga Restaurant** ((053) 711062. Sporting a choice

little place directly opposite called the **Thala Cafe**, and live music nightly at **Heuan Kao** (The Old House) on Suksathit Road.

What to See

Chiang Rai is the setting-off point for many river trips to visit the hill tribes and the landing stage, opposite the island, is a photogenic place worth a visit even if you're proceeding north or west by other means. Otherwise a much-venerated statue and two temples are all that need detain you.

Chiang Rai was once the capital of the independent Lanna kingdom, only becoming Thai territory in 1786 after having been under Burmese control. The **Monument to**

King Mengrai at the intersection of Uttakit Road and Singhakai Road commemorates the town's 13th century founder and is rarely without its incense-burning and flower-laying devotees.

Wat Phrasingh and **Wat Phra Keo**, the latter distinguished by once having been home to Bangkok's celebrated Emerald Buddha, are each worth a quick look.

Trekking

A number of establishments in Chiang Rai offer treks to visit hill tribes. Among these

seems very full and the driver unusually reckless.

CHIANG SAEN

Fifty-nine kilometers (37 miles) from Chiang Rai, this riverside town is quite simply the nicest little place imaginable.

Sited on the bank of the broad Mekong river, with views across its waters to Laos, Chiang Saen, now hardly more than a village, has a placidity and charm that expresses all the ease and geniality that

are the **Chiang Rai Travel and Tour Company** ((053) 713314 FAX (053) 713967 and **Golden Triangle Tours** ((053) 711339.

It has to be mentioned that in the past there have been armed attacks on river boats carrying tourists on the Kok River, with passengers and boatmen killed. Armed police patrols have now made the area much safer but it's not advisable to go trekking on your own into remote areas.

It's safer to travel by unpretentious public bus. It's the tourists' money bandits are after, and the humble local vehicles are rarely held up. They may, of course, become overloaded and crash into the river, drowning all occupants. The answer here is simply to get off and wait for the next one if the bus

life in Laos not so long ago used to be famous for.

Chedis crumble in a swirl of morning glory, and hollyhocks and roses bloom smilingly round the temples. Along the waterfront, stall-holders sell fruit on wooden balconies high out above the stream, while over on the Lao shore flame-of-the-forest trees blossom an astonishingly luminous scarlet.

OPPOSITE: Pastoral cool by the Kok River. Northern Thailand consists of agricultural land following the rivers as they wind through forested hill country. ABOVE: There is something very special about Chiang Saen. As a modern town it's insignificant, but its extensive ruins surrounded by tenuous contemporary economic activity on the banks of the Mekong give it a rare poignancy.

The Great River

Laos-watching is Chiang Saen's distinctive pleasure. The Mekong is very wide, but people can be clearly seen, girls bathing, monks strolling, and children playing with a dog. Buffaloes roam at will along the shore.

It is the presence of the Mekong that makes Chiang Saen so magical. The brown surface of the river is luminous in the heat, and there is ample space for both countries to ply their water-borne trade along their respective channels. It's one of the world's great rivers, and, with its combined docility

of Chiang Rai's King Mengrai it was almost certainly an important place. Its northerly situation, however, meant it became an inevitable victim of Thai-Burmese rivalry. The Burmese successfully seized the city in 1558, the Thais retaking it in the early 19th century, sacking it in the process.

At the end of the century, however, King Chulalongkorn, the great restorer of things lost, had descendants of the former residents sought out and brought back to the site. The place has thrived, albeit in a modest way, ever since.

and strength, and a summery haze over the distant reaches, its beauty entirely envelops the little town.

A Long History

The origins of this ancient settlement are lost in the celebrated mists of antiquity, mists that gather rather more readily in this part of the world than elsewhere. But even before the town's refounding in 1328 by a grandson

Akha men ABOVE pursuing their life of ease on a remote road in the north. Despite their insistent cultivation of the opium poppy, the relaxed and amused life of the hill tribes adds an incomparable air of charm to northern life. OPPOSITE: Northern markets are characterized by the freshness of their produce and the greater variety afforded by the upland climate. This market is in Chiang Rai.

What to See

One kilometer before you get to the river, on your right, stands the **museum**. It contains a small collection of Buddhas and stone-carvings and is open from 9 AM to 4 PM, Wednesdays to Sundays (closed Mondays, Tuesdays and public holidays. You may also find it shut between 1 and 2 PM).

The temples of Chiang Saen are picturesque but not of major importance. The most striking temple in the immediate area is **Wat Phra That A-Kgao**, dramatically sited on a hilltop south of the town, four kilometers (three miles) along the road to Chiang Khong.

Where to Eat

An essential item in any visit to Chiang Saen

is a meal at the **Sala Thai Restaurant**. It's located at the T-junction where the road from Chiang Rai meets the river. As far as roads go, all Chiang Saen is a T-junction, and Sala Thai is at its very heart. You're right on the river, and you can gaze across at Laos over a bottle of Kloster while the excellent sour chicken soup is being prepared. It's one of the nicest places in Thailand, but unfortunately not unknown to the coach-tour operators.

Where to Stay
There are several small guesthouses in

Chiang Saen. The **Lanna Guest House** (10 rooms; inexpensive) on the river is well located though very simple, while the imposing-looking **Poonsuk Hotel** (10 rooms; inexpensive), on your right as you approach the river, just before the Sala Thai Restaurant, is actually rather basic.

THE GOLDEN TRIANGLE

The evocative phrase "The Golden Triangle" suggests both legends and an arcane mystery. What it actually means here on the borders of Burma, Laos and Thailand

is a rather large area of land, shaped roughly like a triangle with its long base south of Chiang Mai and its apex somewhere in Burma, where the majority of the world's opium crop is grown.

But the colorful words have proved too good a tourist magnet to be resisted, and it's hard to market an ill-defined area of land stretching over international borders. Hence a specific location had to be promoted as the legendary triangle itself. The point where, at the confluence of the Sop Ruak and Mekong rivers, Thailand, Laos and Burma meet was the inevitable choice.

This Golden Triangle, then, is a joke. What you see when you arrive at the village, **Sop Ruak**, is a fairground of souvenir stalls along the top of a 10-m- (33-ft)-high river bank. What they overlook, and what all the fuss is purportedly about, is a perfectly flat, treeless, shrubless island the size of a small sports stadium that an increase of a couple of meters in river level would immediately innundate.

Its interest is that it belongs to none of the three countries. Somebody cultivates it, however, as it is neatly raked over and shows signs of a green crop — lettuces, someone said euphemistically "for the tourist restaurants here on the Thai bank". The only other notable sight is a new resort, on the Burmese side of the river confluence, which is being built by a wealthy Thai. At the time of writing, it is still unfinished.

A Viewing Point
Even so, the river scene is on a grand enough scale to be beautiful despite the tourists. The best place to view it is a small hill, close to where all the coaches park, where there's a pavilion attached to a monastery, **Wat Phra Thai Pukhao**.

Accommodation
Two new luxury resorts have taken advantage of this bizarre spot's reputation — the **Le Meridien Baan Boran Hotel** ((053) 716678 FAX (053) 716702 managed by the same company as the Phuket Yacht Club, and the **Delta Golden Triangle Resort Hotel** ((053) 777031 FAX (053) 777005 (74 rooms; expensive). Things, it seems, are all set to change in this once remote corner of the country.

ABOVE: A poppy head is cut to extract the potent sap. OPPOSITE: Akha hill tribe.

How to Get There

You can get to Sop Ruak from Chiang Saen by *songthaew* or boat. The *songthaews* leave several times a day for the 11-km (seven-mile) ride beside the bank of the Mekong. Boats can be hired in either direction for about 400 baht.

MAE SAI

Once you reach Mae Sai, you really are at the end of the road. It continues on across a bridge into Myanmar (Burma). Foreigners can enter Burma by this route for a one-day visit (US$5 payable at the border crossing) or for a four-day trip to Kengtung.

Mae Sai is a shabby, dusty town that feels more Burmese than Thai. The frontier, anyway, is merely a stream children have no trouble kicking a football over, and during daylight hours a throng jostles busily in each direction over the border bridge.

Still, with hill tribe children in costume posing for photos against the border sign-posts — 5 baht a shot is the usual fee they ask with the only English words they know — and mounds of strawberries on sale throughout the dry months, the place does have a character all of its own.

The strawberries achieve the status of a cult at the height of the season, in mid-February. They are on sale everywhere, not only in the town but also from stalls along the main road, together with bottles of lethal-looking strawberry juice. There is even a Strawberry Festival in Mae Sai, with processions, brass bands and a beauty contest. Check with TAT in Chiang Mai or Bangkok for the dates.

Over the frontier stream is hilly country, and Burma peers down on Mae Sai, its lights and fires flickering in the cold nights. For a view of the town, the river and Burma beyond, climb the 206 steps that ascend to a *chedi* on a hilltop from **Wat Phra That Doi Wao** in the center of town.

Where to Stay

There are plenty of places to stay in the town, but they vary a lot in the value they offer. The good places are reasonable enough, but the bad ones are really very bad indeed.

There are two reasonably clean hotels on the main street, the **Sin Watana** ((053) 731950 (30 rooms; moderate) and the better **Tai Tong** ((053) 731975 (14 rooms; moderate). There are several bungalow hotels down by the river — of these, the **Northern Guest House** ((053) 731537 (30 rooms; inexpensive) has new air-conditioned rooms as well as simpler, cheaper rooms, while **King Kobra Guesthouse** (/FAX (053) 733055 (inexpensive) is run by an enterprising American nicknamed Kobra Joe who also organizes tours to Burma.

A Gigantic Cave

For the **King's Cave**, turn left off the main road five kilometers (three miles) before Mae Sai at a prominent sign. Two and a half kilometers along a sideroad you come to the entrance. Drinks, and strawberries in season, are on sale, and you can hire a flashlight for 15 baht.

The cave extends an astonishing seven kilometers (four miles) into the limestone mountain. In the rainy season, only the first 500 m (one-third of a mile) is accessible. This first section, though, gives a good idea of the cave's general character. The way is always roomy and never cramped. The floor is sandy — where it becomes rocky, concrete steps have been built. The usual limestone cave characteristics, stalactites, stalagmites and "rock fountains" can be seen.

The second 500 m is even easier than the first, but after that the route becomes very difficult. Thus a kilometer (two-third of a mile) is as far as the ordinary visitor can go.

DOI THUNG

This mountain of 2,000 m (6,600 ft) with a temple, Phra That Doi Tung, on the summit, is a popular destination with local people. Get off the Chiang Rai — Mae Sai bus at **Huai Khrai**, 19 km (12 miles) before Mae Sai, and from where the bus puts you down mini-buses leave up the hill road. The fare to Doi Thung from here is 30 baht.

The wind sounds in the pine trees and bells of various sizes tinkle. The buildings were rebuilt in 1973 and are not spectacular, but the location is magnificent and the views, when free of cloud, splendid.

The temple is much revered because it contains remains of the Lord Buddha. The road up is metalled all the way. You pass half a dozen hill tribe villages en route, Akha and Lahu. The unofficial **Akha Guest House**, on your left on the way up, has some inexpensive rooms where you may be able to stay, but take along a mosquito net as none arc provided.

The Doi Thung area is in the process of becoming a major resources development district, with the aim primarily reforestation. The project is linked to a palace and health center being built for the Thai Princess Mother.

MAE SALONG

This is the mountain village close to the Burmese border settled by a group of Chinese Kuomintang refugees.

From **Mae Chan**, a small town 28 km (17 miles) north of Chiang Rai, take the road for Mae Sai, and after two kilometers turn off at a sign on the left to the Hill tribe Development Center and Mae Salong.

After 12 km (seven miles) you reach the **Hill tribe Center**, a large establishment employing 200 people in the attempt to show the hill tribes a more enlightened way of life than growing opium poppies in temporary forest clearings.

Another 24 km (15 miles) and a good climb further on is Mae Salong, settled by a group of Chinese Nationalists after their defeat by the Communists in China in 1949. The views, and the flowers in season, are magnificent, though the houses with their corrugated-iron roofs are less impressive. But it's a unique place, neither Thai nor hill tribe, the home of people stranded by history in wild frontier territory.

Should you want to stay, there's accommodation at the **Mae Salong Resort** (/FAX (053) 714047 (average at weekend; inexpensive on weekdays), and at a few cheaper guesthouses.

A NOTE ON THE HILL TRIBES

The following information is extracted from the booklet *The Hill Tribes of Thailand,*

published by the Technical Service Club Tribal Research Institute in Bangkok.

Evidence of language puts the hill tribes into two groups, one originating from the Tibetan plateau, the other more locally. In the former, Sino-Tibetan, group are the Karen, Meo, Yao, Lahu, Lisu and Akha tribes. In the latter, Austro-Asiatic, group are the Lua, H'tin, Khamu and Mlabri tribes.

The agricultural practices of the tribes vary, but it's the tribes that practice shifting cultivation — moving on to another patch of land when one has been temporarily

exhausted — that cause the problems to the authorities. Not only is it these people who cultivate opium (which, incidentally, only grows well at altitudes of 1,000 m or 3,280 ft — and over) but their slash-and-burn methods are leading to extensive deforestation in the northern hills.

See THE SIAMESE WORLD; A LIFE IN THE HILLS page 74 for more on the hill tribe question. If you're interested in buying hill tribe crafts, see AROUND CHIANG MAI; SHOPPING FOR CRAFTS (page 188).

KAREN Far and away the largest tribe, these people largely occupy areas close to the Burmese border. They are happy to live at a lower altitude, are monogamous, trace kinship through the mother, and have adopted opium recently rather than cultivating it as a traditional crop.

MEO, or H'MONG A people widespread in southern China, they trace kinship through the father and the men can have more than one wife. They live at high altitudes, and are more extensively engaged in opium production than any other hill tribe.

LAHU This tribe lives only at high altitudes, is monogamous, and cultivates opium among other crops in slash-and-burn agriculture. Though they worship their ancestors, they believe in a single god called Geushu.

YAO Cultivating dry rice and corn, these people are polygamous, and the adoption of children is common. They show great influence of Chinese culture, and popular Taoism has influenced their religion.

AKHA Thought to have arrived in Thailand in the 1880s, they are shifting cultivators, monogamous, with complex rituals associated with spirit propitiation and ancestor worship.

LISU Subdivided into the Flowery Lisu and the Black Lisu, they engage in shifting cultivation at around 1,000 m (3,280 ft) and grow opium for sale. They have strong social cohesion and have a reputation as individualists.

LUA Unlike the other tribes, the Lua are found only in Northern Thailand and have largely been absorbed into Thai society. Those remaining in the hills have the reputation of being conservation-minded.

KHAMU These are a small group found mainly in Nan Province. They are part cultivators, part hunters. Their shamans are very highly regarded as religio-magical practitioners in Laos.

HTIN This tribe consists of migratory slash-and-burn farmers and is only found in Nan Province. They are animists, though some villages have Buddhist temples.

MLABRI This tiny group, numbering only about 150, are hunter-gatherers. They have no fixed settlements and move their camp-site every three or four days.

PRECEEDING PAGE and OPPOSITE: Yao tribe women.

Off the
Beaten
Track

THE SOUTHWEST

For anyone intent on discovering "new" palm-fringed islands, Thailand's southwest is its last frontier. It's lightly populated, entirely rural, and the coast is scattered with what are still for the most part untouristed islands.

How much longer this will remain so is anyone's guess, but if Thai tourism continues to expand at the current rate it won't be very long. The situation at present is rather like that in Greece in the 1960s and 1970s — every season the spotlight falls on a new island, and what begins as "undiscovered" very quickly becomes the name that's on everyone's lips. Needless to say, the locals waste no time in erecting the necessary facilities to channel the unforeseen wealth that is suddenly coming their way — if, that is, the big commercial concerns don't get in there before them.

Nevertheless, the three southwestern provinces of Krabi, Trang and Satun contain a wealth of peace and simple pleasure.

KOH JUM

Thirty-five kilometers (22 miles) from Krabi Town and on the way out to Phi Phi Island is **Koh Jum**. This inshore island is very like the others in this area, featuring limestone caves and coral reefs, with fine views of high marine stacks. The difference is Jum boasts a small bungalow hotel, **Jum Island Resort** (40 rooms; inexpensive; bookings via Krabi ((075) 611541). A boat leaves Krabi for Jum every morning at 9 AM, returning every afternoon. You can also get there from Laem Gruad to the south.

TRANG TOWN

Trang, 864 km (540 miles) south of Bangkok, is a typical Thai provincial town, with few Western visitors in evidence. It is larger and considerably more attractive than Krabi. It's 25 km (16 miles) from the coast. Trang has, however, several very reasonable hotels and one superb up-market hotel, and is clearly gearing up to handle a whole new wave of

tourism, and in the meantime is hosting all kinds of media events to draw attention to its charms.

An elegant, but remarkably inexpensive, upmarket hostelry is the **Thumrin** ((075) 211011 FAX (075) 218057 (120 rooms; moderate but with average and above suites), close to the train station. There is also an older and rather basic hotel, the **Queen's** ((075) 218522 (48 rooms; inexpensive).

Trang has two parks, the **Praya Rasadanupradit Monument Park** and the **Sa Kapangsurin Park**, each only a kilometer (two-third of a mile) west from the town center. The latter features a small lake.

Trang Airport ((075) 218224, is a small affair, but there are three direct flights a week to Bangkok, as well as flights to and from Phuket and Surat Thani. Contact **Thai Airways** ((075) 218066, in Trang.

There is also a **railway station** ((075) 218012, on a branch line that leaves the main line at Tung Song (half way between Surat Thani and Hat Yai) and runs down to the coast at Kantang.

Trang has an autumn **Vegetarian Festival**. Like that of Phuket's, its dates are fixed according to the lunar calendar, but fall sometime in late September or early October.

There is a **Tourist Service Center** at the Police Station ((075) 218019 ext. 191, and there are several travel agents on Thanon Wisatekoon.

TRANG PROVINCE

This quiet region offers the usual southwest Thailand mix — open country rising to low mountains inland, limestone caves and hot-springs, and a largely untouched coast featuring spectacular rock formations, exceptionally clear water, and innumerable sandy beaches.

Haad Pak Meng is the most accessible beach from the provincial capital, some 35 km (24 miles) to the west. The beach is about five kilometers (three miles) long and faces out towards the extraordinary profile

Going places — A "motorbike-bus", an enlarged and mechanised version of the traditional pedicab.

of precipitous Koh Meng. Backed with pine trees, it's a popular beach with campers.

Two boats per day leave Pak Meng regularly for **Koh Hai**. The island is five square kilometers (two square miles) in size and currently has two resorts with restaurants and fan-cooled bungalows. Excellent coral reefs extend for two kilometers (just over a mile) about 400 m (440 yards) from the shore. You can reserve a room at the resorts in Trang, at **Koh Hai Villa Travel Agency** ((075) 210496.

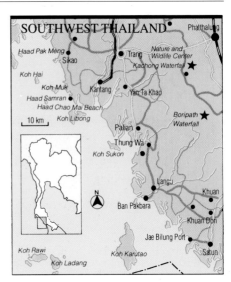

Kantang

Kantang harbor, 25 km (16 miles) from Trang town, is where boats can be found going to most of the province's off-shore islands, it's the end of the branch rail line and a small commercial port. Otherwise there's nothing to see there except the remains of a country residence of King Rama VI, **Tamnak Jan**. Set on a hill, it's now part of a public park.

Koh Libong

The largest island off the Trang coast, Koh Libong has three villages, a headland (Cape Juhoi) famous for its migrant birds and now a protected zone, and a long west-facing beach, Haad Thungyaka. Ornithologists are offered free accommodation — enquire at the Tourist Service Center in Trang town. Boats leave for Koh Libong from Kantang.

A Choice of Islands

Slightly further afield is **Koh Kradan**, often called Trang's most beautiful island. There's commercial rubber and coconut cultivation on the island, and accommodation is available.

Further south, lying 10 km (seven miles) off the coast of the sub-district of Palian, are **Koh Lao Lieng** and **Koh Petra** with their rich submarine life and swallows' nests. Nearer inland is the larger **Koh Sukon** (also known as Koh Moo. Inhabited mostly by Thai Muslims, the island has many good beaches and is famous for the quality of its watermelons.

Mainland Beaches

Back on the mainland, there are beaches at **Haad San**, **Haad Yong Ling**, and **Haad**

Chao Mai, this last also featuring a cave. These are all in the area west of Kantang. Further south, and 49 km (33 miles) from the town of Trang, there is **Haad Samran** beach, backed by thick pine woods. And close to the small town of Palian, there is **Hyongstar Cape**, a local beauty spot.

Inland

Trang Province boasts a number of waterfalls, as well as caves bearing either the usual royal initials cut into the rock or sweetly smiling reclining Buddhas. You can see an example of the latter at **Wat Tham Soratpradit** (locally known as *Wat Tham Iso*) to the right of the main road running north out of Trang, just before you reach Huai Yot.

The waterfalls are all in the upland area to the east of Trang town. The nearest to the Trang to Had Yai road is the **Kachong Waterfall**, 20 km (13 miles) east of Trang. Near the waterfall there is also a small Nature and Wildlife Center. A number of initials commemorating royal visits are carved on a large stone.

Before you reach Kachong there is a swampy lake known for its teal — look out for a sign on the right of the road to **Noknam Khlong Lamchan Park**.

A Waterfall Tour Route links a number of waterfalls south of Kachong in the **Mount Banthat** area, ending up on the Palian to Sathun Road, not far from Palian. It's a sound route for vehicles.

Near the **Chaopha Waterfall** at the southern end of this trail you might be able to meet members of the Sakai, a migrant tribe of the Mount Banthat region.

Bullfighting

This is a popular entertainment in southern Thailand generally. It is totally unlike the Spanish variety — instead it's a test of strength between two bulls. The fights usually take place on Sunday afternoons, and are worth catching if you get the chance.

Rawi. Basic accommodation is available on Koh Adang.

THE NORTHEAST

Invariably known as "Esarn" by Thais, after the pre-Angkor kingdom that flourished in this area and in neighboring Cambodia, the northeast is Thailand's despised, rejected, neglected and almost forgotten region.

Esarn is an upland plain, a vast rice-growing plateau constantly under threat of

KOH TARU TAO

This is the main island of a group of 51 forming the **Taru Tao Marine National Park**. Limited accommodation is available from the Park authorities (16 rooms; reservations in Bangkok, ℂ (02) 579-0529). There's also provision for camping. Access to the island — 25 km (17 miles) off the coast — is from Pak Bara Pier, near La-gnoo, halfway between Palian and Satun. During the dry season, there are weekend trips which can be booked through travel agents in Hat Yai.

Forty kilometers (25 miles) west of Koh Taru Tao is the island cluster of **Adang-**

drought. If the monsoon is inadequate, poverty, with its attendant horrors of starvation and disease, quickly slips into its accustomed place.

This is the part of Thailand where leprosy continues to elude the under-funded attempts of the authorities to stamp it out, where in desperation the people take to masquerading as monks and nuns to become "false-beggars", and where the hunting of toads to sell to the manufacturers of wallets and handbags for one baht per four animals is common.

The tranquility of Thailand's far south — skies shine, a fish jumps, and heat reflects off the surface of the water.

Yet this huge area is, despite everything, routinely considered by Thais as the "real" Thailand. Here Westernization has had least effect (except during the Vietnam War when the Americans set up three huge bases there). Very few tourists visit the Great Plain, but if you're keen to get away from other foreigners, and don't mind the lack of Western comforts, this could well be the direction in which to head.

The area has strong links with Laos to the east. Lao, or a Thai dialect very close to it, though looked down on elsewhere in the country, is the true language of the region. The historical remains and art here tend to be Khmer rather than Thai.

Getting There

Getting to this region is not a problem. You can fly from Bangkok to Udon Thani, Ubon Ratchathani, Khon Kaen or Sakon Nakhon, and there are overnight trains from Bangkok north to Udon Thani and Nong Khai, and east to Khorat (Nakhon Ratchasima), Buri Ram, Surin and Ubon Ratchathani.

The main route through the region is the road running north from Bangkok to Udon Thani. It's essentially the communications link between Bangkok and Vientiane, the Lao capital, and will become increasingly important as trade and tourism links between the two countries develop.

PHIMAI

Nakhon Ratchasima, usually known as "Khorat", has a TAT office ((044) 213666 at 2102 Mittaphap Road. Khorat's big attraction are the 12th century Khmer ruins at Phimai, 60 km (37 miles) further along the road — there's also a small museum attached. Nakhon Ratchasima is remarkably prosperous, and the young citizens parading its central square in the early evening quite as elegant as their Bangkok counterparts. One of the nicest hotels is the **Chomsurang** ((044) 242940 FAX (044) 252897 (119 rooms; moderate), though the **Sima Thani** ((044) 213100 FAX (044) 213121 (135 rooms; expensive) is the deluxe choice in town.

OPPOSITE: Serenity above the jostle near Nakhon Ratchasima (Khorat).

PHANOM RUNG

Standing magnificently on a hilltop near **Burirum**, these remarkably intact Khmer remains are, like Phimai, a fortress and temple in one. Phanom Rung is much visited by Thais on account of a carved lintel, recovered from the United States in 1988 after much diplomatic activity. It had allegedly been smuggled out of Thailand, and its return was a source of considerable national pride.

UDON THANI

This important city close to the border with Laos is a good base from which to explore the region. Despite the fact that it has no taxis in the normal sense, and transport within the city is by the three-wheeled pedal-powered *samlor*, Udon has all the appearance of being a prosperous place. Its new park, **Nong Phra Jak**, and clean, wide streets testify to farsighted local government policies.

The best hotel, the **Charoen** ((042) 248115 FAX (042) 246126 (120 rooms; moderate), has a sophisticated restaurant and a rather basic swimming pool. Air-conditioned rooms are also available at the **Charoensri Palace** (/FAX (042) 222601 (70 rooms; moderate), the all air-condiationed **Udon Hotel** ((042) 248160 FAX (042) 242782 (100 rooms; moderate), and the friendly **Prachaphakdi** ((042) 221804 (inexpensive).

There are attractive outdoor restaurants overlooking the park — the fashionable **Rabieng Patchanee** ((042) 241515, can be recommended. Slightly further out of town, the **International Bar Steak House** ((042) 245341, specializes in Western food and has pleasant outdoor seating.

BAN CHIANG

This archaeological site (closed Mondays and Tuesdays) makes a convenient half-day trip out of Udon Thani — take one of the direct buses that leave several times a day. The fare is 25 baht. Be sure not to miss the last bus back, which leaves in the late afternoon.

Artifacts found here show that between 3,600 BC and AD 200 there existed in this region an advanced civilization whose accomplishments included the making of bronze and iron tools and utensils, pottery and glass beads, weaving, and the cultivation of rice. The implication is that metallurgical technology was not imported from India or China, as had previously been thought, but was evolved here independently, and earlier.

Entrance to the **Museum** is 10 baht. It is of an international standard and very informative — Ban Chiang is a major site and was excavated between 1972 and 1975 with the help of the University of Pennsylvania.

At another site, half a mile to the left on coming out of the museum, an actual excavation site is preserved, with some objects in place, in the grounds of a temple. Produce your museum admission ticket and there is no further charge.

NONG KHAI

Buses leave Udon Thani for Nong Khai from the New Bus Station; the fare is 15 baht and the trip takes just over an hour.

On arriving, take a *samlor* to the Mekong where there are restaurants and a fine view from the **Nong Khai Boundary Post**. Small riverboats ferry locals across the majestic Mekong to Tha Deua on the Lao bank. Foreigners have to use the Friendship Bridge (opened in 1994) three kilometers (one-third of a mile) west of town. You can get visas for Laos in Bangkok or Nong Khai within one to two days for about 2,500 baht.

The best of the riverside restaurants in Nong Khai is the **Udomrod (** (042) 412561, immediately to the left of the frontier post. The little menu proudly proclaims "Mekong River fish you eat today slept last night in the bottom of the Mekong River".

From **Wat Haisok**, just under one kilometer (half a mile) away up-river, you can take an hour-long river trip for 20 baht; departure is from the floating restaurant at 5 PM daily.

The best central hotel is the **Phanthavy (** (042) 411568 to 69 FAX (042) 421106 (51 rooms; moderate). Among the new rash

of upmarket hotels there's the **Holiday Inn Nong Khai** ((042) 420024 FAX (042) 421280 (average and above) by the Friendship Bridge.

And at the full moon in June, the **Rocket Festival** — Bun Bang Fai — is celebrated at Wat Po Chai, next to the bus station.

Wat Kak

This extraordinary Hindu-Buddhist garden is a fifteen minute drive from Nong Khai. A motorbike bus will take you there and wait to bring you back.

To the sound of the latest Thai pop successes, gigantic mythological figures gesticulate in impeturbable magnificence against the blazing sky. The effect is quite extraordinary, and unique (though there is another such garden at Tha Deua on the Lao side). It is all the work of followers of the local yogi-priest-shaman Luang Pu Buenleuca-Surirat and was begun in 1978. Additional figures, made from wire, brick and concrete, are being constructed on all sides.

LOEI

West of here is the province of Loei, chiefly celebrated for being the only place in Thailand ever to record frost. It's a mountainous, remote and beautiful region that would repay the attentions of the adventurous

ABOVE and OPPOSITE: Khmer ruins at Phimai. Thailand's northeast has been profoundly influenced by the culture of the Khmers, the people whose great empire, based in modern Cambodia, once dominated the region.

traveler. TAT does produce a leaflet on it, but they currently have few takers. You might begin your explorations with the **Phu Kradung National Park**, a lush plateau at an elevation of 1,325 m (4,350 ft), with accommodation available. But you *must* check with TAT before going as the park is frequently and inexplicably closed for extended periods.

WAT THAT PHANOM AND SURIN

In the far east of the region, **Wat That Phanom**, 50 km (32 miles) from **Nakhon Phanom**, has a huge *chedi* that is famous all over the country. And back in the south, **Surin** has an annual **Elephant Round-Up** in November, organized by TAT. It may seem a tourist-oriented show to some, but the people handling the animals are professionals who are with them permanently. "Elephant football", only one item in a two-day event, is a typical example of the ingenuous Thai sense of humor.

MONSOON COUNTRY

Valuable adjuncts to any trip to the North-East, and indeed to any trip to Thailand, are the books of Thai author Pira Sudham. He was born of peasant parents in Esarn and, with the help of a string of scholarships, studied first in Bangkok, then in New Zealand and London. Writing in English, his two little books of short stories — *People of Esarn* (1983) and *Siamese Drama* (1987) — tell of the agonies of poor country people going to work in Bangkok. His full-length novel, *Monsoon Country* (1987), tells what is virtually his own life story.

It so happens that this author sometimes organizes weekend trips for small groups of invited guests to his home village in Buri Ram Province. He drives the parties himself in a mini-bus or his own car, and the tours include a visit to the Khmer remains at Phanom Rung. Accommodation is in his own house in the village of Napo.

These private tours offer an excellent insight into northeastern village life. For further details, contact the author at (/FAX (02) 258-1975 or write via G.P.O. Box 1534, Bangkok 10501.

Lastly...

A GENIAL INSOUCIANCE

As recently as the mid-Eighties, Relax Bay on Phuket was a mysterious little hideaway accessible only by motorbike from Patong. You bumped down the sandy road, past strange talismans nailed to trees, to find a perfect beach on which the blue sea broke in near-silence. Palms nodded, and under them an aging *farang* slept in a faded deck chair, a worn paperback open on his knee. Somewhere in the shadows a Thai in a *sarong* raised an eyebrow to ask if he could fix you a drink. A swing creaked. This, you felt, was the ultimate entranced place, magically seductive, if a bit spooky after dark.

Now, all that has been swept away. The place is today dominated by Le Meridien Phuket hotel, with sunbathing on "the white sands of your own private beach". For better, for worse, the world is moving on, and Thailand with it. In faraway Pattaya, oriental lookalikes are prancing to the music of the hit numbers of Madonna, Michael Jackson, and Cher.

The Thais are enthusiastic participators in the modern world. This shows itself in the shining new stereos in the buses and the astonishingly eclectic architecture being put up by the new bourgeoisie (such as the white gothic of Suan Phlu Gardens, near the Immigration Office on Bangkok's Soi Suan Phlu).

But for all the plastic-and-neon aesthetic that characterizes so much of urban Thailand, not to mention the ubiquitous manifestations of the international Coca Cola culture, the inescapable charm of old Thailand almost everywhere somehow manages to prevail.

In a country of holy caves and night markets, there's hardly a subterranean Buddha, a *tuk tuk* or an open-air food stall, let alone a picture of old King Chulalongkorn, that isn't draped in that most loved of all Thai decorations, a string of fairy lights. And in the early hours boys who in the daytime sell the strings of honey-scented jasmine buds that drivers everywhere hang inside their vehicles emerge, like phantoms from the darkness, to sell roses wrapped in banana leaves to late-night lovers.

Of course it's the Thais themselves that are the real delight. There can be few nations on earth where the people are so extensively amiable, gentle and long-suffering. For someone to come up and ask if they can help you is the most ordinary thing in the world. And everywhere there is the same genial softness, whatever hardships and deprivations it is covering.

Among themselves the Thais are immensely gregarious. Students or city workers on

a brief holiday at the beach sleep together in piles on the floor, and they find it very difficult to believe that anyone is by choice alone. If you tell them that that's indeed what you are, their response is invariably, "I'm sorry".

This is connected with the extraordinary lack of solemnity in Thai affairs. Life is to be enjoyed, and this is most easily done by taking it easy, and giving the beautiful things in life time to bloom.

Dreams of another life — OPPOSITE cooling off in Bangkok and ABOVE a pedi-cab driver — he will spend the night curled up in his vehicle.

An abbot lies in state in his temple. The flowers around his coffin are illuminated by pink neon, and outside children fly their kites, and a radio plays the newest love songs in the late sunlit afternoon.

STREET THEATER

A narrow *soi* is crowded with chairs. The two-story wooden houses, some with elegant balconies, face each other across the

audience, and a stage has been set up at the end of the lane.

Behind the spectators, a Chinese temple is lit up, while at the far end of the *soi* a film is being projected onto a screen that fills the entire width of the alley. In a brilliant stroke of invention, the screen is so arranged that the audience can watch the film from either side.

The film is well under way when the theater play begins. Boys with heavily made-up eyes and dressed in period glitter (but with modern watches still in place) make slow ritual movements to a basic musical accompaniment. The two musicians sit at the side of the stage, one playing drums, the other a wooden xylophone. Lighting consists of neon tubes and large unidirectional bulbs.

The audience keeps up a perpetual chatter throughout, though some people watch and listen with close attention. Children swing from the edge of the stage.

It isn't long before a comic interlude takes over the show. In a manner reminiscent of Hamlet's complaints about the liberties taken by actors, the performers improvise at inordinate length in increasingly bawdy fashion. The love scenes consist of women trying to inveigle themselves into the company of a particular man and being rudely repulsed. This scenario quickly descends into obscenely erotic horseplay, and the five-year-olds in the audience squeal with laughter at the mock copulations.

A ritual knife-fight ensues—but the final impression is made up less of the songs and music, the fights and slap-stick farce of the play than of the elements of the scene in the *soi* itself this hot Bangkok night — the crowds of people, the smell of the drains, the light breeze, the TVs flickering in the houses, the percussive music, the actors shouting into their microphones, the children with pink sausage-shaped balloons tied round their heads.

This is *likee*, the popular Thai traveling theater. It's almost impossible to discover it except by following the crowds down some poorly lit back-street to where the light spills off from the stage onto a mass of upturned faces. If you do discover one, sit down and enjoy it. No one will mind — indeed, the humble audience will be honored that you've come. It's a spectacle very close to the heart of Thailand.

ABOVE and OPPOSITE: Ancient and modern mix easily in the carefree, relaxed ambiance of the popular Thai street theater.

Travelers' Tips

VISAS

Your passport must be valid for at least six months beyond your intended period of stay in Thailand.

Many nationalities may enter Thailand without a visa for stays of up to 30 days as long as they enter at the international airports of Bangkok, Phuket, Hat Yai or Chiang Mai.

For a longer stay, you need to obtain a visa in advance from a Thai consulate. These are usually processed within 48 hours.

Most visitors will opt for a tourist visa. This is valid for 60 days, officially renewable once for a further 30 days when you are inside Thailand. In practice, further renewals are usually possible. Fees for Tourist Visas are the equivalent of 500 baht for the initial visa, and 500 baht for each extension.

If you are going to Thailand on business, you can apply for a non-immigrant visa, valid for 90 days. A letter from a company, organization or institution guaranteeing your repatriation must be included with your application.

Thirdly, transit visas are available, valid for 30 days, theoretically for people "traveling in transit through the Kingdom to other countries."

All visas must be taken up within 90 days of their being issued.

The Immigration Office in Bangkok, for visa renewals, is on Soi Suan Phlu, off Sathorn Tai Road. There are also offices in other major centers such as Pattaya and Phuket.

CUSTOMS ALLOWANCES

Foreign visitors may bring in unlimited amounts of foreign currency, but need to declare if the total value exceeds US$10,000.

On leaving the country, an amount over US$10,000 must again be declared, and in this case you will only be allowed to take out a sum equivalent to that which you brought in. Foreign visitors can take with them 50,000 baht per person when leaving Thailand without prior authorization.

It is forbidden to bring into the country narcotics (e.g. marijuana, hemp, opium, cocaine, morphine, heroin), obscene literature or pictures. Firearms or ammunition are prohibited unless a permit has been obtained from the Police Department.

CURRENCY

Thai baht come in banknotes of 500, 100, 50, 20, and 10. Coins come in 1, 2, 5 and 10 baht.

The baht is subdivided into 100 stang. There are coins for 50 and 25 stang.

At the time of going to press, the exchange rate for US$1 is 33 baht.

BANKS

Thailand's banks are open 8:30 AM to 3:30 PM, Mondays to Fridays.

The head office of **Thai Farmers Bank** ((02) 270-1122 and 270-1133 FAX (02) 273-2226 is at 400 Phahon Yothin Road, Bangkok 1040. It has branches all over the country and overseas offices in London, Hamburg, New York and Los Angeles.

The headquarters of **Bangkok Bank** ((02) 231-4333 are at 333 Silom Road, Bangkok 10500. It has overseas branches in Hamburg, Hong Kong, Jakarta, London, Los Angeles, New York, Osaka, Singapore, Taipei and Tokyo.

FROM THE AIRPORT

Bangkok's new International Airport, Don Muang, is a great improvement on the quaint but increasingly inappropriate old one. There's a Tourist Information Office run by TAT, and, of course, a Customs and Excise. Try to avoid extended contact with the latter: it may be full of peasants pleading against levies on tattered carrier bags full of vegetables, but, as a foreigner, you are automatically bigger game.

Taxi fares into Bangkok are now fixed to prevent overcharging. Go to a central taxi desk (turn left after you leave the customs area) and you'll be given a slip of paper with your destination in Thai and the fare written on it. The fare to central Bangkok will be about 250 baht. You will have to pay an extra 30 to 40 baht toll fee for the expressway into Bangkok.

Ignore any touts who may approach you offering cheaper fares — they are rarely genuine offers.

It's almost as easy to catch an ordinary Bangkok bus (N° 29 to N° 59) on the motorway outside the airport, and then get a taxi in Bangkok to your ultimate destination. The bus costs three-and-a-half bahts and will give you an instant taste of Thai life at the grassroots. You'll almost certainly have

In CHIANG MAI Avis Rent a Car ((053) 221316, 14/14 Huay Kaew Road; **Queen Bee** ((053) 275525, 5 Moon Meuang Road. In PHUKET Avis Rent a Car ((076) 311358 at the Phuket Airport; **Phuket Car Center** ((076) 212671 to 73, Takuapa Road; **Pure Car Rent** ((076) 211002, 75 Ratsada Road.

HEALTH

There are no obligatory vaccinations required for entry into Thailand, other than for

to stand for the 25 km (15 miles) into town. There are also more expensive air-conditioned buses — (N° 4, N° 13 and N° 29) — which are more comfortable.

CAR HIRE

Touring Thailand in a rented car is a good way of seeing the country. You'll need an International Driving Licence, and then you can rent cars from, among others, the following companies.
In BANGKOK Avis Rent a Car ((02) 233-0397 or 255-5300, 16/23 North Sathorn Road; **Hertz International Co. Ltd.** ((02) 251-7575, 1598 New Phetburi Road.

yellow fever if you have been in an infected area during the previous six days. It's a good idea, though, to consult your doctor, and to have an anti-tetanus injection anyway before leaving home.

Malaria is a real danger, however. It's now on the increase as resistant strains develop worldwide. Koh Samet, for instance, only two and a half hours from Bangkok, is in a malarial area. You should therefore take prophylactic tablets from before you leave home until several weeks after you leave a danger area — to all intents

It's just an 80-minute hop on a Bangkok Airways plane to Koh Samui's busy little airport ABOVE, which has vastly increased the island's tourism business.

and purposes the whole of Thailand. Your doctor should have up-to-date information on the most effective brands. It's also sensible to sleep under a mosquito net where your accommodation hasn't got anti-mosquito mesh over the windows, to burn mosquito coils during the night, and to put repellent on exposed skin from late afternoon onwards. Note that mosquitoes begin to bite well before dark.

Your main enemy is probably the sun. Get into the habit of wearing a hat, avoid sunbathing in the middle of the day, and only lie on the beach for short periods during your first few days. Suntan oils with a high protection factor will help, but better is simply to find your own tolerance levels, and not expect to look as if you've been there a month after your first afternoon.

If you do get seriously ill, contact the **Bangkok Nursing Home** ((02) 233-2610 to 19 or the **Seventh Day Adventist Hospital** in Bangkok, or the **Chang Puck Hospital** ((053) 220022 in Chiang Mai. Otherwise, go to the best hotel near you and ask to see a doctor.

Minor cuts should be attended to promptly as they will become infected very quickly in this climate. Even mosquito bites tend to become septic almost as a matter of course. Hydrogen peroxide solution and basic antiseptics are widely available and you should carry one of each around with you for these, and other minor abrasions.

Lastly, medical professionals traveling in Asia will want to carry a private medical kit for first aid to the cases of often severe skin disease inevitably encountered.

CLOTHING

It's going to be hot, sometimes very hot, so make sure you bring light-weight things with you. Remember that 100 percent cotton is coolest. You will only need more up in the north between November and January, when it does get cool at night. Of course, clothes are so cheap in Thailand it isn't really necessary to bring much — you can kit yourself out very nicely your first day there. You'll certainly lose out financially if you

buy a lot of clothes specially for the trip just before you leave home.

One useful tip is that if there's anything that makes you feel uncomfortable when temperatures are high it's hot feet. Try wearing soft shoes or sandals, and no socks — you'll be astonished at the difference it makes.

As for decorum, and doing as the Thais do when in Thailand, you'll notice that few adults, other than manual workers, wear shorts in the cities, unless, of course, they're off jogging at sundown in Lumpini Park. Innumerable tourists do, though, and nobody seems to mind.

TRAVELING CONDITIONS

Getting around is remarkably painless in Thailand.

Flying within the country is very good value. Thai Airways offer a **Discover Thailand Fare** on its domestic routes — you buy coupons which you then exchange for tickets at a bargain rate. As they are intended to encourage foreign visitors to see more of the country, these coupons are sold only outside Thailand, so check with your travel agent before departure. Price at the time of writing is US$240 for four coupons — the minimum number you can buy.

Trains and buses are comfortable, they run on time and are very rarely double-booked. The ordinary long-distance buses, with their plastic flowers, shining new cassette players, whirring fans, stainless steel interiors, and food and drink sellers visiting at every major halt, are a joy. The air-conditioned buses are less colorful and obviously more comfortable, but you should try the ordinary kind at least once. You may well become addicted to them. Enquire, too, about the **Thailand Rail Pass**.

In the country, Thais rarely travel by road after dark. In compensation, the buses begin very early in the morning, frequently at, or even before, first light.

There's only one set-back — as in most Asian countries, safety precautions leave something to be desired. In the poorer areas such as the northeast, accidents due to old and unmaintained vehicles are unfortunately not rare, and in multiple-occupancy taxis — where you may have no alternative but to occupy the front seat — seat-belts are unknown.

ACCOMMODATION

The best Thai hotels are excellent and can be judged by the most exacting international standards. Their prices, however, will come as a pleasant surprise. Hotels in the "average and above" category will differ little

from those marked as "expensive". They will perhaps have one or two restaurants instead of four, and a more limited range of sports facilities.

Accommodation in the "moderate" bracket ranges from comfortable, Western-style hotels in areas where international tourism has yet to make an impact to simpler hotels in Bangkok, some of whose rooms may not have air-conditioning or hot water.

Places in the "inexpensive" category can be anything from an idyllic wooden chalet literally on the beach in Koh Samui to a plain, commercial-travelers' hotel up-country in Mai Hong Son or Chiang Saen. This is the category in which there's the greatest

range, and where you can never quite be sure what you'll find. Inclusion in this book, however, guarantees certain minimum standards.

The rates for hotels mentioned in this book are based on the price of an average double room, double occupancy:
Inexpensive: under 660 baht (US$20)
Moderate: 660 to 2,000 baht (US$20 to $60)
Average and above: 2,000 to 3,300 baht (US$60 to $100)
Expensive: over 3,300 baht (US$100).

RESTAURANT

There is a huge range of restaurants and eating places in Thailand, from open-air night markets where you'll find some of the cheapest and tastiest fare in the country, to deluxe air-conditioned hotel restaurants serving international cuisine with all the frills. On a tight budget, you could spend little more than 130 baht (US$4) a day on food if you eat simple rice dishes at market stalls or cheap noodle or curry restaurant dining (minus alcoholic drinks, of course, a large bottle of beer immediately adds on another US$2).

Our price categories are based on the average cost of a standard Thai-style one-course meal per person excluding drinks:
Cheap: Less than 130 baht (US$4)
Medium: Less than 330 baht (US$10)
Expensive: over 330 baht (US$10).

Nearly every region in Thailand has its culinary specialties (The northeast is famous for its especially spicy salads, for instance, while seaside resorts in the south concentrate on a fantastic array of seafood), but you'll find that spices and chilies, fresh ingredients and chili sauces characterize most Thai dishes everywhere. In restaurants, you can always request cooler versions of a particular dish if you can't take the heat, or stick to more Chinese-style dishes. Drinking tap water is not advisable, bottled water or fresh fruit juices are available everywhere. Find out more in the section of GALLOPING GOURMETS, page 44.

ABOVE: Ready for anything — Thai police in dress uniform.

SECURITY

All Southeast Asian hotels make special security provision for valuables, for which no charge is ever made. The reason for this is that it is in the hotel's interest that temptation is not placed in the way of its employees. Cash that a Westerner might leave round his room without a second thought could easily represent wealth a room-boy might have to work months, if not years, to accumulate. Accusations and subsequent investigations can do nothing but harm to a hotel which, though anxious to acquire your money, has no interest whatsoever in any of its minor employees doing so.

MAIL

Thai postal rates at the time of going to press are as follows:

To Singapore and Malaysia: postcards 6.25 baht; letters under 5 g 8.75 baht; letters under 10 g 9 baht.

Elsewhere in Asia: Postcards 7 baht; letters under 5 g 9.50 baht; letters under 10 g 10.50 baht.

Europe and Oceania: postcards 8 baht; letters under 5 g 10.50 baht; letters under 10 g 13 baht.

North America: postcards 9 baht; letters under 5 g 11.50 baht; letters under 10 g 16 baht.

South America: postcards 9.50 baht; letters under 5 g 12 baht; letters under 10 g 16 baht.

Africa: postcards 8.50 baht; letters under 5 g 11 baht; letters under 10 g 13.50 baht.

The main Bangkok Post Office is on New Road, close to the Swan and Oriental hotels. If letters are addressed to you c/o Poste Restante, Bangkok, this is where they will arrive.

The various counters at the General Post Office are all open at different times. Poste Restante is open from 8 AM to 8 PM on weekdays, 8 AM to 1 PM Saturdays, Sundays and public holidays. International Express Mail

is open 8:30 AM to 3 PM weekdays, 9 AM to noon Saturdays. For telegrams, the Telegraph Office is open 24 hours. Faxes can be sent from the main telephone office, next to the GPO, or from private fax booths in town.

TELEPHONE AND AREA CODES

Thailand's telephone service is improving very fast now. IDD (International Direct Dialing) has been set up, and direct-dial calls to other parts of the country are available from public kiosks in some places.

It's always possible to make international calls from the bigger hotels, but usually with a rather hefty surcharge.

Public offices where such surcharges can be avoided are still rather thin on the ground. The place to go in Bangkok is the main telephone office, next door to the General Post Office on New Road. The service is reasonably efficient and is open 24 hours. You can send your faxes here or from private fax booths in town.

Also there are now over 15 countries with Home Direct service which gives you instant connection to your home country operator. Home Direct telephones are available at the main telephone offices in Bangkok and other major cities.

AREA CODES INSIDE THAILAND:
Central Region
Ang Thong   035
Ayutthaya   035
Bangkok   02
Kanchanburi   034
Lopburi   036
Nakorn Pathom   037
Nonthaburi   02
Pathum Thani   02
Phetchaburi   032
Prachuap Khri Khan   032
Prachinburi   037
Rachaburi   032
Samut Prakarn   02
Samut Sakhon   034
Samat Sungkhram   034
Saraburi   036
Sing Buri   036
Suphanburi   035

OPPOSITE: Golden devotion — veneration of a Buddha image on a float in the Silom Parade, Bangkok.

Eastern
Chachoengsao 038
Chanthaburi 039
Chonburi (including Pattaya) 038
Rayong 038

Northern
Chiang Mai 053
Chiang Rai 054
Kamphaengphet 055
Lampang 054
Lamphun 053
Mae Hong Son 053
Nakhon Sawan 056
Phetchaboon 056
Phayao 054
Phitsanulok 055
Phrae 054
Phichit 056
Sukhothai 055
Tak 055
Uthai Thani 056
Uttaradit 055

Northeastern
Buriram 044
Chaiyaphum 044
Kalasin 043
Khon Kean 043
Loei 042
Maha Sarakham 043
Nakhon Phanom 042
Nakhon Ratchasima 044
Nong Khai 02
Roi Et 043
Sakon Nakhon 042
Sisaket 045
Surin 045
Ubon Ratchathani 045
Udon Thani 042
Yasothon 045

Southern
Chumphon 077
Hat Yai 074
Koh Samui 077
Krabi 075
Nakhon Sithammarat 075
Narathiwat 073
Pattani 073
Phang Nga 076
Phuket 076
Ranong 077

Satun 074
Songkhla 074
Surat Thani 077
Trang 075
Yala 073

NEWSPAPERS

There are two English-language papers published in Bangkok, the *Bangkok Post* and *The Nation*. There's not a lot to distinguish between them — indeed, they often carry

the identical foreign news stories. Both are available wherever tourists are found, though far from Bangkok they're often a day or so out-of-date.

TV AND RADIO

Television's almost entirely in Thai. There is, though, what purports to be a simultaneous translation of the main evening TV news on one of the radio stations, but the degree of detail you get has been questioned.

There's an all-English radio station, and two hours of Western classical music are put out every week night from 9:30 PM by enthusiasts at Chulalongkorn University.

Programs and wavelengths are in the English-language newspapers.

RELIGION

The overwhelming majority of Thais are Buddhists, but there are plenty of other places of worship dotted around the country, mosques in the south, and Christian churches, especially Catholic ones, almost everywhere. Ask at your hotel for details.

TAT

The **Tourism Authority of Thailand** ((02) 266-0060 or 226-0070 or 226-0085 FAX (02) 280-1744, is the government agency responsible for helping tourists and hence increasing tourism into the country. Its central office is at 372 Bamrang Muang Road, Bangkok 10100.

TAT also has offices in the following places:
Cha-Am ((032) 471005 FAX (032) 471502, at 500/51 Phetkasem Road.
Chiang Mai ((053) 248604; FAX (053) 248605, at 105/1 Chaing Mai–Lamphun Road, Amphoe Muang, Chiang Mai 50000.
Chiang Rai ((053) 717433 FAX (053) 717434, at Singhaclai Road.
Hat Yai ((074) 243747 and 245986 FAX (074) 245986, at 1/1 Soi 2 Niphat Uthit 3 Road, Hat Yai, Songkhla 90110.
Kanchanaburi (/FAX (034) 511200, at Saeng Chuto Road, Amphoe Muang, Kanchanaburi 71000.
Khon Kaen ((043) 244498 FAX (043) 244497, at Klang Muang Road.
Nakhon Ratchasima ((044) 255243 FAX (044) 255244, at 2102-2104 Mittraphap Road, Tambon Nai Muang, Amphoe Muang, Nakhon Ratchasima 30000.
Nakhon Si Thammarat (/FAX (075) 356356 at 1180 Bowon Bazaar, Ratchadamnoen Road.
Pattaya ((038) 428750 and 429113 FAX (038) 429113, at 2461/1 Moo 9 Beach Road, South Pattaya.
Phitsanulok ((055) 252743 FAX (055) 252742, at 209/7-8 Surasi Trade Center, Boromtrai-

lokan Road, Amphoe Muang, Phitsanulok 65000.
Phuket ((076) 212213 and 211036 FAX (076) 213582, at 73-75 Phuket Road, Amphoe Muang, Phuket 83000.
Rayong (/FAX (038) 611228, at 300/77 Liang Muang Road.
Surat Thani ((077) 281828 FAX (077) 282828, at 5 Talat Mai Road, Ban Don, Amphoe Muang, Surat Thani 84000.
Ubon Ratchathani ((045) 243770 FAX (045) 243771, at 264/1 Khuan Thani Road.

TAT maintains offices abroad in the following cities: Chicago, Fukuoka, Frankfurt, Hong Kong, Kuala Lumpur, London, Los Angeles, New York, Osaka, Paris, Rome, Seoul, Singapore, Sydney, Taipei and Tokyo.

AIRLINES

Bangkok's Don Muang is a major international airport and is on the schedules of a large number of airlines. The following are their telephone numbers in Bangkok (02):
Aeroflot (251-0617 and 251-1223 to 25
Air Canada (233-5900 to 09 ext 11 to 14
Air France (234-1330 to 39
Air India (256-9614 to 49
Airlanka (236-4981
Air New Zealand (233-5900 to 09
Alia Royal Jordanian Airline (236-8609 to 17 and 236-0030
Alitalia (233-4000 to 01
Aloha Airlines (251-1393
Bangladesh Biman (235-7643 to 44
British Airways (236-8655 to 58
CAAC (235-1880 to 82
Cambodia International Airlines (229-3387
Canadian Airlines (251-4521
Cathay Pacific (233-6105
China Airlines (253-4242
Delta Airlines (237-6855
Dragonair (237-6161
Eastern Airlines (253-9097 to 99
Egypt Air (231-0505
Finnair (251-5012
Garuda Indonesia (285-6470
Gulf Air (254-7931 to 34
Hawaiian Airlines (236-9513 to 19
Indian Airlines (233-3890 to 92
Iraqi Airways (235-5950 to 55

Japan Airlines (233-2440
KLM Royal Dutch Airlines (235-5155 to 59
Korean Airlines (234-0957
Kuwait Airways (251-5855 to 60
Lao Aviation (236-9822
Lauda Air (233-2544 and 233-2565 to 66
LOT — Polish Airlines (235-2223 to 27
Lufthansa (255-0370
Malaysia Airlines System (236-4705 to 09
Myanmar Airways (233-3052
Northwest Airlines (253-4822
Pakistan International Airlines (234-2352 and 234-2961 to 65
Philippine Airlines (233-2350 to 52
Qantas (236-9193 to 95
Royal Brunei Airlines (235-4764
Royal Nepal Airlines (233-3921 to 24
Sabena (238-2201
SAS Scandinavian Airlines System (260-0444
Saudi Arabian Airlines (236-9400 to 03
Singapore Airlines (236-0440
Swissair (233-2935 to 37
Tarom Romanian Air Transport (253-1681 to 85
Thai Airways (domestic) (234-3100
Thai International (233-3810
Trans World Airlines (233-1412
Union de Transport Ariens (UTA) (233-9477
United Airlines (253-0558 to 59
Vietnam Airlines (251-4242
Yemenian Yemen Airways (253-9097 to 99
Yunnan Airways (216-3328

Other useful telephone numbers inside the airport:
Don Muang International Airport (535-1254.
Airport Limousine Service (277-0111 to 13.
Airport Bus Service (523 6121 Ext 138 or 267.

ETIQUETTE

Thailand is a very easygoing country, but there are nonetheless aspects of life where you need to take care not to give offence.

The monarchy is revered by almost all Thais, and for a foreigner to speak ill of members of the royal family is likely to be offensive as well as dangerous. And when the national anthem is played, such as at 8 AM and 6 PM in public places under government administration, such as railway stations or city parks, or in the cinema, you should stop talking and stand still.

In temples, dress respectfully. In many temples you will be denied entry into the room where the main Buddha image is kept if you're wearing shorts. You'll also have to take your shoes off to go into this area. Buddha images, even if they're ruined, are considered sacred and you shouldn't climb on them or show lack of respect in any way.

In mosques, men should wear hats, women should be well-covered, wearing slacks or a long skirt, with a long-sleeved blouse buttoned to the neck and a scarf over their hair. Everyone should take their shoes off, and not enter a mosque at all if there's a gathering of any sort taking place.

Don't touch Thais on the head, even children. Don't point your feet at people, and at least make the gesture of trying to keep your head lower than those of people "senior" to you.

You'll notice Thais almost never lose their temper. They'll carry on smiling even when they're feeling like hitting you. Try to go along with this tradition, and conversely understand that a Thai smile is not an absolute indication that all is well — there may be problems still to be resolved.

The Thai form of greeting, the *wai*, is also a gesture of respect. Don't be afraid to try it. Keeping your elbows tucked in, hold your outstretched palms together (as in Christian prayer) and bow slightly with your head to the person you're meeting or parting from. Hold your hands at chest level for a child, at your chin for an equal, by your upper lip for someone senior to you, and at your forehead for a monk, the king or a Buddha image.

Sex may be a national industry in Thailand, but public "displays of affection" aren't considered very tasteful.

Lastly, you're quite likely to be called by a Thai "Mr. John" or "Mrs. Sally". This is the way the Thais address each other, and in talking to you in the same way they are merely translating their own polite form of address into English.

CONSULATES AND EMBASSIES

These are the telephone numbers of the consulates and embassies in Bangkok (02):

Consulates
Dominican Republic (552-0675 and 521-5000
Iceland (249-1300 and 249-1253
Ireland (223-0876 and 233-0304
Jordan (391-7142
Mexico (246-0206
Peru (260-6243
Senegal (252-5692
Sri Lanka (254-9438 to 39

Embassies
Argentina (259-0401 to 42
Australia (287-2680
Austria (287-3970 to 72
Bangladesh (392-9437
Belgium (236-7876
Brazil (256-6023 and 255-6043
Brunei (391-6017
Bulgaria (513-9781
Canada (238-4452
Chile (391-8443 and 391-4858
China (PRC) (245-7030 to 44
Czech Republic (266-7500
Denmark (213-2021
Egypt (253-0160 and 253-8131
Finland (256-9306 to 69
France (266-8250
Germany (213-2331
Greece (251-5111
Hungary (391-2002 to 03
India (258-0300 to 06
Indonesia (252-3135 to 40
Iran (259-0611 to 13
Iraq (278-5335 to 28
Israel (252-3131to 34
Italy (285-4090
Japan (252-6151 to 59
Korea (247-7537
Laos (287-3963
Malaysia (286-1390 to 92
Myanmar (233-2237
Nepal (391-7240
Netherlands (254-7701 to 05
New Zealand (251-8165
Norway (253-0390 to 92
Oman (236-7385
Pakistan (253-0288 to 89

Philippines (259-0139 to 40
Poland (251-8891 to 93
Portugal (234-0372
Romania (279-7902
Russia (234-9824
Saudi Arabia (237-1938
Singapore (286-1434 and 286-2111
Slovak Republic (256-6663
South Africa (253-8473
Spain (252-6112 and 252-6368
Sri Lanka (251-2789 and 251-8399
Sweden (254-4955
Switzerland (253-0156 to 60
Turkey (275-6173
United Kingdom (253-0191 to 99
United States (252-5040 to 49; 252-5171 to 79
Vietnam (251-5838

VOCABULARY

Geographical Terms and Place Names
The following words occur very frequently in place names and so a knowledge of them will be especially useful to visitors travelling round the country:
Amphoe — district
Amphoe muang — downtown district
Aow — bay
Baan — village
Chedi — stupa, or tower
Doi — peak
Haad — beach
Hin — stone
Khao — mountain
Klong — canal
Koh — island
Laem — cape
Maenam — river
Muang — place
Nakhom — town
Nam — water
Sapan — bridge
Soi — lane
Soon — city center
Thale sap — large lake
Thanon — road
Wat — Buddhist temple

Numbers
Nueng — 1; *sorng* — 2; *saam* — 3; *see* — 4; *haa* — 5; *hok* — 6; *jet* — 7; *paet* — 8; *kau* — 9; *sip* — 10.

Teens are formed by adding the numbers 1 to 9 after 10 (eleven is an exception, as *"et"* is used instead of *"nueng"*). So: *sip et* — 11; *sip sorng* — 12; *sip saam* — 13, and so on. Another exception is twenty — *yee sip*. Then it's straightforward. *Yee sip et* — 21; *yee sip sorng* — 22; *yee sip saam* — 23, and so on. Thirty is *saam sip*, forty is *see sip*, and so on.

The word for "hundred" is *"roi"*, *neung roi* — 100; *sorng roi* — 200, and so on.

So 170, for example, is *"nueng roi jet sip"* (one hundred seven ten). And 465 is *"see roi hok sip haa"* (four hundred six ten five).

The word for "thousand" is *"phan"*; *neung phan* — 1,000. 2,483 is therefore *"sorng phan see roi paet sip saam"*.

Greetings

Thais very frequently add the words *"khrap"* and *"kha"* to their speech. They are terms of politeness, and you use *"khrap"* if you're a man, *"kha"* if you're a woman. So: *"sawatdee khrap"* — hello (if you're a man speaking), *"sawatdee kha"* — hello (if you're a woman speaking).

Useful expressions

"Khorp khun khrap" — thank you (man speaking), *"khorp khun kha"* — thank you (woman speaking).

These two words are also used alone to mean "yes". So a man saying "yes" says *"khrap"*, a woman *"kha"*.

And "no" is *"mai khrap"* (man speaking), *"mai kha"* (woman speaking).

A common (and typical) Thai expression is *"mai pen rai"* — "never mind". It's used to cover all kinds of difficulties.

The following phrases might be useful in taxis/*tuk tuks*, or on the back of a motorbike:
chaa chaa noi — slow down
trong pai — straight on
liaw sai, kwaa — turn left, right
yut trong nee — stop here
yuu klai nit diaw — very near;
yuu klai — far away;
khaa rot thau rai — how much is the fare?
thueng ... bork duay — tell me when we get to ....

Other Useful Phrases

farang — foreigner (a 17th-century corruption of *français*, French);

wan nee — today; *muea waan nee* — yesterday
phrung nee — tomorrow
phaeng pai — very expensive
yai — big
lek — small;
thau rai — how much?
praisanee — post office
sataem — stamps; *sorng* — envelopes.

TAX CLEARANCE CERTIFICATES

Tax clearance certificates can be a problem. Basically, if you have derived income while staying in Thailand, you will need to have a Tax Clearance Certificate before you are allowed to leave the country.

Applications for certificates should be made to the Tax Clearance Sub-Division, Central Operation Division, Revenue Department, One Chakrapongse Road, Phranakorn District, Bangkok. For more information, call (216-5332.

DEPARTURE TAX

Departure tax is now 200 baht to foreign destinations and 20 baht to domestic ones.

Further Reading

ANON *An Englishman's Siamese Journals 1890-1893* (1895). Reissued by Siam Media International (now Shire Books). Fascinating account of trips upcountry to the north – Chiang Mai, Chiang Saen and Laos. Easily obtainable at Elite Books in Bangkok. Recommended.

AYLWEN, Axel *The Falcon of Siam* (1988). Methuen. A lengthy historical novel, teeming with the exotic of every kind, on the rise to power of the Greek adventurer Constantine Phaulkon in seventeenth century Thailand.

BOONTAWEE, Kampoon *A Child of the Northeast* (1976) DK Books. Set in rural Esarn, this realistic novel offers many insights into pre-war life in the region.

BOWRING, Sir John *The Kingdom and People of Siam* (1856). Oxford in Asia Historical Reprints, 2 vols, 1969. The official account of the country by the British envoy to the court of Rama IV. Based on a very short time in the country, but solid and voluminous nonetheless.

BURUMA, Ian *God's Dust* (1989) Jonathan Cape. Politically aware pieces on several Asian destinations, including a sardonic section on Thailand.

CADET, John *Occidental Adam, Oriental Eve* (1981) Asia Books. Maugham-like stories of modern Thai life by a writer who has spent many years teaching English in Chiang Mai.

COOPER, Robert and Nanthapa *Culture Shock – Thailand* (1982). Times Books International, Singapore. An excellent little guide to the pitfalls awaiting the uninformed foreigner blundering over-confidently into Thailand.

GEDDES, W. R. *Migrants of the Mountains* (1976). Oxford University Press. A survey of the hill-tribes.

IYER, Pico *Video Night in Kathmandu* (1988), Bloomsbury. Brilliant and amusing pieces on travel in SE Asia by this intelligent young writer. Highly recommended.

KEYES, Charles F. *Thailand: Buddhist Kingdom as Modern Nation-State* (1987). Westview Press, Boulder, Colorado & London. An excellent general outline of recent Thai history.

The author researched relations between the Thais and the hill-tribes in Mae Hong Son Province.

MAUGHAM, W. Somerset *The Gentleman in the Parlour* (1930). Heinemann, London. An account of a journey from Rangoon in Burma to Haiphong in Vietnam, made in the days when such trips were still possible.

SMITH, Malcolm *A Physician at the Court of Siam* (1957). Reissued in paperback by OUP, 1982. Partly memoirs of practice as an English court doctor in the early years of this century, partly a reconstruction of palace life during the earlier reigns of kings Mongkut and Chulalongkorn. Absorbingly interesting and crammed with bizarre and hardly credible detail.

SUDHAM, Pira *Siamese Drama* (1983), *People of Esarn* (1987), *Monsoon Country* (1987). All Shire Books, Bangkok. The first two are short pen-portraits of North-Eastern Thais caught up in the metropolitan labyrinth of Bangkok. The last is a novel closely following the author's own experiences as a scholarship boy transplanted from the impoverished North–East to Bangkok, and later London and West Germany. A successor to *Monsoon Country* will deal with life in Thailand during the 1970s.

TETTONI, Luca Invernizzi and WARREN, William *Thai Style* (1988), Asia Books. A sumptuously-produced book that both illustrates the finest in modern Thai styles, notably domestic decor, and comments intelligently on them.

VERAN, G. C. *Fifty Trips Through Siam's Canals* (1979). Editions Duang Kamol. Following these at water level will give you an authentic view of what's left of what was once the "real Bangkok".

WINTLE, Justin *Paradise for Hire* (1984). Secker & Warburg. A novel set in a Bangkok love hotel written by a distinguished British scholar in a moment of surrender which an age of prudence can never retract.

YOUNG, Ernest *The Kingdom of the Yellow Robe* (1898). Reprinted in paperback by OUP, 1982. A comprehensive overview of Thai life in the late nineteenth century. An authoritative work, and a classic of its kind.

Quick Reference A–Z Guide
to Places and Topics of Interest with
Listed Accommodation, Restaurants and
Useful Telephone Numbers

A accommodation
  backpackers 28
  camping 28
  general information 227
  pricing in this guide 227
airlines
  Aeroflot (251-0617 and 251-1223 to 25 230
  Air Canada (233-5900 to 9 ext 11 to 14 230
  Air France (234-1330 to 39 230
  Air India (256-9614 to 19 230
  Air New Zealand (233-5900 to 9 230
  Airlanka (236-4981 230
  Alia Royal Jordanian Airline (236-8609 to 17
    and 236-0030 230
  Alitalia (233-4000 and 233-4001 230
  Aloha Airlines (251-1393 230
  Bangladesh Biman (235-7643 to 44 230
  British Airways (236-8655 to 58 230
  CAAC (235-1880 to 82 230
  Cambodia International Airlines (229-3387 230
  Canadian Airlines (251-4521 230
  Cathay Pacific (233-6105 230
  China Airlines (253-4242 230
  Delta Airlines (237-6855 230
  Dragon Air (237-6855 230
  Eastern Airlines (253-9097 to 99 230
  Egypt Air (231-0505 230
  Finnair (251-5012 230
  Garuda Indonesia (285-6470 230
  Gulf Air (254-7931 to 34 230
  Hawaiian Airlines (236-9513 to 19 230
  Indian Airlines (233-3890 to 92 230
  Iraqi Airways (235-5950 to 55 230
  Japan Airlines (233-2440 231
  KLM Royal Dutch Airlines (235-5155 to 59 231
  Korean Airlines (234-0957 231
  Kuwait Airways (251-5855 to 60 231
  Lao Aviation (236-9822 231
  Lauda Air (233-2544 and 233-2565 to 66 231
  LOT — Polish Airlines (235-2223 to 27 231
  Lufthansa (255-0370 to 79 231
  Malaysia Airlines System (236-4705 to 9 231
  Myanmar Airways (233-3052 231
  Northwest Orient Airlines (253-4822 231
  Pakistan International Airlines (234-2352 and
    234-2961 to 65 231
  Philippine Airlines (233-2350 to 52 231
  Qantas (236-9193 to 95 231
  Royal Brunei Airlines (235-4764 231
  Royal Nepal Airlines (233-3921 to 24 231
  Sabena (238-2020 231
  SAS Scandinavian Airlines System 260-0444 231
  Saudi Arabian Airlines (236-9400 to 3 231
  Singapore Airlines (236-0440 231
  Swissair (233-2935 231
  Tarom Romanian Air Transport
    (253-1681 to 85 231
  Thai Airways (domestic) (243-3100 231

  Thai International (233-3810 231
  Trans World Airlines (233-1412 231
  Union de Transport Ariens (UTA) (233-9477 231
  United Airlines (253-0558 to 59 231
  Vietnam Airlines (251-4242 231
  Yemenian Yemen Airways (253-9097 to 99 231
  Yunnan Airways (216-3328 231
airport
  Airport Bus Service (523-6121
    Ext 138 or 267 231
  Airport Limousine Service (277-0111 231
  Don Muang
    information (535-1254 231, 224
Ao Nang 164
Ao Wongduan
  access 128
architecture
  terminology of Buddhist temple architecture 69
Ayutthaya 36, 91, 95, 105-108
  attractions
    Bang Pa-In 106
    Chao Sam Phraya National Museum 106
    Mong Kol Bo Phit temple 106
    Wat Na Pramane 106
    Wat Panan Choeng 106
    Wat Phra Maha That 106
    Wat Phra Sri Sanphet 106

B backpacking 28
Bang Pa-In 106
Bang Saen 115
  accommodation
    Bangsaen Beach Resort ((038) 381675,
      reservations in Bangkok
      ((02) 253-6385 115
    Bangsaen Villa ((038) 282088, reservations in
      Bangkok ((02) 253-4380 to 81 115
  attractions
    Bangphra golf course 116
    Khao Kheo Open Zoo 116
    marine aquarium 116
Bangkok 79, 81-104, 105, 108, 110
  accommodation
    Ambassador ((02) 254-0444 84
    budget 82, 86
    Dusit Thani ((02) 236-0450 to 59 84
    Executive Penthouse ((02) 235-2642 86
    Grace Hotel ((02) 253-0651 97
    Grand Hyatt Erawan ((02) 254-1234 84, 96
    Landmark ((02) 254-0404 84
    Mansion Kempinski ((02) 255-7200 84
    Meridien President ((02) 253-0444 84
    Montien ((02) 234-8060 86
    Nana Hotel 97
    Narai ((02) 233-3350 84
    New Peninsular ((02) 234-3910 to 17 86
    Oriental Hotel ((02) 236-0400 30, 84, 91
    Regent Bangkok ((02) 251-6127 30, 84
    Reno Hotel ((02) 215-0026 to 27 86

Royal Orchid Sheraton Hotel ((02) 234-5599 84
Royal ((02) 222-9111 to 26 84
Shangri-la Hotel ((02) 236-7777 30, 84
Sukhumvit Crown ((02) 253-8401 86
Swan ((02) 234-8594 86
Y.M.C.A. Collins International House
  ((02) 287-2727 86
administrative area 82
attractions
  Chao Phraya River 82, 91
  Chinatown 100
  Democracy Monument 82
  Dusit Zoo 82
  Erawan Shrine 84, 96
  floating markets 98
  Grand Palace 88
  Jim Thompson's House 36, 96
  klongs (canals) 97, 98
  Kuan-Im Palace 100
  Lumphini Park 33
  Lumphini Stadium for Thai boxing 49
  Lumpini Park 84, 100
  Marble Temple, Wat Benchamabophit 94
  National Assembly 82
  National Museum 95
  National Theater, ((02) 224-1342 95
  Oriental Hotel 91
  Patphong 84
  Ratchadamnoen Stadium 98
  Reclining Buddha (Wat Pho) 90, 91
  river trips 98
  Royal Barges 94
  Senam Luang 95, 96
  Siam Society 96
  Snake Farm 82, 97
  Suan Pakkad Palace Museum 36
  Sukhumvit Road 82, 97
  Surawong Road 82
  Thonburi 94
  traditional massage at Wat Pho 18
  Wat Arun (Temple of the Dawn) 36, 82, 92
  Wat Benchamabophit (Marble Temple) 94
  Wat Mahathat 94
  Wat Pho 36, 82, 90
  Wat Phra Kheo (Temple of the Emerald
    Buddha) 34, 88, 90
  Wat Santiasoke 73
  Wat Traimit (Temple of the Golden
    Buddha) 36, 95
  weekend market 33, 98
city layout 82
environs
  Ancient City 33
  Ayutthaya 105
  Bang Pa-In 106
  Crocodile Farm 104
  day trips 108
  Rose Garden 33, 77
  Samphran Elephant Ground and Zoo 33, 104
  The Rose Garden 104
Grand Palace 82
nightlife
  Diana's 31
  Dusit Thani disco 31
  massage parlors 100
  Nana Plaza and adjacent area 100
  Nasa Spacedrome ((02) 314-3368 31, 100
  Paradise 31
  Patphong Road 100

Shangri-La disco 31
Silom Road 82
Soi Cowboy 100
Surawong Road 82
Patphong 88
public transport
  buses 102
  Ekamai Bus Terminal ((02) 391-2504 for
    buses to Pattaya and the east coast 103
  micro buses 103
  Northern Bus Terminal (279-4484 to 87 103
  rail, Bangkok Noi Station
    ((02) 223 0341 ext. 713 103
  rail, Hualamphong Station ((02) 223-3762
    or 224-7768 103
  Southern Terminal (Phrapinklao Road)
    ((02) 434-5558 or 391-9829 for
    southern destinations 103
  taxis 102
  trains 103
  tuk tuks 102
restaurants
  Akbar's ((02) 253-3479 88
  Baan Khun Luang ((02) 241-2282 87
  Bei Otto (02) 242-6836 87
  Bussaracum ((02) 246-2147 32, 87
  Cabbages and Condoms 87
  Cafe India ((02) 234-1720 88
  central area restaurants 87
  Dunkin' Donuts 88
  La Brasserie ((02) 251-6127 87
  La Paloma ((02) 233-3853 88
  Lemongrass ((02) 258-8637 87
  MacDonald's 88
  Maharaj ((02) 221-9073 87
  Moghul Room ((02) 253-6989 88
  Nasir Al-Masri ((02) 253-5582 88
  Ngwanlee Lungsuan ((02) 251-8366 87
  Normandie ((02) 236-0400 87
  Paesano 1 ((02) 252-3592 87
  Pan Pan (02) 258-5017 87
  riverside restaurants 87
  Ruen Thep ((02) 235-8760 88
  Sala Rim Nam ((02) 437-9471 32, 88
  Shaharazade ((02) 251-3666 88
  Spice Market ((02) 251-6603 87
  Sukhumvit Road and sois 87
  Tasaneeya Nava (Banya) ((02) 437-7329 87
  Tum-Nak-Thai ((02) 276-7810 88
  vegetarian 88
  Whole Earth ((02) 252-5574 87
shopping
  Amarin Center 101
  amulets near Wat Mahathat 94
  antiques 100
  department stores 82
  Elite Used Books 97
  floating markets 98
  gold jewelry in Chinatown 102
  hotel shopping arcades 102
  Jim Thompson's Silk shop 102
  Mah Boon Krong department store 101
  Patphong 84
  Robinson's department store 97, 101
  Siam Center 101
  Siam Square 101
  Silk 102
  Silom Road 102
  Sogo department store 101

Sukhumvit Road for inexpensive clothes, crafware and leather goods   97
Sukhumvit Road   82
Thieves' Market (Nakhon Kasem)   100, 102
tourist items   97, 101
weekend market, Chatuchak Park   98
Thonburi   82
tourist information
TAT office ((02) 226-0060 or 226-0072   103
transport
river boats   91, 92
where to eat
Bangkok Gourmet Guide, for dining suggestions   87
eating at food stalls   88
Ram Food Center   88
Villa Market, supermarket for western ingredients   88
banks
Bangkok Bank ((2) 231-3333   224
Thai Farmers Bank ((02) 270-1122 and 270 1133   224
birdwatching   22, 52, 210
Borsang   189-190
shopping
Hilltribe Handicrafts Center ((053) 331977   189
Lanna Lacquerware ((053) 331606   189
Nanna Thai craft center ((053) 331426   188
Silk Factory ((053) 331959   189
Suwan House teak furniture workshop   189
Wat Bauk Pet   189
Brahminism   69
Buddhism   57, 66, 68, 72, -74, 230
attitude to sex   74
history of   68
monasteries   73
monastery retreats   72
retreats
Boonkanjanaram Meditation Centre at Jomtien Beach   48
temple architecture   69
visiting temples   73
Buddhist monks   68, 72
bullfighting   168, 211
Buriram   28, 212
attractions
Phanom Rung Khmer remains   212
bus travel in Thailand   226
C   car rentals
Bangkok
Avis Rent A Car ((02) 233-0397   225
Hertz International Co. Ltd. ((02) 251-7575   225
Chiang Mai
Avis Rent A Car ((053) 221316   225
Friend's Service ((053) 275525   225
Phuket
Phuket Car Center ((076) 212671 to 73   225
Cha-am   115, 140-142
access   140
accommodation
Dusit Resort and Polo Club ((032) 520009   142
Regent Cha-am Beach Hotel ((032) 471480 reservations in Bangkok ((02) 251-0305   142
Chaiya   144

Chantaburi   132
accommodation
Chantaburi Riversidee Hotel and Resort ((039) 311726   133
attractions
Roman Catholic Church   132
sapphires and rubies   132
environs
Pliew Waterfall   132
shopping
gems   132
Chao Phraya River   82
Chiang Khan   28
Chiang Mai   16, 32, 37, 182-188
access   182, 186
by air   186
by coach   186
by rail   186
accommodation
Chiang Inn ((053) 270070   183
Chiang Mai Orchid ((053) 222099   183
Chiang Mai Plaza ((053) 270040   183
Dusit Inn ((053) 251033 to 36   183
Gold River Side ((053) 244550   183
Happy House ((053) 252619   183
Hollanda-Montri ((053) 242450   183
Je T'Aime ((053) 241912   183
Kent Guest House ((053) 217578   183
Montri ((053) 211070   183
New Chiang Mai Hotel ((053) 236561   183
Pornping ((053) 270100 to 7   183
Rincome ((053) 221044   183
River View Lodge ((053) 271110   183
Sumit Z/fax (053) 214014   183
Top North ((053) 213900   183
Westin Chiang Mai ((053) 275300   31, 183
attractions
Chiang Mai National Museum   184
golf   186
Night Bazaar   184
Wat Chedi Luang   37
Wat Chiang Man   37, 184
Wat Je Dee Luang   184
Wat Jet Yot   184
Wat Phra Singh   37, 184
Wat Suan Dok   184
environs
Chiang Dao Cave   188
Chiang Dao Young Elephant Training Center   188
Doi Suthep Temple   186
Khru Ba Siwichai Statue   186
Lamphun   188
Mae Sa Elephant Camp   188
Meo village   187
Royal Winter Palace   187
Sai Nam Phung Orchid Nursery   188
Wieng Goomgarn   188
zoo and arboretum   186
festivals   43, 186
general information
Chiang Mai Motorcycle Touring Club ((053) 210518   186
Post Office   186
TAT Office ((053) 248604-5   186
Thai Airways office ((053) 211044 to 47   186
khantok dining   184
Library Service ((053) 210518   184

nightlife
Bubbles in the Pornping *184*
Club 77, in the Chiang Mai Orchid *184*
Crystal Cave, in the Empress *32, 184*
Honey Massage *184*
Plaza Disco, Chiang Mai Plaza *184*
The Brasserie *32*
Vanda Massage and Coffee Shop, Muang Mai
   Hotel *185*
restaurants
Baan Suan ((053) 242116 *184*
Bier Stube ((053) 210869 *184*
Chiangmai Lakeside Ville
   ((01) 510- 0258 *184*
Daret's House ((053) 235440 *184*
Khumkaeo Palace ((053) 214315 *184*
Musashi Restaurant ((053) 210944 *184*
Riverside ((053) 243239 *184*
Tha-Nam Restaurant ((053) 275125 *32*
The Cafeteria ((053) 235276 *184*
The Chalet ((053) 236310 *183*
The Gallery ((053) 248601 *32*
Whole Earth ((053) 232463 *183*
shopping
arts and crafts *184*
D.K.Books *184*
hill tribe handicrafts *16*
Night Bazaar *184*
Suriwong Book Center *184*
tours around
Ox Cart Tours ((053) 222019 *186*
transport
motorbike rentals Daret's ((053) 235440 *186*
motorbike rentals Pop's ((053) 276014 *186*
trekking *37, 40, 182, 186*
Singha Travel Ltd ((053) 233198
   in Bangkok ((02) 258-0160 *186*
Chiang Rai *16, 40, 194-197*
access
by air *196*
by bus *196*
accommodation
Dusit Island Resort ((053) 715989-997 *31, 196*
Wangcome ((053) 711800 *196*
Wiang Inn ((053) 711533 *196*
attractions
Monument to King Mengrai *196*
Wat Phra Keo *197*
Wat Phrasingh *197*
restaurants
Bierstube *196*
Cabbages & Condoms
   ((053) 719167 *196*
Hownaliga Restaurant ((053) 711062 *196*
Thala Cafe *196*
shopping
hill tribe handicrafts *16*
trekking
Chiang Rai Travel and Tour Company,
   ((053) 713314 *197*
Chiang Rai Travel Information Center
   ((053) 711062 *197*
Chiang Saen *197, 198, 200*
accommodation
Lanna Guest House *200*
Poonsuk Hotel *200*
attractions
Chiang Saen Museum *198*
Wat Phra That A-Kgao *198*

restaurants
Sala Thai Restaurant *200*
Chonburi *115*
attractions
buffalo races *115*
Wat Dhamanimita *115*
Wat Sam Yot *115*
Wat Yai Intharam *115*
Chumphon *27*
churches *230*
classes and courses
Buddhism *48*
cuisine *47, 48*
Bussaracum *48*
Chiang Mai Thai Cookery School *48*
scuba diving *11*
Thai language *48*
Thai massage
Old Medicine Hospital *48*
Suan Samoonprai *48*
climate *57*
clothing *226*
consulates *232*
Dominican Republic (*552-0675 and*
   521-5000 *232*
Iceland (*249-1300 and 249-1253* *232*
Ireland (*233-0304* *232*
Jordan (*391 7142* *232*
Mexico (*246-0206* *232*
Peru (*260-6243* *232*
Senegal (*252-5692* *232*
Sri Lanka (*254-9438 to 39* *232*
coral reefs *77*
cuisine (food and drinks)
classes and courses *47*
drinks
juices *47*
local beer *47*
food stalls *18*
general information *45*
ingredients *45*
local drinks *46*
local fruits *46*
night markets *18*
sauces characteristic in Thai food *45*
Thai dishes to try *46*
vegetarian *46*
Western *46*
currency *224*
D **Damnoen Saduak** *98*
attractions
floating market *98*
departure tax *230*
diving in Thailand
Ang Thon Marine Park, near Koh Samui *148*
Pattaya *122*
Phuket *156*
Doi Inthanon *21*
Doi Suthep *186*
temple
Wat Doi Suthep *186*
Doi Thung *203*
accommodation
Akha Guest House *203*
Donsak *144*
ferry to Koh Samui *144*
dress code *226*
E elephant training centers   *12*

Embassies   226
  Argentina (259-0401 to 2   232
  Australia (287-2680   232
  Austria (287-3970 to 72   232
  Bangladesh (392-9437   232
  Belgium (233-0840 to 41   232
  Brazil (256-6023 and 255-6043   232
  Brunei (391-6017   232
  Bulgaria (314-3056   232
  Canada (238-4452   232
  Chile (391-8443 and 391-4858   232
  China (PRC) (245-7030 to 44   232
  Czech Republic (266-7500   232
  Denmark (213-2021   232
  Egypt (253-0160 and 253-8131   232
  Finland (256-9306 to 9   232
  France (234-0950 to 56   232
  Germany (213-2331   232
  Greece (251-5111   232
  Hungary (391-2002 to 3   232
  India (258-0300 to 6   232
  Indonesia (252-3135 to 40   232
  Iran (259-0611 to 3 232
  Iraq (278-5225 to 8   232
  Israel (252-3131 to 4   232
  Italy (285-4090   232
  Japan (252-6151 to 9   232
  Korea (247-7537   232
  Laos (287-3963   232
  Malaysia (286-1390 to 92   232
  Nepal (391-7240   232
  Netherlands (254-7701 to 05   232
  New Zealand (251-8165   232
  Pakistan (253-0288 to 89   232
  Philippines (259-0139 to 40   232
  Poland (251-8891 to 93   232
  Portugal (234-0372   232
  Romania (279-7902   232
  Russia (234-9824   229
  Saudi Arabia (237-1938   229
  Singapore (286-1434 and 286-2111   229
  Slovak Republic (256-6663   229
  South Africa (253-8473   229
  Spain (252-6112 and 252-6368   229
  Sri Lanka (251-2789 and 251-8399   229
  Sweden (254-4955   229
  Switzerland (253-0156 to 60   229
  Turkey (275-6173   229
  United Kingdom (253-0191 to 99   229
  United States (252-5040 to 49   229
  USSR (234-2012   229
  Vietnam (251-5838   229
entry formalities   224
Esarn   211
  access
    by air   212
    by train   212
  etiquette   231
F family entertainment   32
festivals
  Asalha Puja, July usually   44
  Bun Bang Fai, May   44
  Chiang Mai Flower Festival, February   43, 186
  Chinese Vegetarian Festival, Phuket   44, 156
  Chulalongkorn Day, October   44
  Constitution Day   43
  Coronation Day, early May   44
  Elephant Round-up, Surin, November   42, 77, 214
  His Majesty the King's Birthday   43

  Loi Krathong   42
  Magha Puja   43
  Nong Khai Rocket Festival   214
  Ok Phansa, October usually   44
  Ploughing Ceremony, early May   44
  Queen's Birthday   44
  Songkran, April   43, 186
  Vegetarian Festival   209
  Visakha Puja   44
floating markets
  Damnoen Saduak   98
flora and fauna   22
fruit and drinks   47
G game fishing   24
gardens
  orchid gardens   22
  tropical gardens   22
geography   57
Golden Triangle   200
golfing   116, 137, 153-55, 168, 186
H Hat Yai   27, 166-169
  access
    by air   167
    by rail   167
  accommodation
    Grand Plaza ((074) 243760   167
    JB Hotel ((074) 234300 to 18   167
    Laem Thong Hotel ((074) 244433   167
    Montien ((074) 245593   167
    President ((074) 244477   167
    The Regency ((074) 234400 to 9   167
  attractions
    bull fighting arenas   168
    Kho Hong Army Camp Golf Course   168
  environs
    Ton Nga Chang Waterfall   169
  general information
    Hat Yai Bus Station ((074) 232789   167
    Railway Station (244362   167
    TAT office (243747   169
    Thai Airways (245851 to 52   167
  night markets   167
  nightlife
    Cetus Night Club   168
    Disco Palace   168
    Inter Disco Club   168
    Metropolis Disco Club   168
    Palm Court   168
    Pink Lady Massage and Coffee Shop (
      244095   168
    Zodiac Disco   168
  restaurants
    Krua Luang   167
    Sukhontha Bakery and Coffee Shop   167
  shopping   168
  where to eat
    markets   167
health   225
  emergency contacts
    Bangkok, Seventh Day Adventist
      Hospital   226
    Bangkok, Nursing Home
      ((02) 233-2610 to 19   226
    Chiang Mai, Chang Puck Hospital
      ((053) 220022   226
  malaria precautions   132
  traditional Thai medicine   91
  traditional therapeutic massage   18, 101

health spas
  Chiva-Som ((032) 536536   *30*
hill tribes   *11, 76, 187, 196, 200, 202, 203, 204, 211*
  general information   *203, 204*
Hua Hin   *26, 137-139*
  access 137
  accommodation
    Chiva-Som ((032) 536536   *30*
    Hotel Sofitel Central ((032) 512021,
      reservations in Bangkok
      ((02) 541-1463   *30, 137*
    Jed Pee Nong Hotel ((032) 512381   *138*
    Royal Garden Resort ((032) 511881 to 4) or
      (02) 251-6859 or 252 4638 or 252 8252   *138*
  environs
    Khao Takieb   *139*
    Khao Tao   *140*
    Sing Toh Island   *140*
    Suan Son   *140*
  general information
    Post Office   *138*
    Tourist Information Service Center
      ((032) 512120   *138*
  nightlife
    Harbor   *138*
    Night Market   *138*
  public transport
    Bus Station   *138*
  restaurants
    Bann Tappikaew (032) 512210   *138*
    Euro Seafood and Steak Garden
      ((032) 922-0154   *138*
    Le Chablis ((032) 531499   *138*
    Meekaruna Restaurant (032) 511932   *138*
    Saeng Thai Restaurant ((032) 512144   *32, 138*
    Sailom Hotel (032) 511890 to 1   *138*
    Thai-German Restaurant (032) 512536   *138*

J **Jomtien** *119, 122, 124*
  restaurants
    Nang Nual   *32*

K **Kanchanaburi** *40, 109-110*
  accommodation
    Kwai Yai Garden Resort ((02) 251-5223   *110*
  attractions
    Bor-Ploy Sapphire Mines   *110*
    Chungkai War Cemetery   *109*
    Erawan Waterfall and National Park   *110*
    Kanchanaburi War Cemetery   *108*
    River Kwai Bridge   *108*
  general information
    TAT office ((034) 511200   *110*
  Kanchanaburi Province *108-110*
  attractions
    Khao Poon Cave   *110*
  see also separate entry for Nakhorn Phathom   *110*
Kantang
  boats to offshore islands in Trang Province   *210*
Karon Beach *151*
khantok dining, specialty of Chiang Mai   *184*
Khao Sam Roi Yod National Park *142*
  access   *142*
  attractions
    Bang Pu village   *143*
    Haad Laem Sala Beach   *143*
    Kaeo Cave   *143*
    Phraya Nakhon Cave   *143*
    Sai Cave   *143*
    Sam Phraya Beach   *143*

  tours
    enquire at National Park Headquarters *144*
    enquire in Khao Daeng Village   *144*
Khao Sok National Park *42*
Khao Takieb *139*
Khao Tao *140*
Khmers *58*
Koh Adang *211*
Koh Chang (Chang Island) *26, 133*
  accommodation
    Rooks Ko Chang Resort (01) 329-0434,
      reservations in Bangkok
      ((02) 277-0482   *133*
  attractions
    Hat Sai Khao beach *133*
  getting there   *133*
Koh Hai *210*
  accommodation
    Koh Hai Villa Travel Agency
      ((075) 210496   *210*
Koh Jum *209*
  access   *209*
  accommodation
    Jum Island Resort, bookings
      ((075) 611541   *209*
Koh Koot Island *133*
Koh Kradat Island *133*
Koh Laan (Coral Island) *125*
  ferries from Pattaya   *125*
  Tavan Beach   *125*
  Tion Beach   *125*
  Tong Lang Beach   *125*
Koh Lor Island *116*
Koh Ngob Island *133*
Koh Pha-Ngan (Pha-Ngan Island) *27, 147-148*
  access
    arrival at Haad Rin Beach   *147*
  accommodation
    Laem Son   *148*
    Laemthong   *148*
    Pha-Nga Central Hotel ((077) 377068   *148*
    See Thanu   *148*
    Thong Yang   *148*
  attractions
    Baan Khay   *148*
    Haad Rin Beach   *148*
    Thong Sala   *147*
  restaurants
    Rin Beach Resort Kitchen and Bakery   *148*
Koh Samet (Samet Island) *26, 115, 126-132*
  accommodation
    Ao Phai Inn   *129*
    Dhom ((01) 321 0786   *132*
    Diamond ((038) 321 0814   *129*
    Malibu Garden Resort, ((038) 651292   *129*
    Naga ((02) 321-0732   *129*
    Nop's Kitchen ((01) 211-2968   *129*
    Nui's   *129*
    Pudsa Beach   *129*
    Ratana's   *132*
    S.K.Hut   *132*
    Sai Kaew Villas ((01) 321-0975   *129*
    Samet Resort   *129*
    Samet Villas   *129*
    Sea Breeze ((01) 321 1397   *129*
    Sun Sand   *129*
    Tantawan ((01) 321 -0682   *129*
    Tarn Tawon   *129*
    Toy ((01) 321 0975   *129*

Tub Tim   *129*
Tub Tong   *129*
White Sand (038) 321734   *129*
Wongduan Resort ((038) 651777 or in
  Bangkok ((02) 250-0423 to 26   *129*
Wongduan Villa ((01) 321-0789 and 211-0509
  or (02) 525 0220   *129*
arriving in Nadeen   128
attractions 129
  Ao Cho   *129*
  Ao Phai Beach   *128, 129*
  Ao Phrao Beach   *132*
  Ao Wongduan   *128*
  Hat Sai Kaeo Beach   *128*
  National Park   *128*
  Sai Kaew Beach   *129*
  viewpoint near Wongduan   *132*
Koh Samui   *26, 27, 144-147*
access
  arrival in Nathon   *144*
  from Ban Don Pier, Surat Thani   *144*
  from Thatong pier, Surat Thani   *144*
attractions
  Bophut   *146*
  Chaweng Beach   *146*
  diving   *11*
  Maenam Beach   *146*
Bophut
  accommodation
    Samui Palm Beach ((077) 421358   *147*
Bophut   147
Chaweng
  accommodation
    Blue Lagoon Hotel ((077) 422037   *146*
    Chaweng Cabana ((077) 421377 to 9   *146*
    First Bungalows ((077) 423444   *146*
    Imperial Samui Hotel ((077) 422020   *146*
    J.R. Palace ((077) 421402   *146*
    Matlang Resort (Z/fax (077) 421141   *146*
    Montien   *146*
    Moon Bungalows   *146*
    O.P. Bungalow   *146*
    Pansea ((077) 422384   *146*
    Samui Cabana   *146*
  nightlife
    Arabian   *147*
    Madonna   *147*
    Reggae Pub   *147*
environs
  Pha-Ngan Island   *147*
general information
  Guide Map of Koh Samui   *146*
  Paradise Seagull Tours   *144*
  Songserm Travel Center ((077) 421228,
    421078 and 421316 to 19   *144*
Lamai
  accommodation
    Aloha Resort ((077) 421418   *147*
    Best Resort   *147*
    Coral Cove Resort   *147*
    Lamai Inn Bungalows
      (/FAX (077) 421427   *147*
    Rose Garden Bungalows
      ((077) 421410   *147*
  nightlife ·
    Flamingo   *147*
  restaurants   *147*
nearby islands
  Ang Thong National Marine Park   *148*

Koh Nangyuen   *148*
Koh Tao Island   *148*
Koh Wua Koh Wua Ta Lap Island   *148*
Mae Koh Island   *148*
tours to   *149*
Tongsai
  accommodation
    Imperial Tongsai Bay Hotel and Cottages
      ((077) 425015   *147*
watersports
  diving   *148*
  snorkeling   *148*
Koh Sichang (Sichang Island)   *166*
access   116
accommodation   116
attractions
  Chakrapong Cave   *116*
  Haad Tampang Beach   *116*
  Haad Tawang Beach   *116*
  summer palace   *116*
Koh Tao   *27*
Krabi   *27*
Krabi (Ao Nang Beach)   *164-165*
accommodation
  Ao Nang Villa ((075) 612431   *165*
  Dusit Rayavadee ((075) 620740, reservations
    in Bangkok (02) 236-0450   *31, 165*
  Krabi Resort ((075) 612160 reservations in
    Bangkok ((02) 208-9165   *165*
  Krabi Seaview Resort ((075) 611648   *165*
attractions
  Shell Cemetery   *165*
Krabi Town   *166*
access
  by bus   *166*
accommodation
  Riverside Hotel (075) 612128   *166*
  Vieng Thong Hotel ((075) 611188   *166*
general information
  onward travel through Chan Phen
    Travel   *166*
  onward travel through P P Family Co
    ((075) 611717   *166*

| L | **Laem Ngob cape**   *133*
Lampang   *37, 181-182*
accommodation
  Tip Chang ((054) 224273   *182*
attractions
  Elephant Training Centre   *13, 181*
  Wat Phra That Lampang Luang   *37*
Lamphun   *188*
attraction
  Wat Jamathevi   *188*
  Wat Prathard Haripoonchai   *188*
lifestyle
  authoritarianism   71
  displays of Thai country life   77
  fishermen of the south   77
  hill tribes   74
  standards of living   71
  the monarchy   72
  the monastic life   72
  the pastoral life   76

| M | **Mae Chan**   *203*
Mae Hong Son   *26, 40, 190-194*
access
  by air   *190*
  by road   *190*

accommodation
Baiyoke ((053) 611486   *190*
Holiday Inn Mae Hong Son
((053) 611390   *190*
Mae Hong Son Resort ((053) 611504   *190*
Maetee Hotel ((053) 611141   *190*
Rim Nam Klang Doi Resort ((053) 62142   *190*
Siam Hotel ((053) 612148   *190*
attractions
Wat Chong Klang   *192*
Wat Phra Non   *192*
Wat Phra That Doi Kong Mu   *192*
environs
Forest Park   *194*
Hot Springs at Pha Bong   *194*
Rim Nam Klang Doi Resort
((053) 612142   *40*
The Fish Cave   *193*
restaurants
Bai-Fern Restaurant ((053) 611374   *192*
Bua Tong Restaurant ((053) 611187   *192*
Sunny Coffee Shop   *192*
transport
motorbike rental   *193*
trekking
Bua Tong Restaurant ((053) 611187   *192*
Don Enterprises ((053) 612236   *192*
Mae Sai   *202-203*
accommodation
in Watana ((053) 731950   *202*
King Kobra Guesthouse
(/FAX (053) 733055   *202*
Northern Guest House ((053) 731537   *202*
Tai Tong ((053) 731975   *202*
attractions 14
view from above Wat Phra That
Doi Wao   *202*
environs
Hill tribe Development Center   *203*
King's Cave   *202*
Mae Salong   *203*
Phra That Doi Tung   *202*
festivals   202
Mae Salong   *203*
accommodation
Mae Salong Resort ((053) 714047   *203*
attractions
Hill tribe center   *203*
Mae Sot   *14*
attractions
trips into Myanmar (Burma)   *14*
mail and postal rates   *228*
maps for traveling in Thailand   *25*
media   *229*
Mekong River   *18, 28, 198*
monsoons   *57, 58*
Moslem Thai community   *70*
motor bike rentals   *29*
music and dance
traditional Thai music   51
where to see performances   51
Myanmar (Burma), trips from
across the Thai border   *14*
N | **Nakhon Ratchasima**   *212*
accommodation
Chomsurang ((044) 242940   *212*
attractions
Phimai Khmer ruins   *38, 212*

general information
TAT office ((044) 213666   *212*
Nakhon Si Thammarat   *27, 38*
attractions
Wat Mahathat   *38*
Nakhorn Phathom   *104*
attractions
Jeath Museum   *109*
Kanchanaburi War Cemetery   *108*
Phra Phathom Chedi Buddhist
monument   *108*
River Kwai Bridge   *108*
Wat Chaichunphon   *109*
restaurants
Luan Poi ((034) 511897   *109*
Nan   *37*
attractions
Wat Phumin   *37*
Nathon   *144*
general information 144
national parks
Ang Thong National Marine Park   148
camping   28
Doi Inthanon   21
Erawan   21
Forestry Department's National Park Division in
Bangkok ((02) 579-0529   21
Khao Sam Roi Yod National Park   142
Khao Sar Ban National Park   132
Khao Sok National Park   21, 42
Khao Yai National Park   34, 77
Khao Yai   21
Koh Samet National Park   128
Marine National Parks   22
Nai Yang National Park   153
Phu Kradung National Park   214
Similan Islands marine national park   156
Taru Tao Marine National Park   211
Nong Khai   *28, 42, 213-214*
accommodation
Holiday Inn Nong Khai ((042) 420024   *214*
Mut-Mee Guesthouse   *42*
Phanthavy ((042) 411568 to 69   *213*
attractions
Laos frontier post   *213*
Mekong River   *213*
river trips   *213*
Rocket Festival   *214*
Wat Kak   *214*
restaurants
Udomrod ((042) 412561   *213*
North East Thailand, tours of   *214*
P | **Pa La-u**   *142*
attractions
Pa La-u Waterfall   *142*
environs
Karen villages   *142*
Pai   *26*
attractions
river rafting   *26*
Paknam Incident   *64*
pastimes
kite flying   49
Thai games   49
Patphong   *84*
Pattani   *172*
attractions
Panare Beach   *172*
town mosque   *172*

Pattaya   *26, 33, 113-125*
  access   *118*
  access to offshore islands   *125*
  accommodation
    Ambassador Resort Jomtien
      ((038) 231501 to 40, reservations in
      Bangkok ((02) 254-0444   *120*
    Jomtien Hill Resort ((038) 422378   *119*
    Marine Beach Resort ((038) 231129   *119*
    Montien Pattaya ((038) 428155 to 6
      or (02) 476-0021   *119*
    Novotel Tropicana ((038) 428645 to 48,
      or (02) 234-3818   *119*
    Royal Cliff Beach Resort ((038) 428613 to 16,
      or (02) 282-0999   *119*
    Sea Breeze ((038) 231056   *119*
    Surf House International
      ((038) 231025 to 26   *119*
    Wong Amat Hotel ((038) 426999,
      or (02) 476-0021   *119*
  attractions
    diving   *11*
    Pattaya Park   *124*
    Wong Amat beach   *118*
  Elephant Village   *77*
  environs
    Koh Khrok Island   *125*
    Koh Laan (Coral Island)   *125*
    Koh Pai Island   *125*
    Koh Sak Island   *125*
    Mini Siam   *33, 124*
    Nong Nooch Village (cultural
      show)   *77, 125*
    Pattaya Elephant Village   *124*
    Siam Country Club ((038) 428002   *120*
  general information
    City Telecommunications Center for IDD
      calls   *125*
    Immigration Office ((038)429409   *125*
    tourist information TAT
      ((038) 428750   *125*
    tourist magazines, Explore Pattaya and
      Pattaya Tourist   *125*
  golfing
    Cherry Tree Golf Tours ((038) 422385   *24*
  Jomtien Beach   *125*
  nightlife
    Alcazar Cabaret ((038) 428746   *31, 120*
    Disco Duck   *122*
    Marine Bar   *122*
    Marine Disco   *122*
    Sarabu Café (Karaoke)   *122*
    Tiffany's ((038) 428746   *31, 120*
  Pattaya boatmen   *125*
  public transport
    air-conditioned bus station   *118*
  restaurants
    Al-Sheikh ((038) 429421   *120*
    Dolf Riks ((038) 428269   *120*
    Flying Vegetable   *120*
    Green Bottle Pub ((038) 429675   *120*
    Krua Suthep ((038) 422722   *120*
    Lobster Pot   *32*
    Rim Talay Restaurant
      ((038) 231683   *120*
    Somsak (038) 428987   *120*
  shopping
    Siam Art Shop ((038) 429045   *124*
    Watchaimongkol Market   *118*

  watersports
    diving   *23, 122*
    sailing   *23*
    swimming pool complex   *124*
    waterskiing   *122*
    windsurfing   *23*
    yachting   *117*
Phang-Nga   *160*
  accommodation
    Phang-Nga Bay Resort Hotel
      ((076) 412067-70 or in Bangkok
      (2) 398-2543 to 44   *160*
  attractions
    Khoa Ping Gun   *160*
    Pang Yee Muslim village   *160*
    Tam Lod Cave   *160*
Phanom Rung   *28, 38, 212*
  environs
    Buriram   *212*
Phetchaburi   *140*
  attractions
    Khao Luang Cave   *140*
    Rama IV's Summer Palace   *140*
    Wat Khao Bandai It   *140*
    Wat Tra Keow   *140*
    Wat Yai   *140*
Phi-Phi Island   *160-164*
  accommodation
    Krabi Pee Pee Resort ((075) 612188   *162*
    P.P. International Resort reservations in
      Bangkok (255 8790 to 98   *162*
    PP Island Cabana (/FAX (075) 612132   *31, 162*
    PP Paradise Pearl (01) 723-0484   *162*
  attractions
    Long Beach   *162*
    Phi-Phi Lay birds nests cave   *162*
    snorkeling   *162, 164*
  boat hire   *164*
  express boats to Krabi   *164*
  restaurants
    Mama's ((075) 620078   *32*
Phimai   *28, 38, 212*
Phitsanulok   *25, 177*
  access   *177*
  accommodation
    Amarin Nakhon Hotel ((055) 258588   *177*
  attractions
    Wat Phra Si Rattana Mahathat   *177*
  general information
    TAT office ((055) 252742   *177*
Phu Kradung National Park   *214*
Phuket   *26, 149-157*
  access   *149*
  accommodation
    Amanpuri ((076) 311394 reservations in
      Bangkok ((02) 250-0746   *30, 153*
    Banyan Tree Club ((076) 324350   *30, 153*
    Boat House Inn and Restaurant
      ((076) 381557   *30, 151*
    Chedi Phuket ((076) 324017   *30, 152*
    Club Andaman ((076) 340530 reservations in
      Bangkok ((02) 270-1627   *152*
    Club Med ((076) 381455 reservations in
      Bangkok ((01) 253-9780   *30, 150*
    Coral Beach Hotel ((076) 340106   *151*
    Dusit Laguna Resort ((076) 311174   *30, 153*
    Holiday Inn Phuket ((076) 3401608
      reservations in Bangkok
      ((02) 254-2614   *152*

Holiday Resort ((076) 340119   152
Kata Beach Resort ((076) 330530   150
Kata Thani Hotel ((076) 381417
   reservations in Bangkok
   ((02) 235-5120   151
Le Meridien Phuket ((076) 321480   30, 151
Metropole ((076) 214020   154
Patong Beach ((076) 340611 reservations in
   Bangkok ((02) 233-0420   152
Patong Merlin (076) 321070 to 74 reservations
   in Bangkok ((02) 253-2641   152
Pearl Hotel ((076) 211044 reservations in
   Bangkok ((02) 260-1022   154
Pearl Village ((076) 327006   153
Phuket Arcadia Hotel ((076) 381038   151
Phuket Island Resort ((076) 381010   150
Phuket Island View ((076) 381919   151
Phuket Merlin ((076) 212866 to 70
   reservations in Bangkok
   ((02) 253-2641 to 42   154
Phuket Yacht Club ((076) 381156   30, 150
Royal Paradise Hotel ((076) 340566 to 70
   reservations in Bangkok
   ((02) 260-3254 to 55   152
Sheraton Grande Laguna Beach
   ((076) 324101   30, 153
Thavorn Hotel (211333 to 35   154
Thavorn Palm Beach
   ((076) 381034   30, 151
attractions
   Aquarium and Butterfly Farm   155
   Bangtao Beach   153
   Banyan Tree Golf Club   154
   Blue Canyon Country Club   155
   Boxing Stadium   154
   Chinese Vegetarian Festival   156
   Gibbon Rehabilitation Centre   155
   golf courses   154
   Kamala Beach   152
   Karon Beach   151
   Kata Beach   150
   Kata Noi Beach   150
   Khao Rang Hill, Phuket Town   154
   Marine Biological Research Center   154
   Nai Harn Beach   150
   Nai Thorn Beach   154
   Nai Yang Beach   153
   Nai Yang National Park   153
   Patong Beach   151
   Phuket Town   154
   Rawai Beach   150
   Surin Beach   152
   Tarzan's Bungy Jump   155
   Ton Yai Waterfall   155
      Wat Chalong   155
      Wat Phra Thong   155
diving   11, 156
   best dive spots   156
   Holiday Diving Club ((076) 321166   156
   Marina Divers ((076) 381625   156
   Santana ((076) 381598   156
   Siam Diving Centre   156
   Songserm Travel ((076) 222570   156
   South East Asia Yacht Charter Co.
      ((076) 340406   156
environs
   Phi-Phi Island   160
   Suwan Ku Ha Caves   160
festivals   44

general information
   Immigration Office   154
   Post Office   154
   TAT Office ((076) 212213   154
golf courses   154
public transport   154
restaurants
   Salaloy Restaurant (81297   150
   Shalimar ((01) 723 0488   152
   The Boathouse Wine & Grill
      ((076) 330015   32, 151
watersports
   diving   156
Pranburi   142
public holidays   44
public transport in Thailand   29, 226
   bus travel   226
   domestic flights   226
   general information   226
   rail travel   226
R rail travel in Thailand   226
   Rayong   115, 125
   access   125
   accommodation
      Ban Phe Cabana ((01) 211-4888, reservations
         in Bangkok ((02) 2801820   126
      Ban Phe Resort ((01) 211-7763, reservations in
         Bangkok ((02) 250-0928   126
      Ko Saket Phet ((01) 319042, reservations in
         Bangkok ((02) 319-9929   126
      Novotel Rim Pae Rayong (/FAX (038) 614678,
         reservations in Bangkok
         ((02) 247-0247   126
      Palmeraie ((01) 211-7763 reservations in
         Bangkok ((02) 213-1162   126
      Pines Beach Hotel ((035) 651636, reservations
         in Bangkok 02) 332-0805   126
      Rayong Resort ((038) 651000, reservations in
         Bangkok ((02) 255-2392   126
   attractions
      Hat Sai Thong Beach   125
      Koh Saket Island   126
   religion   230
   restaurants in Thailand
      cost of eating out in Thailand   227
      pricing in this guide   227
   river rafting   12
   Rose Garden (near Bangkok)   77, 104
S **Sam Muk**   115
   attractions
      wild monkeys   115
   scuba diving, where to learn   11
   security precautions   228
   shopping in Thailand
      antiques   39
      Chiang Mai for hill tribe handicrafts   16
      gems   39
      handpainted umbrellas   189
      hill tribe handicrafts   16, 39
      lacquerware   184, 188
      nielloware   39
      painted umbrellas   184
      silk   38, 184, 188
      silver   184
      tailor-made goods   39
      teak furniture   189
      weaving   189
   Si Racha   116

Surin *42, 214*
  attractions
    Elephant Round-Up, November *13, 77, 214*
Suwan Ku Ha Caves *160*

T *takraw* *16*
Taru Tao Marine National Park
  access *211*
tax clearance certificates *230*
telephone service in Thailand
  Home Direct and IDD service *228*
  telephone dialing codes inside Thailand *228*
temples
  see under each location (temple is wat *in Thai)* *90*
Thai boxing *49*
Thai people, origins of *58*
Thailand
  history
    Ayutthaya period *59*
    Bang Chiang *213*
    Burmese invasions *59, 60, 95*
    Chakri dynasty *62*
    Chulalongkorn *64*
    European influences *60*
    King Bhumipol *65*
    King Bumipol and modern Thailand *72*
    King Mongkut *64*
    modern era *65*
    Old Siam *58, 178*
    Sukhothai era *178*
    the Khmers *58*
    Treaty of Friendship and Comerce *64*
    World War II *65*
Thale Luang Waterbird Sanctuary *170*
Thaton *26*
Thonburi *82*
tour operators offering Thailand trips *52*
tourist information and TAT offices
  Don Muang Airport
    TAT office *224*
  TAT Nakhon Si Thammarat
    (/FAX (075) 356356 230
  TAT Bangkok ((02) 282-1143 to 47 230
  TAT Chiang Mai ((053) 248604 230
  TAT Chiang Mai ((053) 248604 230
  TAT Chiang Rai ((053) 717433 230
  TAT Hat Yai ((074) 243747 and 245986 230
  TAT Kanchanaburi ((034) 511200 230
  TAT Khon Kaen ((043) 244498 230
  TAT Nakhon Ratchasima ((044) 255243 230
  TAT Pattaya ((038) 428750 and 429113 230
  TAT Phitsanulok ((055) 252743 230
  TAT Phuket ((076) 212213 and 211036 230
  TAT Rayong (/FAX (038) 611228 230
  TAT Surat Thani ((077) 281828 230
  TAT Ubon Ratchathani
    ((045) 243770 230
traditional Thai massage *18*
traditional Thai medicine *91*
Trang Province *209-211*
  access
    by air *209*
  accommodation
    Queen's ((075) 218522 209*
    Thumrin ((075) 211011 209*
  attractions
    Vegetarian Festival *209*
  environs
    Chaopha Waterfall *211*

    Haad Chao Mai beach *210*
    Haad Samran beach *210*
    Haad San beach *210*
    Haad Yong Ling beach *210*
    Hyongstar Cape *210*
    Kachong Waterfall *210*
    Koh Hai *210*
    Noknam Khlong Lamchan Park *210*
  general information
    railway station ((075) 218012 209*
    Tourist Service Center at the Police Station
      ((075) 218019 ext. 191 209
    Trang Airport (075) 218224 209*
  offshore islands
    getting there *210*
    Koh Kradan *210*
    Koh Lao Lieng *210*
    Koh Petra *210*
    Koh Sukon (also known as Koh Moo) *210*
Trat Province *133*
  getting to the offshore islands *133*
  Koh Chang Island *133*
  Koh Koot Island *133*
  Koh Ngob Island *133*
  Laem Ngob cape *133*
Treaty of Friendship and Commerce *64*
trekking *11, 24, 192, 197*
  Chiang Mai, Chiang Rai and
    Mae Hong Son *192*

U **Ubon Ratchathani** *28*
Udon Thani *212*
  accommodation
    Charoen Hotel ((042) 248155 212*
    Charoensri Palace ((042) 242611 to 13 212*
    Siriudorn ((042) 221804 212*
    Udon Hotel ((042) 248160 212*
  attractions
    Nong Phra Jak *212*
  environs
    Ban Chiang archaeological site *212*
    Nong Khai *213*
  public transport *212*
  restaurants
    Rabieng Patchanee ((042) 241515 212*
    the International Bar Steak House
      ((042) 245341 212

V visas *226*
vocabulary *229, 23*

W war cemeteries in Thailand *109*
Wat That Phanom *214*
  attractions
    huge *chedi* *214*
watersports (see also under sports)
  game fishing *24*
  river rafting *26*
  sea canoeing *24*
water in Thailand *227*
Wieng Goomgarn *189*
  Chiang Mai, environs *188*
wildlife
  birds *22*
  dolphins *21*
  elephants *77*
  gibbons *21*
  hornbills *21*
  monkeys *115*
  turtles *21*
  wild elephant *21*

windsurfing
  Siam World Cup championships
    (part of the Asian World Cup Series) 23
Wongduan *129*
  accommodation
    Sea Horse (01) 323-0049 *129*

Y | **Yala Province** *172*
  Pattani 172